P9-CLS-574

TRYING OUT
THE DREAM

Books by PAUL WILKES

Trying Out the Dream
These Priests Stay
Fitzgo: The Wild Dog of Central Park
You Don't Have to Be Rich to Own a Brownstone
(with Joy Wilkes)

TRYING OUT THE DREAM

A Year in the Life of an American Family

by PAUL WILKES

J. B. LIPPINCOTT COMPANY
Philadelphia and New York

Copyright © 1975 by Paul Wilkes
All rights reserved
First edition

Printed in the United States of America

"Crippled Inside" by John Lennon
Copyright © 1971 Northern Songs Ltd.
All rights for the USA, Canada, Mexico & The Philippines
controlled by MACLEN MUSIC, INC. c/o ATV Music Group
Used by Permission All Rights Reserved
International Copyright Secured

"I Can't Get Started" by Vernon Duke and Ira Gershwin
Copyright © 1935 by Chappell & Co., Inc.
Copyright renewed.
Used by permission of Chappell & Co., Inc.

"Mr. Tambourine Man" by Bob Dylan, quoted on p. 304.
© 1964 M. Witmark & Sons
All Rights Reserved
Used by permission of Warner Bros. Music

U.S. Library of Congress Cataloging in Publication Data

Wilkes, Paul, birth date
    Trying out the dream : a year in the life of an
American family.

    1. Family—United States—Case studies. 2. United
States—Social conditions—1960–   I. Title.
HQ536.W54   301.42'0973   74–22272
ISBN–0–397–01079–6

For all my brothers and sisters

Who is my brother?
Who is my sister?
I'm yours.
You're mine.

And especially for Joy

Contents

The threshold for excitement is low, and for many, excitement is identified with conflict, crisis, and deprivation. Most Levittowners grew up in the Depression, and remembering the hard times of their childhood, they want to protect themselves and their children from stress.

—Herbert J. Gans
The Levittowners

My subject is the American Protestant small-town middle class. I like middles. It is in the middle that extremes clash, where ambiguity restlessly rules. Something quite intricate and fierce occurs in homes, and it seems to me without doubt worthwhile to examine what it is.

—John Updike

Foreword

ON THIS MORNING in mid-January, 1972, newspaper headlines tell us that an AWOL Army private with a Ph.D. in psychology is suspected of planting bombs in bank safe deposit boxes; a woman has been informed by the courts that she can be a baseball umpire; Howard Hughes denies that a biography of him is authentic; an Appalachian woman is surprised that her homemade quilts are being sold for hundreds of dollars. On this morning we turn on our television sets to see George Wallace in a wheelchair, declaring his candidacy for President; a doctor telling about the adverse side effects of a vasectomy; an elderly couple showing how they wrap old papers and rags around themselves to keep warm now that their electricity has been shut off.

The significant and the passing, the warp and woof of human existence and activity. We know, through word and image, about a lot of different Americans. But often it seems as though those who capture headlines or stand before television cameras are not real people, not really like us. They are too rich or poor, too powerful or disenfranchised, perhaps too eccentric or publicity conscious. The people we know, we ourselves, don't live like that. Of course our lives are filled with peaks and valleys, of course we have our high moments, but, admittedly, more times of no moment.

After all, who is interested in the millions of workaday Americans undistinguished by birth or profession, by money or lack of it? Even those who want their vote, or want to determine how to

11

manipulate them to buy this detergent or that after-shave lotion, are interested in "average Americans" en masse, not as individuals.

Writers have described the rich and the poor, but little has been told of the lives of the so-called average people in America. Statistics? Yes. Stereotypes? Yes. What their lives are really like? No. That is why this book is in your hands today. It is based on a simple concept: that it would be interesting and possibly educational to follow an average American family for a year and then report on it.

The study of one family will not show us what is going on in America today. This will be no distillation of human experience so that we can look at the boiled-down essence and say, "Aha, that's what we're all about!" No, looking at it that way, the family would be raw material, raw data. But they are human beings, with the range of expectations and dashed hopes, laughter and tears, fears and successes that many of us experience. I felt when I embarked on this project, and I feel now, that in looking at the members of one American family and what they are going through in the 1970s, we may all be able, through them, to hold up a mirror to ourselves. In watching five faces in the blur of two hundred million, we may better understand how other ordinary people try to make sense out of their lives. Perhaps we can learn something from people who are neither more nor less than we are.

At the end of the book I will describe how I went about finding the right family. It was not an easy job; the Average American Family exists in only one place: as a set of sterile facts at the bottom line of a U.S. Census Bureau computer printout. There is a father who is a middle-echelon manager and a mother who is primarily a homemaker, although she has occasional part-time work. They are in their early forties and have 2.4 children, whose average age is in the teens. They live in a suburban area and, like most suburbanites, have migrated from a city.

The real-life embodiment of those statistics turned out to be a family of five we'll call the Neumeyers. They live in a suburban community some thirty-five miles from the center of the city from which they moved in 1959. We'll call their community Mariposa and the surrounding county Mohawk. On this particular day Art and Betty Neumeyer and their three children, Martha, Richard and Joan, are going about their individual lives at the places they have chosen, society has imposed or necessity has dictated.

Art Neumeyer, age forty-three, is at work. He is a foreman at Rabinowitz Diecutting, Inc., and divides his time between supervising workers in the factory and giving estimates to potential customers on the phone in the office. Art started at Rabinowitz over twenty years ago, wearing patched jeans, sweeping floors and earning 55 cents an hour. He now wears a tie to work and earns $15,000 a year. His wife, Betty, who is forty-two, is at home. Betty occasionally works for a woman who does catering and has a sprinkling of other activities—most of them church-related—that take her outside the house. But most of the time she is at home, as she is today. She has been a full-time homemaker all her married life. With her children either at school or working, Betty might be expected to find more things to do outside the house, but Betty does not drive, and the Neumeyers live deep within a section of Mariposa called The Knolls, where public transportation is over a mile away.

Martha, the oldest Neumeyer child, is twenty and majoring in English Education at Hillcrest College in Kansas. A bright student at Mariposa High School, she is now holding a B average at Hillcrest. She is a sorority member and active in many campus groups. Her brother, Richard, age eighteen, did poorly at Mariposa High and, after dropping out of a local junior college, is now working at a metal fabricating shop, doing semiskilled work and earning $2.25 an hour. He eats and sleeps at home, but most of his free time is spent outside the house, riding around with one of his friends, hanging out at the Gulf station, or visiting one of the many singles bars in Mohawk County. Joan, the youngest Neumeyer, is ten and in the fifth grade at Pawnee Elementary. Although she is not an especially good student, she is talented in arts and crafts, enjoys cooking and is involved in Camp Fire Girls, cheerleading, piano lessons and many other activities.

Art and Betty are what many people would call a hardworking, diligent couple. They are both active in the local Methodist church, and Betty has been a Camp Fire leader, Art a coach in Little

League, although both of them come from lower-income homes and from families whose lives were uncomplicated by outside commitments. Art is conscientious at his job and is considered quite knowledgeable in the diecutting field. Betty is a meticulous housekeeper whose house is always clean, with the dishes put away, fresh towels available and the evening meal ready when her husband walks in the door. Martha and Richard attended Sunday school or youth groups well into high school, and Joan is currently enrolled in a Sunday school class and sings in the children's choir.

Art and Betty have come a long way from their humble beginnings. Art, who spent over nine years in an orphanage, and Betty, whose parents ran a series of fruit markets that eventually went under, could easily be considered a couple that has modestly fulfilled the American Dream. They are well thought of in their community, and when their old friends from the city visit them, they come away impressed that Betty and Art have provided their children with a clean, safe place to live, good educations and material comforts. To people of their upbringing, how well parents take care of their children and, in turn, how well those children produce in society are the criteria by which the parents are judged. For Art, who left school after the tenth grade, it is quite an accomplishment to have worked himself into management at Rabinowitz; for him and Betty, who was not encouraged to go beyond high school, to have a child in college and heading for a degree is even more important. Conversely, having a son in a menial factory job is an embarrassment.

The outcome of their children's lives is crucial to Art and Betty because their married life has been centered around them. More money for Art meant better clothes for the children or a down payment on a house in the suburbs. The move to Mariposa was prompted by the threat of busing in their old neighborhood in the city, called the North End. Now the push is to get Martha through college, get Richard back into college or otherwise settled in some worthwhile profession and continue to help Joan through her formative years.

When the Neumeyers moved from the city in 1959, they first lived in a $14,750 home on Tulip Lane in a hastily built develop-

14

ment in Mariposa called Clinton Park, where the houses, as Betty has said, "were crackerboxes, but you could have a yellow crackerbox, a pale green or a white one." So, in the eyes of their city friends as well as their old neighbors in Clinton Park, the Neumeyers have not only made it to suburbia, they have taken still another step: they have moved into a house in a better section of town.

They live in an area called The Knolls, which has a few older homes—twenty or twenty-five years old—interspersed among newer ones like the Neumeyers', which was constructed twelve years ago when the area was rapidly built up. The Neumeyers paid $25,000 for their house in 1967. It is one of the more modest homes on the street; some are in the $60,000 category. The Knolls, on a county map, looks like a labyrinth—cul-de-sacs and winding streets that change names frequently proliferate. The Neumeyers live at 97 Birchwood Street in a house covered with green-painted shake cedar shingles and some red brick facing. It is called a "high ranch" because of its two-story design, in which the basement is at ground level and the living area upstairs. This type of architecture is dictated by the high water table in this area; since excavated basements are not possible, construction is on a cement slab. There are no birches on Birchwood, but medium-sized locusts and evergreens are abundant. It is a pleasant, quiet street with no through traffic.

Before the 1950s, many city people thought of this part of Mohawk County as a no-man's-land, inhabited by rustic folk, a pleasant-enough place to drive to but who would want to live there? The earliest recorded history of the area, in the seventeenth century, shows it was a wilderness sparsely populated by Indians, not very good for hunting or farming because of the poor soil.

In the 1950s—an era of burgeoning families leaving crowded cities, low down payments on tract-built houses and the biggest building boom America had ever seen—Mariposa's population grew from 2,000 to 20,000. Some defense plants had been located in Mohawk County during the war, but the 1950s and 1960s saw mammoth plants, one of them employing 24,000 people at its peak, rise out of the marshes and grassy plains. Lucrative federal con-

15

tracts, first because of the Korean War and then for the aerospace age, created jobs and pumped money into the local economy.

The Neumeyers were happy to be one of the homogeneous families that peopled Tulip Lane: school-age children, mother at home, big mortgage but manageable payments. Crime, crowding, noise were left behind in the city, as were litter and fear. Shopping centers were built; new stores opened weekly; ground was broken for new schools. The real estate man who sold them their house promised that "minority" people would not be allowed to buy, and in fact the 1960 census listed only twenty-eight blacks in Mariposa. By 1970 that figure had been cut to nine.

The 1960s were good years for the Neumeyers and for Mariposa. There were the incumbent problems of growth, but the community was constantly bettering itself, filling vacant land with houses and buildings, making huge gains in population. The Neumeyer children went to clean, new schools, worshiped in a new church, ice-skated at a new rink. And Betty was happy in her new home, with her children around her and friendly neighbors to talk with.

But now, in 1972, middle age has come to Art and Betty and, without much warning, has descended on Mohawk County. The wide-open spaces are suddenly gone. Where construction was once heralded as a sign of progress, it is now condemned; 96 percent of Mohawk's residentially zoned land is already occupied. In only twenty years, the quickly built houses and stores have aged badly. Already there are abandoned, boarded-up buildings along Main Line Drive and Cedar Crest Drive, the two main roads that go through Mariposa. House foundations are cracking, more lawns are being allowed to go to weed, houses with peeling paint are becoming noticeable.

An economic bust came in the 1970s when the aerospace industry shriveled. Outcries were loud. Workers who had left the "dying" city suddenly found the situation reversed. Mohawk County finally humbled itself, admitted its unemployment rate was higher than the city's and asked the federal government to separate its statistics from those of the city so the county could receive emergency funds to help the sagging economy.

16

Welfare, always considered a city problem, has also been exported to the suburbs. Mohawk County added three times as many people to its welfare rolls as the city did last year. The crime rate is still higher in the city, but crime is growing at double the city rate in the county. One out of every five people in Mohawk County experienced a theft or a more personal assault last year. And drugs are readily available from junior high on up.

In their middle age, Art and Betty are proud of what they have achieved. They are aware that their lives and their community are not perfect, but, as Betty has said, "Better than most, way better than most." Where once they had to scrape together $600 for a down payment on their first house, they paid more than that amount in cash two years ago for Joan's piano. "To outsiders—and I've heard this myself—we're close to the perfect family," Art has said. "We're not the most successful; we don't have the most money, but we are a happy family. Sure, we have our problems, but the outside world never knows about them. Just let them believe like they do right now: the Neumeyers are doing just fine."

1

"The Best Jogger in the Business"

ART NEUMEYER ADMITS he gets up grouchy every weekday morning. "At quarter to six, what do you expect, a tap dance?" is his stoical way of putting it. On this particular Monday morning in February his bad mood is intensified by the greasy smudge he finds on the beige living room rug. Also, he and Betty didn't sleep well last night, each keeping the other awake until Richard came home. It was well after midnight when their son returned, and Art knows he did not go directly downstairs to his room. The greasy smudge says two things: Richard spent another night at the Gulf station on Main Line Drive, and for some reason he went up into the living room before going to bed.

Art does nothing about the smudge except stew over it. Betty will clean it, he is sure. If she hasn't seen it by the time he calls her today, he'll tell her about it then.

The Neumeyers' 1968 red four-door Chevrolet starts easily in the garage, and Art backs out of the driveway at 6:40 and starts the nine-minute drive down deserted streets that will take him to the railroad station and the same parking spot he fills each workday. At the station, other men are buying the morning papers, but Art walks past them and climbs the stairs to the platform. Many of the other men carry briefcases—newly found status symbols for some of them. Art has a hard-cover book tucked under his arm.

He knows exactly where to stand on the platform so that a nonsmoking car of the 6:55 will open in front of him. It is a mild

19

morning for February, but the wind that gusts across the platform is raw as it rattles the gum wrappers in the tiny refuse containers attached to the platform's pillars.

As the doors of the 6:55 open, Art steps into the train. His gaze fixes on a seat a few rows from the door, and he heads for it.

Art Neumeyer and hundreds of other men and a few women who must be at work early ride this train every day. Some of the commuters exchange greetings; some have built up relationships that revolve around traveling gin rummy games that have gone on for years during the fifty-eight-minute ride to and from the city. Art bids good morning to no one. It is not that he is an unfriendly man. It is just that the morning and evening commutes are the only times Art has to himself, and he jealously preserves them.

One might think Art Neumeyer is constantly angry, his look is so stern, his dark eyes so penetrating, but he is merely a reserved man. He is of average height—about 5 feet 9 inches—and slender build. His black hair has some gray intermingled, enough to frost the top and his sideburns, which reach the bottom of his ears. As a young man he had a bad case of acne—a problem his son is suffering from now—but the years have muted the scars. Art's most distinguishing characteristic is his right hand. He lost two fingers, the index and middle, in a diecutting press accident in 1959. Covering the gap is a skin graft from his stomach; the patch supports a growth of soft, short black hair which is strangely out of place on the otherwise smooth skin.

On the train Art often reads paperback mysteries or potboilers that one of the salesmen at the office buys and then gives to him. On Friday he finished *Hate Is for the Hunted*, a book, according to the cover, about "the most exclusive club on earth. . . . Staying in is risky. It means submitting to an incredibly bizarre variety of sadistic sexual appetites." Today he begins a book Betty got from the Mariposa Public Library, *The Mafia Is Not an Equal Opportunity Employer*, by Nicholas Gage. Reading lasts for about fifteen minutes, and then Art dozes off until he is awakened by a jerk as the train reaches his destination, the city terminal. A short subway ride takes him a block from Rabinowitz Diecutting, which is in a rundown section of the city where the printing trades have for years been centered.

The air is already pungent with the odors of printing inks and tenement incinerators as Art steps gingerly over the gray slush in the curb and makes his way through a litter-filled alley alongside Rabinowitz and then up the metal ramp that leads to the loading platform, which is gnarled and rusted from years of nudging by trucks.

"Mort, Tony, how you doing?" Art says in a flat voice as he hangs up his topcoat, hat and sports jacket in the office.

"OK, Artie. Hey, while I'm thinking of it, we need to get sixty-five samples of the Peerless job over to Fairfax," Tony says. "They want to see how those corners came out and play around with all that stuff that goes in the package."

"Freddie was supposed to have that out yesterday afternoon. When did they call, this morning already?" Art asks, his brows closer together.

"Freddie says he never saw them," Tony says, looking up again from the stock pages of the *Wall Street Journal*.

"All he has to do is look behind him. I pulled that pallet in there myself yesterday. OK, OK, I'll see Freddie in a couple minutes." Art makes himself a cup of instant coffee, takes one of the glazed doughnuts that are brought in for the office staff each morning and settles down behind his desk to read the morning paper, also paid for by Rabinowitz Diecutting.

The office at Rabinowitz, a quiet refuge that has been partitioned off from the noisy factory, has desks for eight people: Tony Napoli and Mort Stern, two of the owners; Sidney Stern, Mort's twenty-eight-year-old son; Miriam, an unmarried woman in her late forties or early fifties who is secretary/bookkeeper; a receptionist/switchboard operator; two salesmen; and Art, who is an estimator and the foreman for the second floor of the shop. Tony's brother, Angelo Napoli, is the third owner and serves as foreman on the first floor, where most of the machines are located. Angelo, in nineteenth-century sweatshop fashion, has his desk backed against a wall in the factory, raised off the cement floor so he can see to every corner and behind the low barriers that separate the workers.

Art is middle management at Rabinowitz—a long way from a bench worker, a longer way from ownership of this multimillion-dollar business. Rabinowitz, like most diecutting houses, does a variety of jobs, such as taking a printed page, mounting it on cardboard and trimming the edges or scoring lines. A March of Dimes counter display would be a good example of a diecutting job.

Most of the jobs in the shop are tedious and routine. Even the highest paid and most skilled men operate automatically or manually fed diecutting machines. An operator might work for weeks watching the same two lines being cut halfway through a cardboard backing so that the display will fold into thirds and stand upright once it reaches the store. Art knows that routine, for he once operated the machines and has now escaped them. He and other young men from poor, often immigrant homes did all the menial jobs years ago. Now the new low-paid workers are almost all Puerto Rican. Rabinowitz hires as few blacks as possible; Puerto Ricans are felt to be easier to handle and more productive. The higher-paid jobs—machine operators—are almost all held by whites.

It is not yet eight thirty when the first call of Art's working day comes in. "Art, pick up eighty," the switchboard operator calls over to him. Art answers with "Hello" and then listens for the better part of a minute, scribbling down figures and a rough sketch on a pad. "No, no, hold on, I can figure it for you right now. . . . When, by Thursday? Let me see if they have a free press for it. Hold on."

Art picks up the other phone on his desk.

"Angelo, Inkblot is on the phone and they have a small job, about five hundred pieces, that will need backing and trimming and they want it by Thursday. How do we look back there? Late Thursday? OK."

Art punches the Japanese-manufactured electronic adding machine on his desk.

"George, a small run like that will cost. Going to be about

22

fifty-five cents a unit, packaged and ready to go Thursday, late Thursday."

Art drums his fingers on the sports page and looks at the basketball box scores.

"I know it's high; I'm sorry. If you can get a better price, you'll break my heart, but I'll forgive you." He smiles and looks up toward the wall. "OK, I'll tell the guys in shipping to look for it. Get it right over here so we can get going."

Art swallows the rest of his coffee, leafs quickly through the rest of the paper, then walks out into the plant and up to the second floor. The ceilings and walls are like the hide of some huge, molting animal. Large, suspended clumps of peeling paint seem to defy gravity. Curds of dust and dirt as big as softballs dot the floor and collect near the walls. A dingy firehose hangs forlornly off its rack. Scraps of paper from today's and last week's work litter the floor.

Art is neatly, conservatively dressed and crisp from eight o'clock, when he arrives, until five, when he leaves. Today he is wearing a pale-green shirt, dark slacks and striped clip-on tie as he walks toward the work area. Most of the Puerto Rican work force is earning a fourth of Art's pay, but their clothes do not show it. Plastic, wet-look midi coats and fur-trimmed cloth coats hang along the peeling walls. The women wear wildly striped and printed blouses and color-coordinated slacks, or trim-fitting polyester double-knit midi-length dresses finished off with laced boots. The men, like the floor manager, Alex, wear silky shirts, dress slacks and patent leather shoes with silver- or gold-colored buckles. Compared with Art's relatively simple life, the low-paid workers live with, if not excitement, at least a good measure of upheaval. Alex, for instance, who is called "The Cat" because of his prowess with the "Kittens" he supervises and often dates, is twenty-six and has been married three times. The dark-skinned woman assembling displays is out on bail after killing her husband.

Alex speaks good Spanish and broken English, so he is Art's translator. Art calls Alex over to him and points out the bubbles that are showing up in the puppet displays that were worked on

23

yesterday. The displays look like a small stage, and later puppets will be added, giving the effect of a performance being under way.

"These can barely make it, so watch the girls closer. Check the glue machine every fifteen minutes to make sure the distribution is even. Even, yes?"

Alex nods and says nothing.

"And those other girls that are bundling the mailers; they're still fighting them. Set them up with weights, like I showed the girl on the end two weeks ago."

Alex smiles a toothy grin, showing that two of his front teeth are missing, punched out by a jealous husband unwilling to share his wife. The smile is a knowing one and one of respect. Art can see shortcuts, and he often shows workers how to tie the first bundle, put in the first staple, or oil a creaking machine.

Art leans against a cement pillar and lights a cigarette. Out here in the factory as well as in the office, he is known to be a quiet, calm person, never flustered or rattled. It is a rare occasion when Art erupts in the office; usually it happens if he feels his bosses are pushing him too hard or expecting him to cover up for mistakes that they or the shop people have made. But most of the time he accepts orders from Tony or Mort with an expressionless face and then goes to the second floor to see the job through. It would surprise many people at Rabinowitz's to find out what is going on beneath that seemingly expressionless surface.

ART: For openers, Mort is an idiot. He married Rabinowitz's daughter and got the business. If Tony and Angelo hadn't bought in, he'd be broke today. He alienates customers; he never gets new business; all he ever does in the office is talk about stupid things or make fun of his son. More than once I've walked out of that office when I was ready to tell him off. Tony has it but he's not really interested in the business; he loves the stock market. Angelo is the best of all three of them. You can ask him a question and get an answer. The other ones always want you to take all the responsibility but never share in the profits. I don't know how they stay in business. And the kid, Sidney—he couldn't care less. Business Administration degree so he has to cheat. A customer

24

ordered fifty thousand displays, and Sid marked the invoice fifty and sent them forty-five. You can't get away with stuff like that for long. They'll catch you. And these people are backward; they don't want to spend anything for new equipment. When pressure-sensitive tape came in they weren't interested. If I hadn't convinced them it was the coming thing, they wouldn't have done a thing. Now we do thousands of dollars of business with it.

Listen, who loves to go to work? I work here because I've got a house to support, a kid in college. I never had anybody pushing for me; I never had the chance to go to college. I never want my kids to say I wasn't behind them a hundred percent. I don't want them ending up like me. I've got a skill, but I got no education. These days you need education.

Today, Art spends the better part of the morning on the second floor, his refuge when few estimating calls come in. As noon approaches, he walks into the office and tells Miriam he'll have a ham and cheese sandwich for lunch. Another of the fringe benefits for the office force at Rabinowitz is a free lunch. Art recognizes that this gratuity also helps the company, as the lunch period is shortened and no one leaves the office and therefore they are available for business calls. Still, Art is proud of the fact that from the time he gets off the subway until he gets on at night he does not have to spend one cent at work. The company even buys his cigarettes.

Before Art arrived, Tony already had dialed a number and put a device on the telephone cradle. By punching a series of numbers on a keyboard he gets quotations on the fifteen stocks he owns. He writes the day's high and low prices on a sheet he keeps with bookkeeper's precision. He is a handsome man, about five years older than Art. Tony is tanned, having just returned from a week's vacation in the Caribbean; in another week he is going on a package tour of Israel, Turkey and Greece. The secretary, Miriam, acts as if he is a boy going to summer camp. "Here, you take this," she says, giving him a paper bag full of instant coffee packets. "They don't have it over there."

"Miriam, I got a week," Tony says. "Put them in the desk."

"And don't buy any of them goatskins, for Christ's sake," Mort Stern says as he paces around his desk, which is devoid of the papers that clutter the other desks. "They stink like hell every time it rains." He raises his heavy lids to show even more of his bloodshot eyes as he makes a whistling sound through his mustache. "Right, Sid? Stink like hell."

"Yeah," Sidney Stern replies. He has the same drowsy eyes as his father, but his clothes and appearance mark the generational change. Mort's hair is slicked down; Sid's is styled, fluffy and dry. Mort has on a white-on-white monogrammed shirt and wide silk tie; Sid, an expensive-looking knit shirt, open at the neck. Mort wears conservative gray trousers; Sid, blue herringbones with a flared bottom.

"You hear me, Sid?" Mort yells across the office.

"You want me to stand on my head?" Sid looks up angrily. "Goatskins stink in the rain. I heard you, I heard you."

The conversation in the office today, when it isn't about business, centers on subjects that either don't touch Art's life or are, to him, irrelevant. Miriam complains throughout the afternoon that there was too much mayonnaise on her sandwich. That morning she had complained about having her forearm bruised when one of the shop workers opened the office door too quickly. "It's just like your shin; it really hurts."

Tony calls his broker and in a louder-than-usual voice says he'll take the ten-point gain on Control Data and to sell the stock. In another telephone call he commiserates with a friend who caught a marlin in Mexico, left it behind and is now wondering if it looked better than the one he has mounted in his office. To still another friend he says, "Gamble, gamble, gamble, that's all they do on Paradise Island. After a day in the sun it beats drinking all night. Bored. They're all bored."

Angelo won $1,000 in the daily double over the weekend and had to have a relative collect it to avoid paying income taxes. Sid's mother calls to make sure he's keeping his apartment clean.

The only office conversation that has some bearing on Art Neumeyer's life is when Tony laments that his daughter won't return

26

to her home, also in Mohawk County, to teach when she graduates from American University. "Doing her practice teaching in a school where eighty-five percent of the kids are black," Tony says, shaking his head. "Don't know what kids are thinking of today. And she's going to work there, yet. She says coming back to Lonesome Hills would be a dead end." American University and blacks strike resonant chords: Martha wanted to go to American, but the family could not afford it; Martha has also talked about teaching "disadvantaged" students.

Art has tried to call Betty three times this morning, but the line was busy each time. He knows she is going visiting at the nursing home this afternoon and has not tried since lunch. The day has been slow, so Art has spent more time than usual in the shop. On one of his walks through the heavy machine area on the first floor he watches Frank Stepnovich replacing a gear on one of the huge presses. Frank pokes his head out from under the press with a distressed look on his face. It turns to a grin when he sees Art. "There's the best jogger in the business. Art, jog it and let's see if this thing holds." Art Neumeyer jumps onto the platform and punches the black button and releases. Punches and releases. For the first time today Art looks interested. It is a piece of machinery he knows well and respects; one like it deprived him of two fingers. An earlier model, just across the aisle, was the first imported to America, and Art was its first operator. Frank Stepnovich was its second. Frank Stepnovich started the same year Art did and now earns top money in the shop, $180 a week. Art left the machines behind and earns $300.

From four until five o'clock, Art sits in the office, alternately watching the clock, smoking and checking the shipping department on jobs that are supposed to be coming in or going out. At five o'clock a deep-throated buzzer sounds and, as if the electricity were cut off in the shop, all the machines simultaneously hum to a stop. The office staff assembles in moments and files out the door. Sidney switches on the new burglar alarm—the office has been robbed several times of business machines and petty cash—and is the last to leave. There is a grace period of a few minutes and then,

27

if the office is not cleared, the alarm will sound and lights will flash on. Art likes the new alarm. "No excuses to hang around; everybody gets the heck out of there."

With nods and some good-byes, the office people go their separate ways. There has been a detached feeling about the work they did throughout the day, and as they part it is almost with a sense of relief, as if they don't have to play at working any more. Art heads toward the subway, a box wrapped in heavy paper under his arm. The twelve puppets in the box are not his, yet he would not say he is stealing them. "It's one of the benefits you get when you're a boss," he would say if confronted. Art also brings in packages to be mailed, using the company's postage machine. That is not dishonest either. Dishonesty, to Art, is stealing from a person, not from a corporate entity. Freddie the shipping clerk stole from Burt the salesman, in Art's opinion. Burt had some personal mail, and he asked Freddie to mail it at the post office and tell him what it cost. Freddie used company postage but still charged Burt.

Art bypasses a commercial garbage truck that has fish heads and entrails oozing out of its maw and then walks by two men in ragged clothes—one of them white, one black—who are huddled against the side of a building, taking slugs out of wine bottles in brown paper bags. Art does not hurry for his train. If he hurried, he could catch the 5:11, but instead he takes his time and arrives early for the 5:24. That way, he gets a seat.

A Dacron tie and a wash sports jacket instead of cotton work clothes sticky with glue, a commuter train trip to a suburb instead of a subway ride to an apartment—Art Neumeyer has come a long way from the orphanage in which his mother had to place him when he was an infant, a long way from the days when he was a shop worker.

Art went back to live with his mother when he was eleven. He was basically a good boy, although through his teenage years he was often truant from school and was attracted to the dice and card games in the alleys of his neighborhood. Once he met Betty Santangelo and her family, he began to see what he really wanted for himself: to be a father, raise children and give them the attention and the material objects he had missed in his youth.

Art worked hard, sometimes at two jobs, to provide for his wife and children. He was proud when he was able to afford a three-and-a-half-room apartment in the city and to put flowered wallpaper in the kitchen for his Betty. Sometimes it seemed—as it still seems to him today—that although Betty was appreciative, she wanted more. But regardless of their differences, Art invested himself in their relationship and in his children—as no one had done for him. Then, just as the Neumeyers moved out of the city to Mariposa, the accident to his hand occurred that threatened to spoil their modest dream. The painful years that followed were the most difficult of Art's life, as he fought to convince himself he was still a man and that he could still provide for his family.

Art Neumeyer, dozing as he rides the train, is returning to a comfortable house, which proves he has not faltered in his climb up the economic ladder, and to a wife and family he has always been able to support. They mean more than bricks, grass or the "N" on his aluminum storm door; more than his status, his income. Permanence, a family—Art Neumeyer cherishes most what he was deprived of.

As the red Chevrolet pulls into the driveway at 97 Birchwood, Black Beauty, the Neumeyers' cocker spaniel, lets out a low whine and Betty knows her husband is home. Art opens the front door, reaches down to pet the dog, which is frantically wagging its tail, then goes up the stairs to kiss his wife. He balances his book on the post at the top of the stairs, takes off his coat and puts it in the closet. He then goes to the bedroom to remove his sports jacket and into the bathroom to wash for supper, which is already being put on the table.

"Where's Joanie?" he asks.

"She'll be right in; she's playing dolls with Cynthia and I told her to watch for the car," Betty replies. "I can't flush the toilets again, Artie; we've got to get somebody out for the septic system. This is ridiculous."

"Where's Richard?"

"Downstairs. I hope you say something to that kid; I spent an hour getting a spot of oil out—"

"I saw it. Did you tell your son?"

"He just shrugged it off."

Art goes to the top of the stairs. "Rich. Richard," he calls down.

"Is supper on yet?" comes a quiet voice from the lower level.

"This isn't Howard Johnson's." Art raises his voice a bit higher. "I want to talk to you about your dirty feet."

"Yeah, Mom told me already."

"Well?"

"So I'll take off my feet from now on."

Art's face is flushed. "You live here pretty cheap, so the least you can do is respect the carpets." There is silence on the lower level. "Well?"

"A guy at work has been living at home for three years, and he doesn't pay a cent. I'm not getting such a good deal."

"Rich, if you can find a better, cheaper place where you can live like a pig and ruin the carpets and leave your bed unmade, go right ahead."

Richard slowly walks up the stairs. "I might do that," he says in a low voice.

Just then Joan comes bursting through the door. "Cynthia's cat had four kittens last night and—"

"You're supposed to be helping with supper; now get in there and wash up and put the potatoes and beans on the table," Betty says, in a high voice brimming with impatience.

The smile leaves Joan's face. Her chin puckers up and her bottom lip covers the top lip in a pout.

The Neumeyer family gathers around the table in the dining area. Tonight, as during many evening meals in the past months, a strained silence is punctuated by bursts of conversation that lead nowhere or by questions that hang in the air, unanswered. Richard is central to the tension. Three months ago he was midway through his first semester at Mohawk Community College, majoring in farm management, when the slide began that would cause him to drop

30

out at the end of the semester. He was sick of school, he said, sick of the Mickey Mouse courses, and he wanted to go to work, get a decent car, maybe build a race car. Richard Neumeyer talks a lot about doing adventuresome things but often settles for less. When he left school he said he wanted to get a job with the telephone company or one of the utilities. "Something with security and good benefits," he said. "Then I'll build the car." Instead, he settled for a $2.25-an-hour job at the metal fabricating plant, a job with low pay and little future. A few nights a week he fills in as a short-order cook at a hamburger stand. His "hot car" is a lumbering black 1964 Chevrolet.

The meal is simple but one that Art likes and would be happy to eat nightly: salad and a casserole that Betty makes with spaghetti, bottled spaghetti sauce, grated cheddar cheese and ground beef.

"Pass the Italian," Art says, looking at his son.

Richard's eyes are on his empty plate. His feet twitch nervously below the table.

"Rich," his father says, his eyes opening wider, "the dressing; pass the Italian dressing."

The boy passes it without looking up.

Betty dishes up generous portions of the casserole for Art, Richard and herself and a half portion for Joan. "Art, you see in the paper where they found that body over in the marsh wrapped in a plastic sheet?" she says. "Ugly. Young girl, too."

"So what about the septic tank?" Art says. "I just put those chemicals in there and it was working fine. The Roto-Rooter man ain't going to help anything. Let's just see if it settles down by tomorrow."

"Tomorrow!" Betty says, her voice high-pitched. "I've got two days' washing backed up. You want me to walk down to the laundromat?"

"Honey, we'll just wear the clothes again," Art says, smiling across the table.

"Don't be funny." Betty digs into the mound of casserole. "I'll be happy when they get the sewers put in."

"And when the taxes go up and the roads are all torn up."

"Anything is better than this."

31

"That taillight is still out on your car," Art says, looking at Richard. "You're going to get another ticket. So get it fixed."

"Yeah, right," Richard says, rearranging the casserole on his plate but eating little of it.

As Betty and Joan clear the table, Richard gets up to go downstairs. Most of his portion of the casserole is still on his plate.

"Where're you going?" his father calls after him.

"No place. Anyplace. Out."

Richard throws himself on the bed in his pine-paneled room. Posters of motorcycles (one mounted by a scantily clad Brigitte Bardot), racing cars and high-performance cams, pistons and spark plugs cover the walls. On shelves, there is an odd assortment of items: empty champagne, Bufferin and Excedrin bottles; plastic models of an aircraft carrier and a tank; a book on poultry raising. Inconspicuously tacked to the cork bulletin board between scotch- and bourbon-flavored chewing gum wrappers is a card from the Alcan Speedway with two sets of numbers. It bears yesterday's date and marks Richard's first drag race.

RICHARD: Sure, my old man would go crazy, but I just had to do it. My damn Chevy dropped out of gear about half down the stretch, or else I would have won my heat. It's a pig anyhow. A piece of shit. Christ, what a feeling when those yellow lights flash and then you get the green and you stomp down on it and squeal like hell! All my old man can think about is, the insurance don't cover me out there.

Driving me crazy around here. I got to split. Get the hell out of this town and away from them. Can't do nothing. Always complaining I don't make my bed or my feet are dirty. That's all shit, man. If that's where your head is at, you're all fucked up.

A few minutes later Richard gets up suddenly, turns off the stereo, cutting off John McLaughlin in the middle of side two of "Devotion," pulls on a jacket and leaves the room. He says nothing to his parents, who are in the living room. Richard Neumeyer is on his way to the Burger Joint to have a hamburger that is bad for his complexion and budget, and then to spend the rest of the evening at the Gulf station, fully aware he is wasting time.

Betty finishes putting dishes into the dishwasher and is ready to pour detergent into the receptacle when Art walks into the kitchen. "Can't do it, babe. The septic tank is out to lunch."

"This house," she says, waving her hand in the air. "What's with that kid, anyhow? Never seen him this antsy."

"Just thinking about himself. I got to get going; we'll talk about it later."

"Maybe it's Martha coming home for Easter. He always feels she's hot spit and he's nothing when she comes home."

"She's not coming for over a month, Betty."

"Yeah, but Christmas was the worst."

"If he pulls that running-away business again, he's . . . he's . . ."

"He's what?"

"I'll be late for bowling."

A few minutes later, Art is in his car on the way to Strike and and Spare Lanes. And Betty is dialing her mother, who lives a few miles away, for their nightly talk.

As Art goes down to the locker room at the bowling alley to get his ball and change shoes, many of the thirty-two lanes are in use. There is open bowling before the leagues start. Then, as the hour for league competition nears, the men with the blue and red and yellow shirts with this electric company or that construction company emblazoned on their backs take over the lanes. The pins are poised in the racks and the lanes free so the bowlers can take practice throws.

On the wall behind the bowlers, in color photographs, are the Hall of Fame members, men who have had a 300 game or a 700 series. The pose is always the same—it could be the same picture with the heads interchangeable—the eyes riveted ahead, the arm straight down and the ball just touching the polished wood, ready to plummet down the alley and ravage the pins. As the league bowlers toil away, Art, a 148-average man, among them, these, the immortals, gaze past them down the alleys.

Art's team is backed by Rabinowitz Diecutting, although he is the only member who works for the company. Rabinowitz, currently in fifth place in the sixteen-team league, tonight faces the number-two team, Rod's Meat Market.

"Gentlemen, the league competition begins now." A voice booms over the PA system. "Good luck. In commemoration of Washington's Birthday we're using cherrywood pins tonight."

"I don't need that kind of shit; let's go! Who's up?" The speaker is a man in his mid-thirties with a Vandyke beard, hair neatly trimmed with a boxed cut in back, and the beginning of a paunch that presses against his sweatshirt. He wears a black glove on his right hand and fingers a black cigar or fondles a towel, endlessly drying off a hand already encased in a glove. He holds a 168 average and carries himself as if it were at lot higher.

"This damn lane always goes uphill; play for it, Sam," one of Rod's Meat Market men says. "And the slide, jerky as hell."

Art is not one to engage in much talk about the quality of the lanes, the resiliency of the pins or the lighting. As he told Betty last Monday, "It's a lot of crap. Like anything else, when things go bad you look for all kinds of excuses and never look at yourself. I just like to have a good time, get a little exercise, not take it too seriously. Relax."

As the men slide up to the foul line and release their balls, it isn't necessary to watch how many pins go down. The experienced bowler's face reads like a score sheet. The man with the black glove is a good example. If he leaves many pins or a bad split, he comes back after his first ball with eyes downcast or with a tortured look on his face. Or he will grab for his rag as if the ball had slipped or will give a practice slide near the foul line as if his approach had been thrown off by a tacky spot. A strike or a tough-won spare brings him to the bench with shoulders thrust back and eyes fixed on the score table or on the wall, the Hall of Fame. Picking up a habit that originated with black athletes, team members enthusiastically give him a palm-to-palm "soul slap."

Art's bowling style is simple, mostly because his right hand contains only a thumb and the two last fingers and is therefore weaker. He starts closer to the foul line than most bowlers, takes four quick, almost feminine, mincing steps and releases the ball. There is no spin on the ball as it rolls toward the pins at about three quarters the speed of faster bowlers, no curve that gives a ball and the pins it strikes what bowlers call "action." Tonight Art bowls three pins over his average the first game, but the men from Rod's have a 792 series, beating Rabinowitz by 61 pins. Six of the possible seven points for that game in league competition go to Rod's.

"They'll never hold it up, never, never," says Frederick, a dentist with wild eyes and curly red hair, who is a member of Art's team.

"The big boys can't keep going under the pressure; we'll wear 'em down," says Dave Bismark, a pipe-smoking draftsman who is a member of Art's church. The fourth team member, Bill, is a quiet but muscular construction worker who, like Art, bowls without running commentary.

"Fred really a dentist?" Art asks Dave. "I find that hard to believe. He acts like a kid out there. Who cares that much?"

"I do," Dave says somberly. "It's money we're after."

Between turns in the second game, Art goes to the men's room. Two players from other teams sandwich him in, using the urinals on either side. Their conversation goes through him as if the urinal were unoccupied.

"Going into the beer frame and I always have to take a pee."

"Pick up moisture on the floor in here. Hangs you up, and there goes the frame."

"Saw in the pro's shop they have these slippers you wear into the john to keep your soles dry."

"How much?"

"Hell of an idea, no?"

Bowling is Art's only form of recreation and his major personal expense during the week. He pays 75 cents for each of the three games plus $1.60 that goes into a kitty that is divided at the end of the season. Players from the lowest team get $13 each and the number-one team's members each receive $150. Trophies also come out of the kitty money, so the men who bowl at Strike and Spare Lanes largely subsidize their own money prizes and pay for the trophies that are in turn awarded to them. Rabinowitz and other team backers also contribute to the kitty and buy shirts for their team members.

Just before nine o'clock the men of the Rabinowitz Diecutting team walk out the door toward their cars. Frederick, the dentist, has a knowing smirk on his face. "Didn't I tell you, did I not tell you?" he says to no one in particular. "The big boys never hold up." Rod's Meat Market faltered in the second and third games and ended up losing most of the remaining points and finishing 47 pins down, 2,192–2,145.

Art Neumeyer is tired when he gets home, and it is only the first day of the week. There will be four more mornings to face before the weekend. He knows Betty has not been sleeping well for the past few weeks, and when she doesn't sleep she usually wakes her husband. At eleven thirty, as Art is finally falling into a deep sleep, he feels the familiar hand on his back.

"Artie, did we push Rich too hard? What did we do wrong?"

Art groans and rolls over. "Nothing," he breathes.

"Did we make him feel he couldn't do right? Did we keep on comparing him with Martha?"

"He'll grow out of it."

"Artie, what's going to happen to the boy? I have terrible thoughts."

"Tell him to keep Randy Short out of here too. Greasy shoes."

"No, Artie, no!" She is almost pleading with him. "That will push him further away."

"And he's making plenty," Art says, now more awake. "Two jobs. His rent goes up five bucks next week. I'm putting some carpeting in his room and he's paying for it."

"Not now. This isn't the time."

"Tomorrow. Now I want to sleep. And no more arguments about him at the table. It's bad for Joan."

Betty is silent, and Art slips off to sleep a few minutes later. But for Betty, sleep is still an hour and a half away.

2

Nobody Listens

TWO DAYS LATER, on Wednesday morning, Betty Neumeyer sits at her gray Formica kitchen table, staring blankly at a plate of scrambled eggs that are turning light orange at the edges. It is already nine thirty, and by this time Betty usually has her kitchen in order and is about her other duties. Today, there is nothing pressing to do—some cleaning, three loads of wash, a few telephone calls on church business, an evening meal to prepare, a meeting tonight at the church—but Betty is not immobilized because of her light day. She has many of them, and she has learned to fill them.

She looks down at her hands, smooth, almost childlike, pink and plump. She closes her eyes so tightly the lids wrinkle as she recalls last night. Peeved by a new oil smudge on the linoleum and by Richard's surly attitude in general, Art made good on his promise. He told his son that room and board were going from $10 to $15 a week.

Richard blew up. "I didn't ask for that carpet and I didn't ask for all the hassles," he said.

"If you don't like the conditions here, find someplace better," his father retorted.

"I just might: California!" the boy said, and stomped out of the house.

This morning Betty prepared Richard's favorite breakfast—scrambled eggs and English muffins—and called down the stairs that his breakfast was ready. When he came upstairs he looked at the table set for him, mumbled, "I'm not hungry," scooped the muffins off the plate with his gloved hand and was out the door without another word.

Betty's eyes move to the clock. It is now nine forty-five. A scowl covers her face. "Damn kids," she says out loud. She suddenly gets up, takes the plate off the table and moves toward the plastic garbage basket. Black Beauty wags her tail expectantly and gives a guttural whine.

"Shut up, you. You're not getting anything," Betty says as she dumps the eggs into the basket.

She snatches the phone off the cradle, dials, and when the answering party has only said, "Good morning, this is—" Betty interrupts.

"I'm sitting here with toilets running over every time I flush, a dishwasher I can't use; when in the hell is the man coming out? . . . Name? My name is Neumeyer. . . . His first stop, huh? Well, it's ten o'clock; what time do you people start your day over there? Listen, if he's not here by noon, you'll be hearing from me."

Betty plunges her hands into the pockets of her cotton housecoat and heads for the bedroom to change. In a few minutes, dressed in polyester knit slacks and a cotton blouse, she has wheeled out the vacuum cleaner. She looks at the clock again and reaches for the telephone. "Lil," she says after a moment's pause, "what's going on over there this morning? I need some inspiration."

The call is to Lillian Rose, whom Betty considers one of her closer friends and who has teenagers of her own. Lillian's daughter, Phoebe, has even been out with Richard several times.

"Oh, nothing special," Betty says when asked why her voice is so low. "The diet," she says abruptly. "I'm on Dr. Stillman's. Had bouillon for lunch all week, nothing for breakfast, no desserts for three days—I haven't dropped an ounce. Even at Couples Club I passed by the lemon meringue pie. I'm hopeless. But like Artie says, more of me to love."

Betty listens to Lillian and smiles, her first smile of the day. Both Art and Betty were slim when they married in 1950, and while her husband has not gained a pound, Betty has put on quite a few—how many, no one but Betty knows, because she always closes the bathroom door when she weighs herself. Betty is just over five feet tall, heavy in the thighs and arms and ample-breasted, a broad-shouldered, stocky woman but not flabby fat. As Art's look is typically stern, Betty's is typically what it is right now: a smile so broad that the crows'-feet deepen at the corners of her eyes. Her lips part, showing that one front tooth is missing on the bottom jaw and there is a larger space on the top jaw, farther back, where two teeth have been removed. Her skin is pale and smooth, her forehead high. She wears her dark brown hair in a short, lightly curled style that she can set herself, although she prefers to pay $5 a week for a wash and set at Jo's Beauty Parlor. That week is almost over and the hair closest to her neck is straight, having drooped from the rows of curls that Jo arranged masterfully last Thursday.

"You devil," she says to Lillian, "always sex on your mind. He said more of me to love, not more often. OK, got to get going and get on the Roto-Rooter guy. Lot of stuff to do today."

Betty walks to the front window. A breeze swirls and rearranges the light snow that fell last night, uncovering some of the hopscotch lines Art painted on the driveway. The sapling he planted two years ago on the front lawn sways gently as Betty's eyes move up and down the street. There is no one in sight. The snow on the sidewalks is undisturbed. Only tire tracks show there has been some movement on the street.

Betty goes toward her vacuum cleaner, but the ring of the telephone diverts her. At noon when the man comes to work on the cesspool problem the vacuum cleaner still stands untouched. One call was from Doris, a friend who owns a card shop. Business was slow and she had time. Another call was from Bea, a member of their church, Parkside United Methodist, who wanted to make sure the board meeting was tonight. Art called but the conversation was short; both he and Betty were concerned about Richard but neither had much more to say about him. Betty told Art she wanted to get a job. Art said she didn't have to and that she should enjoy herself at home, that she has earned it.

As Betty sits with her cup of bouillon, she hears the repairman coming up from the basement. "Mrs. Neumeyer? OK, all done. Some kind of blockage in there, but it's clear now. I'd be careful what I flush down there. You know, women's things"—he falters —"those napkins and stuff."

"Clear now." Betty huffs. "Had to wait long enough for you people. We hardly even flush water down; don't worry about it."

"OK," he says as if he didn't hear her. "Here's the bill. Call us if anything goes wrong."

"Call and wait a week. You tied up my whole morning."

Finally, at one o'clock, with her first load of washing in the machine, Betty Neumeyer begins her vacuuming, which is a twice-weekly routine. She runs the Hoover across the olive-green rug and, except for the nap being brought up by the suction, the rug looks little different. Betty Neumeyer's house never really gets dirty.

Her off-white living room walls and baseboards are free from any marks and look freshly painted. The furniture is uniformly Italian Provincial, with its characteristic straight square legs, tightly tufted backs and shiny nylon fabric. The sofa is a two-tone brocade, a dark aqua on forest green. In front of it sits the coffee table with two thin pieces of marble embedded on either side of a portion of dull-finished fruitwood. In the dining area, which is an extension of the living room, an Italian Provincial table, also fruitwood-veneered, and six chairs stand in front of a breakfront cabinet. Behind the glass and the web of metal that decorates it are Betty's collector's items: fancy painted plates, teacups and saucers, some crystal, and a set of china which Betty's mother bought at Purdue's Variety Store but which is only used on special occasions.

Betty is proud of her furniture, which was purchased during various warehouse sales and paid for in cash. She is proud of the $700 piano they were able to buy for Joan two years ago and proud of her "distinctive touches"—an antique-style but newly manufactured hurricane lamp with a green base Art bought for her, and a hanging lamp with a gilded pattern of leaves and flowers over a frosted white globe. Because she cannot drive, she cannot leave the house today, but its furnishings and layout—three bedrooms up and one bedroom down, recreation room on the lower level, one and a half baths—are what she wanted in her "dream house," and they offer at least some silent satisfaction to her.

Her vacuuming and dusting completed, the first wash in the dryer and a second sloshing in the machine, Betty is ready for the next part of her day. There are two slips of paper on the glistening countertop in the kitchen. One is a list of chores for Art to do on this and forthcoming Saturdays. Betty picks up the other list and telephones Pastor Firth MacIntosh at the church. Once he answers she begins to check off the items.

"The women's society is going to have a Passover luncheon and we need a bulletin printed," she says. "You can follow last year's; it'll be the same. And how about a short sermon?"

"Check, Betty," he replies.

"Is there still enough grape juice and did we get the communion cloths laundered?"

"I'll find out."

"That chorus is going to have the concert during Easter vacation. Flyers have to be printed to make sure people know it's going to be here."

"Check, Betty."

"Twenty-five church members have to be found who will take two of the chorus members overnight. Better put it in the bulletin."

"Check, Betty."

"We always have a church dinner the night of the concert. Nobody's thinking about it and getting prepared."

"OK, Betty." The pastor begins to laugh. "Got my work cut out for me," he says. "Let me get off here and moving."

Her friends rib her, Art ribs her, the pastor ribs her; they all say Betty is an overorganizer. She likes to plan—church dinners, services, a Saturday's work for her husband—right down to the finest detail, and she doesn't like her plans to go awry. She often overorchestrates minor events in her own life, and when they don't proceed according to plan she gets angry. As one of her friends confides, "I just don't have the kind of time Betty has, so I

41

do the best I can and let the cards fall where they may. It's just not worth it getting worked up over all the trivia. But Betty's one of those people who love the trivia."

For Betty there is a time and place for things and people. Meals must start on time. Groceries must be shopped for on the same night each week. Black Beauty must come no farther than the top step of the stairs because Betty hates to see the dog's long black hairs on the living room rug. Meetings must be scheduled at least a week in advance, preferably longer. For instance, this week on the wall calendar in the kitchen and on her purse calendar there are three commitments which were made last month. Yesterday at ten she helped clean the church kitchen. Tonight at eight the trustees meet. Friday at eight thirty the Neumeyers are going to the Dupreys for drinks and a snack.

Many of Betty's friends from the church now have part- or full-time jobs or are involved in volunteer work or social clubs; still others play bridge or golf several times a week to fill their time. Betty does not want to have to ask for rides, so she devotes most of her out-of-house time to the church, where rides are available for willing workers. Although Betty has talked about getting a job, she has never done anything about it, most often citing transportation and then her own lack of skills as the reasons. She occasionally works for a woman who does catering, earning $30 for a six- to eight-hour day. Another woman, who gives dinner parties, calls upon Betty to help serve and pays her $3.50 an hour.

Betty is not one to constantly bemoan her state; when she and Art sit down and reflect on where they both came from and where they are today—without arguing about it—Betty admits she is living in undreamed-of luxury.

Betty's early life revolved around Anthony Santangelo, her father, who in an afternoon at the track could gamble away a week's profits from his fruit and vegetable stand, and her mother, Joan, who was oblivious to the family's precarious situation. Her father could laugh off a stack of overdue bills, but as Betty grew up she soon found that was not her nature. She liked secure, sure things.

42

Her adolescence was marred by rheumatic fever, a long recovery period and then a continuing stream of prohibitions—"Betty, you can't do that"—so by the time she was out of high school, Betty was all the more sure of what she would do. It would be something no one could ever deprive her of. She would marry; she would have children.

Marriage to Art Neumeyer signaled the beginning of the secure life she had always wanted. Children were conceived who were to be raised in that security, and who would in turn, Betty was sure, love and respect her for her sacrifices and concern.

For Betty, the golden age of the Neumeyer family was lived out in the house she called a crackerbox on Tulip Lane, a house far simpler and less prestigious than the one at 97 Birchwood Street. On Tulip she was busy and happy as the full-time mother of a growing family. It almost seems that the move to this house marked the end of that golden age. The two older children have grown into assertive teenagers; even more painful are the questions she has begun to have about what she is going to do with the rest of her life—when she no longer has children to occupy her. Although her husband now makes $15,000 a year, she lives in a house in The Knolls, and they have the income to buy steak instead of tuna fish, material success has not enhanced Betty in the roles—wife and mother—she so eagerly courted and cultivated.

It is after two o'clock when the phone sounds again at 97 Birchwood. Betty picks up the extension in Richard's room. "Oh, Francine, I was just thinking of you. I was going to call you this afternoon."

"What's going on over there?" says Francine, a woman in her mid-thirties who is Betty's youngest close married friend. "That damn 'Search for Tomorrow'; I've got to be hooked on it."

Betty closes her eyes, then opens them quickly and shakes her head. "Shows you what kind of day this has been," she says with exasperation in her voice. "Missed it. Richard is just driving me—"

"Speaking of kids, did you hear that Boris and Pat Morton's boy is out West someplace, traveling around with some girl? Why don't he marry her if he thinks so much about her?"

43

"Kids aren't like we were—like Artie and me anyhow. It's the new style. Easy sex. Darn Richie wants to—"

"Boris won't let them sleep in the house when they swing through, and I wouldn't either."

"Just wait till yours get older. You'll have to roll with the punches or let ulcers eat your stomach out."

"You mean if Martha brought a boy back from school, you'd let them sleep together?"

"I should be so lucky she'd bring a boy home and *want* to sleep with him," Betty says, affecting the Yiddish accent she learned in her city neighborhood. "I'd make the bed for them!"

There is hearty laughter on both ends of the line. Francine catches her breath and says, "Just be glad you got good kids."

The smile that came quickly to Betty's face leaves just as quickly.

After putting in her third load of wash Betty wanders into the recreation room and looks out into the back yard, where a light, freezing rain has begun to fall. A good-sized locust tree was uprooted by high winds last summer, and the trunk and bare roots lie forlornly on the ground, looking like some wounded animal.

She walks up the stairs, hesitating on each one as if she were out of breath. In the front room she goes to the window and looks out onto the street. There is still no one in sight. Her eyes scan the houses; she knows the names of the people who live in them, but not the people themselves. For the most part they are professionals: a teacher, an engineer, a television reporter. On Tulip Lane, a college degree was a rarity; here it is common. On Tulip Lane, visits by neighbors were common; here they never occur. On Tulip Lane, there was a community of struggling young families; here, people keep to themselves. As Betty Neumeyer stares out the window, many thoughts run through her mind.

BETTY: If I were only closer to the library, I could have new books every week. Take my mind off things. But it's a mile walk, a bus ride to and from, and another mile walk home. Maybe I should go to work. Then everybody around here would have to pick up the slack. They'd learn all the things I do for them. They take so much for granted. I'm the damn slave. Right now I'm

44

supposed to be calling the Camp Fire leader to tell her Joan wants seven boxes of mints and fourteen of pecan clusters. Supposed to check on Richie's loan at the bank. Martha wants us to send her Reese's Peanut Butter Cups. They only care about themselves.

But how would I get to work and who would want me anyhow? Even the department stores out here have their pick of women; they want experience and I don't have it. I came home to an empty apartment when I was Joan's age. I don't want her home alone; that's where trouble starts. There are all kinds of perverts around, too. The waitress jobs I had turned out to be boring and just hard work. I'd really like to open up my own gift shop. I could just visit with people all day and sell pretty scented candles and cards with nice verses and little knickknacks. Artie tells me I'm crazy; we don't have the money to start something like that, and besides, Ben and Doris are going broke with her gift shop.

Sometimes I think I married a jerk. Artie will never let me amount to anything; he's really against me working. Even in the city where there were baby-sitters all over he never would let me work, and we needed the money then too. He wants to bring in the money; that means a lot to him, to his manhood. But we're never going to get any further than we are right now. He never pushed hard enough. I know Martha won't be as dumb as me; she'll get what she wants out of marriage.

Marriage. How sweet that sounds. Artie had the cigars with "It's a boy" even before I went to the hospital for Rich. When he came to visit me he brought a football for his son. Why do we have to have all this friction? How can that kid just quit school and take a crummy job? And now all this talk about leaving. I could cry all day long if I thought about it.

The ring of the telephone jars Betty out of her reverie. It is Mary, another woman from the church. Midway through the conversation Betty says abruptly, "And Pastor is going to miss the appetizer round of the progressive dinner. Has a wedding rehearsal. Now we have to rearrange the whole thing."

Betty listens, then replies irately, "Well, it *is* a big deal. Now I have to shuffle the Dupreys around because they were the fifth couple and the MacDonalds will only have three. People are planning for an exact number; you just can't go changing things at the last minute."

She listens again and rolls her eyes to the ceiling. "I know when it is. I just hate all these last-minute changes. Anyhow, I still have your Corning Ware from a couple Sundays ago. . . ." The conversation momentarily revolves around the Corning Ware: how much it costs, how good it is, how clean it can be kept.

Later, the talk turns to Martha. "I bought her a lavender nightie at Stephen's last night. Going to give it to her at Easter, but it's for her birthday. Mark loves lavender." Betty listens. "Oh, I don't know; one day they're in love and Martha thinks it's the real thing, then she calls and cries and says it's all over. That kid. She couldn't fall in love if she wanted to. She probably opens car doors for him."

There are two other calls this afternoon. The one made by Betty brings Pam Brown over for a late-afternoon cup of tea. Betty's old neighbor, who still lives on Tulip Lane, stops by at least weekly. By the time Pam gets there, Betty has prepared potatoes for baking, washed fresh broccoli, gotten a package of buttered frozen corn from the freezer in the garage and laid out pork chops that she will broil. Also she has spent a few minutes with Joan, who rushed home from school, changed into her Camp Fire uniform and was off. But not before Betty unrolled the top of Joan's skirt, which she had hiked up to mini-length. "Enough time for that," Betty admonished her. "Don't look cheap, honey. Boys will like you better if your behind isn't showing."

Pam Brown is one of Betty's closest friends. They lived across from one another on Tulip Lane, walked their children to school, spent endless hours at one another's kitchen tables. Betty flits from Penney's sales to the cost of ground beef to the threatened strike on the commuter line and then drops what she thinks is a bombshell into the meandering conversation. "Richie's at it. He's always talked about going to California. I think he's serious this time."

Pam reaches for the sugar. "What kind of tea is this anyhow? Kind of bitter. Gerard just got another raise; that kid'll be making more than his father soon."

Betty looks down at her cup and asks glumly, "What is it again that he's in?"

"Steamfitters."

"Bet they have good benefits and retirement."

"The best."

"Artie should have it so good," Betty says, her voice trailing off.

"I don't know what I'm going to do about Sylvia's wedding. Already they're booking for next year and she can't set the date. One year goes like *pfffttt!* Kids don't realize about invitations and showers and fittings and cakes and all."

"Yeah." Betty hesitates. "Martha should only be planning to get married."

"Betty, plan it way in advance. It's a chore."

"Yeah," Betty says, looking down at her empty cup. "You never know what Richie might run into if he goes. What kind of people. While he's at home, at least—"

Pam interrupts. "Oh, my God. It's five thirty and I got to start supper."

"Yeah, I gotta get moving too," Betty says listlessly.

This night Art Neumeyer comes home from work to find his dinner ready but his son gone. Richard showered, changed clothes and was out the front door in less than an hour, saying no more than "Hi" and "Good-bye." Richard is not mentioned at the table, but after dinner, with Joan in Martha's bedroom watching television, Art asks where his son is.

"I'm not the FBI, how am I supposed to know?" Betty says irately.

"You were home, that's how," Art answers back angrily. "Didn't you ask him where he was going?"

"I'm supposed to do everything around here, and I'm sick of it!" Betty's anger is turning to frustration.

"Can't we ask your son where he's going, or will that offend him?" Art says in a mocking tone.

Betty purses her lips. "Don't give me that 'your son' business!"

"Quiet, Joan will hear."

"Let the whole damn neighborhood hear; I'm sick of it!"

"Shut up!" Art shouts.

"You shut up!" Betty shouts back. "I'm late. My meeting is at eight." She goes into the bedroom.

Twenty minutes of relative silence follow in the Neumeyer house, the only sound coming from "I Dream of Jeannie," which Joan is watching on television. When Lillian picks Betty up twenty minutes later, Art is in the basement and they do not bid each other good-bye.

Lillian and Betty find they also have little to say as they drive to the church for the monthly meeting of the Board of Trustees of Parkside United Methodist. The board, which up until recent years was all-male, now has three female members. Because of decreasing church membership, many vacancies had to be filled by women or not filled at all. Tonight, seven of the nine trustees are at the meeting; missing are Percy Martin and Benjamin Morris, the church's only male black member. It is held in the church's "library," a Sunday school room that has three open cases and perhaps five hundred books. Most are solid, older, biblical books, but a few contemporary ones such as *Open Marriage* and *I'm OK— You're OK* are on the shelves.

"Pastor went to the pulpit Sunday to turn on the amplifier, reached down and found it was gone," the chairman begins. "Somebody cut the wires and lifted it right out. OK, what's your pleasure?"

"We have to get a whole set of locks—dead bolts—and isolate the narthex," says one of the men. "Amplifier, two microphones —what else this year?"

"They stole the Bible one week," a woman says.

"Don't forget the cross was stolen, too," Betty says.

"The only way we'll stop it is with guards and dogs," another man says, looking serious.

"The guards we can house-train but I don't know about the dogs," the chairman says. A soft corporate chuckle fills the room.

"If kids come into a *church* and do this, what about private homes?" a man says. "Nothing's sacred any more. Just like when

48

my daughter was growing squash last summer. She was watching it every day, coming up little by little, and then when it looked like it was ready to be picked, somebody came in and ripped out vines and all. And I even got a cyclone fence around my place. Felt like electrifying it."

"These AA people and Al-Anon; they're always leaving doors open," Lillian says. "They've got to be told to shape up or get out. What are we running here, a hall or a church?"

The chairman begins to speak, but Betty overrides him with her high, firm tone. "Why don't we just get a new set of keys and start controlling who gets them? Nobody gets a key who doesn't have a good reason."

The meeting goes on for two hours. At its completion, the amplifier crisis has not been solved. And, with a small congregation and a full-voiced pastor, the immediate need might be questioned anyhow. A rash of other problems, from short-legged tables to unused rooms, have been brought up. One of the last items concerns the appearance of the sanctuary, which has not been painted for ten years.

"Well, I don't like to point any fingers because Benjamin isn't here tonight," Lillian says, her eyes cast down, "but he let the finance committee get that paint amortization fund."

"Now, if we want to get it painted, we have to go for the money on our hands and knees," the chairman adds.

"It's just typical," Betty whispers to Lillian but says no more. Lillian knows the "typical" means "typical of black people." There are many people at Parkside who have their problems dealing with the Morrises, but Betty and Art Neumeyer carry additional psychic baggage. The Morrises' son, Len, dated Martha. That relationship caused a months-long crisis at 97 Birchwood.

The meeting ends in a flurry of dirty choir robes and groups that use upstairs rooms when they are assigned downstairs. On the way home Betty turns to Lillian and says, "Those damn men always criticize us for being the talkers; I thought we'd never get out of there."

"Umm." Lillian nods her head.

"I think Richie's serious about leaving this time."

"Umm." Lillian nods her head again. "God, it's late."

Once home, Betty makes her way to the bedroom and opens the door. With the light from the hall she can see the outline of her husband's sleeping body. "Artie," she whispers. Then louder, "Artie, you awake?"

Her husband does not move.

"Artie?" she says even louder.

Art Neumeyer does not move, so Betty eventually goes into the bathroom to wash for bed. She has been trying to talk about Richard all day, but nobody has listened.

3

"When You're Crippled Inside"

A WEEK LATER, the Neumeyers are at dinner. Art, sipping on a glass of inexpensive white wine that he often has with his evening meal, looks at his son. Richard is drinking a can of beer but not eating. "With two jobs you ought to be buying some of the beer, Rich; you got more money in the bank than I do," he says good-naturedly, trying to smile.

Betty looks at her husband nervously and motions to him quickly before her son can see her. "More salad, Richie? The lettuce was good today."

Her son shakes his head. His salad plate is still full.

"And a couple of things about the room, Rich," Art says in an even voice. "Black Beauty is digging in that new rug, so you better close the door. And you haven't been turning down the heat when you leave. Try to cooperate, OK?"

"It's cold as hell down there," Richard says quietly as he taps his fingers on his knee.

"Don't be smart with the cursing and everything; your sister is at the table," Art says, his voice louder.

Richard Neumeyer almost falls over backward as he slides his chair away from the table. "You won't have to be worrying about anything soon. I'm splitting." He almost runs to his room.

"Splitting?" His father calls after him. "What's this splitting business?" There is no sound for a few moments, then Richard dashes up the stairs and opens the front door as his father continues. "Hold on! Where do you think—"

"That's it. I'm not taking it any more." Richard's words tumble out of his mouth. "Man, I'm getting out of here as soon as I can . . . soon as I get my shit together." The slam of the front door closes the interchange between father and son.

Joan and Betty sit quietly at the table as Art comes back and sits down. "Let's everybody eat. Forget about it and eat," he says.

"I think he means it, Daddy." Joan breaks the stillness and then quickly stuffs a forkful of food into her mouth.

"I think he does too," Betty says somberly.

"Let's eat, please," Art says. Then, after a hesitation, "You might be right."

It has been a tense week, a week of avoidance in the Neumeyer household. Art and Betty made up the day after their shouting match and promised each other not to bother Richard. What followed was a week of uncomfortable silences, uncomfortable smiles from Betty and Art. For Joan it has plainly been confusing. Her parents, who once were so easily set off by her brother, seem not to see him at all. As Joan lays the fork on her plate tonight and props up her chin with her two hands, her look is vacant as she stares across the living room to the tufted back of the brocade couch.

The snow tires on Richard's black Chevrolet bite at the gravel in front of the Neumeyer house and send stones pinging against the trees. The tires hit the asphalt and there is a loud squeal. Two black streaks, each a few yards long, mark his departure. Richard picks up his friend, Ron Bronowski, and a few minutes later they are hurtling down one of the Mohawk County expressways.

"Fucking jig rig won't get over fifty without wobbling," he calls over to Ron, a serene-looking boy with wire-rim glasses and blond hair cut in Dutch-boy style.

"You just missed the turnoff," Ron says calmly.

"Yeah, I'll catch the next one. Man, I need a joint. You got any stuff left?"

"Naw, you?"

"Shit, man, I've been supplying us forever. Naw, I'm out, but I got some schnapps under the seat. Pop me one."

Ron reaches under the quilted, plastic-covered seat and fishes out two cans of Colt 45.

"Good and cold, man; this car is a traveling refrigerator. Hey, how about going to California with me, Ron? Gonna go in a couple days. As soon as I can get my shit together."

"How you going?"

"Hitch, man, down through the South; it's hot as hell down there now. Or else up through Kansas and see Martha."

"I would, but things are pretty bad at home now."

"Come on, man, blow that stuff off."

"When your old man splits after thirty years and your old lady is ready for a nervous breakdown, you just don't blow it off."

"The hell with it. We're still going to Colombia with that guy you work with, right?"

"Yeah, this summer sometime."

Richard and Ron turn into a sprawling parking lot that serves Stephen's Department Store and the small shops that cluster around it.

Richard walks toward Barry's Drugstore in the jerky gait that is much like his father's. He is thin like his father, weighing perhaps 130 pounds. He is his father's height and has inherited his complexion. Through diet and dermatology, the acne has been battled, but the reddish blotches on his face, the fresh swelling on his neck that will soon be a painful boil, show that Richard is losing for now. But even with his bad complexion, he is almost a handsome young man, with dark eyes and, when he grins, a boyish appeal. Inside the store he brushes his hair, which is slightly curly, from his face as he looks at the card rack.

"Here's the best they have, dig it: 'Happy Birthday to a Wonderful Sister.' What crap! Martha's twenty-one; maybe I should get her a sympathy card: 'Heartfelt sympathy in your loss.' Here it is: 'You're one year old already!' I'll change it to twenty-one."

Ron is looking at paperback books when Richard catches up with him. "Nothing," Ron says, "No Hesse, no Kesey. All they

53

got are those sex books. Mind if I rape you and beat you with my nice leather belt, my dear?" he says, leering at Richard.

"Outasight. Got enough sex. Hey, Phoebe Rose is still sick; gotta get her something. Let's see. Should get her joint paper; that chick's into everything." Richard laughs out loud.

"What's she got anyhow?"

"Could have mono or . . ." They laugh together. "As they say, a 'social disease.' "

Soon the boys are back in the car, driving out of the parking lot. For Richard, nights like this have been a habit since he was halfway through his senior year in high school. Complaining that nothing happens at home and that he feels like a caged animal there, he feels he has to go out every night. If nothing happens at home for Richard, very little happens when he goes out. Many nights, like this one, are spent in endless drives for elusive treasures. Ron wants to buy a van and thinks he saw one in a parking lot, and tonight the pair drive thirty miles searching for the van that never appears and is not for sale anyway. When Richard or Ron hear of a new bar opening, they have to check it out. Neither of them being gregarious, the checking out is done by sitting in a corner, sipping on a beer and watching the rest of the people play or live out their lives.

Janis Joplin wailing "Ball and Chain" is vibrating the homemade speaker that rests on the back seat as Richard and Ron speed along Highway 901 on the edge of Mohawk County. "More schnapps. I'm getting a buzz on," Richard says.

A few hundred yards down the road, Richard looks in his rearview mirror and sees a red light flashing. "Man, what is this shit now?" he says, pulling over. He tucks the beer can close to the seat.

A massive patrolman with Marine-style bearing and close-cropped hair walks toward Richard, who is getting out of his car. The patrolman says nothing. He stares at Richard, who, without being asked, pulls out his billfold and shows his driver's license.

"What you been doing tonight?" the policeman asks brusquely.

"Just riding around."

"OK, into the car with you," he says, motioning toward the patrol car.

"What's this all about anyhow?"

"Don't be a wise-ass kid; into the car."

"Just tell me what I did."

"Get in," he says, grabbing one of Richard's slender arms in a paw of a hand.

Two other squad cars, lights flashing and sirens blaring, pull up to block off Richard's car on the side and in front. Four more leather-jacketed policemen hustle out and, after talking with the other policemen, start to search Richard's car.

"OK, what's this about?" Richard repeats, once inside the squad car.

"I'll do the asking, Junior, so shut up." The patrolman questions Richard for a few minutes on where he has been that night, where he was going, how long he's had the car. While one policeman questions Ron the other four rifle the glove compartment, tear up the floor mats and throw rags and tools back and forth in the trunk. The beer can sits, almost invitingly, on the floor in the back, but they pay no attention to it.

When Richard is finally allowed to go back to his car, he is smiling at the policeman who questioned him. The policeman has retained his stern look. "What was all this about anyhow?" Richard asks a third time.

"You fit the description of a kid who robbed a store—long hair and brown jacket," the policeman says, barely audibly.

"Jesus Christ, those guys are wild," Richard says to Ron as they get into the car. "Hungry for a pot bust. Man, that's the fourth —no, fifth—time this year I've been pulled over."

"Good thing they never checked when we were in high school," Ron says. "My locker was like a pharmacy."

The black Chevrolet starts down the highway. Because they have been stopped so many times by the police for a variety of actual and suspected infractions, the incident with the three squad cars is soon forgotten. A generation ago, being questioned by the police was a humiliating experience; today, for young people like

Richard Neumeyer in suburban Mohawk County, it is a common occurrence.

It is eleven thirty when Richard returns home. He goes quietly to his room and to bed. In his parents' bedroom Betty and Art are still awake. Betty rolls over under the electric blanket and says, with a note of resignation in her voice, affecting the Yiddish accent, "He can't come back until he goes already."

"Until it's out of his system, there'll be no peace in him, no peace in this house," Art says.

"He wants somebody to beg him not to go."

"We won't do it, Betty. He's eighteen; if he wants to go, he goes."

"He wants us to cry and beg and give in and let him be a slob and never cut his hair or make his bed."

"He's an adult and he has to learn what it's like to live with other adults. We're not building our life around him."

"Right, Artie. But I'd still beg him to stay."

"Not me."

ART: Rich hasn't learned what love and a home are yet. I just want him to know that he can go but that he'll always be welcome back. But it will be on our terms, not his, when he returns. When I was ten I was in an orphanage and I had to pick potatoes in the fields to earn my keep. He doesn't know anything but luxury. The danger of raising kids today is that we give them too much love and they don't know what it's like to be without it. He doesn't know we're out here in Mariposa because of him. In the city, there's fifty times the chance of getting into trouble, somebody giving him dope. Here he's safe. What do I want back from him? Just that he gets more out of life than I did. I don't have any special ambition for him. Except that he'd be a professional man of some type.

Martha found the easy way out by going to college. That way she could return to the love and ease out of the house slowly. Richie should have done the same. But if Martha stayed at home and commuted to college, I think we would have had the same problems with her. Her senior year in high school was one argument after another.

BETTY: You can only guide children up to a point; then you have to let them go. I would like to tell Richard about the mistakes he's making. It took me a long time to realize that my brother couldn't benefit by the mistakes Art made. He had to make his own. I was a mother to my brother and he never appreciated it. When he got married, his wife used to call me up to see what kind of wax I used because that's the kind he wanted her to get. I always wanted people to look out for me, to give me advice. Nobody ever did. That's why I am this way.

I'm a meddler at times, but I do it for people's good. I search Rich's room to see if he has any drugs there. I watch his appetite and if he's listless, to see if he's on drugs. That's love. More than they had up the street; they were arrested for drugs a couple of months ago. I know that Rich has probably tried some marijuana but he wouldn't really be on it. He doesn't even like to take medicine. People don't see that he's the more compassionate of the older children. One time I had a sore foot and it was Rich who put the medicine in the basin. Never Martha. He will hurt me more because I'm also the one he loves more.

But we just weren't firm enough with Rich, Art especially; he let him stop going to church too easily. If Art would have been firmer years ago, we wouldn't have all this trouble today. I blame a lot of it on Art. But then I think Rich will wake up and live up to his potential some day. Look where his father came from and where he got to.

When the word came from the hospital that his second child was a boy, Art Neumeyer was indeed happy. He had always wanted a boy, a boy to play catch with, a boy to coach, a boy who would go on to college, perhaps to be an engineer or the doctor Art wished he could have been. But right from the start, Richard didn't seem to be that boy. He was an unsmiling child, unco-ordinated and, as Richard would later say about himself, "in a fog."

Richard's teachers felt the boy either couldn't pay attention or that he wasn't interested in school. Betty was often called in for teacher conferences, and she would return home to chastise the boy—comparing his poor showing to the excellent record of his sister. A new term was introduced into Richard's vocabulary at a young age; he never forgot the stigma and the strange comfort of being called an "underachiever."

It hurt to have low marks in tests; it hurt to have teachers say, "Martha's brother? I can't believe it." But Richard also knew that he had an excuse; not much was expected of an "underachiever." He would do half an assignment and then stop. He would day-dream whenever he cared to.

In sports he did no better. He was a pathetic sight on the basket-ball court: his skinny legs, like lollipop sticks, emerging from the shiny satin shorts; the basketball hitting him in the head; his arms flailing as his opponent easily moved around him to score a basket. Richard Neumeyer had a wealth of experience at being a loser. In junior and senior high school his skin erupted furiously, and no sulfur-smelling ointment seemed to work. Richard became more inward, more sullen. Betty and Art were not pleased with the few friends he had, telling him they would get him into trouble. They were the "hoods," the boys more interested in cars than academics.

Through them Richard discovered marijuana before he was fif-teen; he discovered the excitement of getting high between classes or skipping school in the afternoon to drink wine in a parked car. The only major trouble that came to Betty and Art's attention was when Richard and some other boys broke into a house under con-struction and sprayed paint throughout the interior and kicked holes in plasterboard walls. They were caught by police as they were leaving the house, and Art later was forced to pay a portion of the repair costs. Art and Betty smoldered in anger for weeks after the incident, as they would do after each of the automobile accidents Richard would have once he had a driver's license.

Upon graduation, Richard Neumeyer, who had barely passed his senior year, who had taken a healthy share of shop courses, en-rolled in Mohawk Community College. His parents were elated—their browbeating had paid off. But again he disappointed them, by dropping out in the middle of his first semester and going to work in the factory. The boy, encouraged, cajoled and ordered by his parents to do better, seemed to have nothing to show for his life but a continual string of failures.

Richard stays home from work the day after he announced he was leaving, telling his mother he has to get a lot of things together for his trip. He also asks her for the $1,000 that has accumulated in a savings account his parents opened for him when he was a baby. Betty says no; it was for when he married or bought a decent car and not for "a screwy idea like this."

Richard storms out of the house again, saying, "Martha got hers for college; I want mine now."

Betty stomps after him. "Wait, you!" she screams down at him. "Your father wanted to talk to you last night, but you got in so damn late he couldn't. He called from work. Call him!"

"Man, I don't have time for all that."

"Call him!" she screams even louder, as her pale skin takes on a pinkish color.

"All right, all right," he hollers back and pounds up the stairs to the kitchen telephone.

On the phone to his father, Richard is at first defensive; then his voice turns calm. "Yeah. OK. Yeah, I guess that sounds right."

His mother stares at him through the three-minute conversation. He hangs up and starts to leave the kitchen.

"Well, what happened?" she yells at him.

He turns to her and says quietly, "He wants to buy my car for four hundred bucks. He says I can buy it back if I come back. But if I don't, Martha can use it next year for practice teaching. That's all."

"Well, isn't that more than you deserve?" Betty says, her hands on her hips.

"It's a good car. I gotta go."

Richard Neumeyer has some of his mother's traits, one of which is a penchant for overplanning for a coming event. If he wanted to leave immediately, he could do it today; he has $800 saved. Instead, he shops for a sleeping bag, a knapsack, some warm socks. He goes to the bank to check on the $500 education loan he took out for his semester of college and is assured he doesn't have to begin payments on it until nine months after the close of the term. Then he spends the rest of the day trying to find companions for the trip. Ron cannot go because of his mother. Randy Short, who was one of the most ardent supporters of Richard's leaving, backs out, saying he has to get some work done on his car. Sue, a girl who has just taken an apartment, says she would lose a $300 security deposit if she left now. At midnight Richard has all he'll need for the trip except a companion. He decides to spend the night in Sue's apartment. As she sleeps in her bedroom, he struggles to make himself comfortable on the couch.

RICHARD: I got names on pieces of paper, people I can see all over the country. Here's a note from a guy I work with for Muncie, Indiana: 'This is Richie, a friend of mine; if he gets stuck, see if you can't put him up.' Here's one for Canoga Park, California. I didn't even ask people to write these for me.

I'm scared, sure, but I gotta go. I said I wasn't going to be trapped after I dropped out of college. Then I got all these crutches. Jobs, payments; there was always something. I was working in the restaurant and some other people were sitting by the window having a hell of a time blowing J's [smoking marijuana] and I figured the hell with it, I'm going. Not get an apartment around here or anything because then I'd be worse off, trying to pay for that and food and insurance.

Out there on the road it's going to be tough and I'll probably kill myself. I'm not naïve, but I think I'm too naïve to go out on the road. I could get rolled the day I walk out the door. I'm scared, but I'm happy I'm doing it. I'm going to be myself for the first time in my life. Like in these racing magazines. There are tracks all over California. Just gonna go see 'em. Maybe I can earn a couple bucks working at the tracks. Or like Indianapolis for the Five Hundred. I can't get in for the race, but I can get in for the time trials. Cars are my whole life. My parents heard me say it, but they don't believe it.

I got into this rut with two jobs and I want to go. I don't even know if I want to work any more. I'm a hard worker, but I might be happier being a bum.

My parents don't really think I'm going to go. They think if I didn't go right away, I won't go at all. But I'm going. I'm just wondering what they're going to put up next to stop me. Or something else. I had a dream that this cold I have developed into pneumonia and I got stuck here for a couple of months.

I don't know what it'll be like out there. Maybe it's all different colors. I've really never been anyplace. I'm getting all the shit together—traveler's checks and identification—but I'm not making any preparations for destination. I'm just gonna move whenever it feels right. That's the way the whole trip is going to be from beginning to end. I'll be sending cards back to my buddies from all over. One day California, next day Colorado. It'll blow their minds.

Richard goes to work directly from Sue's the next day. After work he returns home only long enough to shower and change clothes. He stays out all night and returns home the next morning bleary-eyed, complaining of feeling cotton-mouthed from his hangover. When his mother tries to fix him some food, he refuses, saying he is going to put in a half day at the factory.

"Then call your father before you go," she says angrily. "He's been wanting to talk with you for days, but the way you run around like a crazy man . . ."

"Got no time," Richard says offhandedly. "See him sometime." He stands there for a moment, at the top of the stairs, his loose-fitting jeans barely held up by his bony hips, his flannel shirt hanging down almost to his knees.

Betty is about to say something to her son, but she stops herself and bites her lip. "You really want to be a bum, don't you?" she says softly.

"Hey, not a bad idea. See ya later."

It is Sunday. Art has gone to church to clear up some discrepancy in the counting of the morning offering when the weekly collect call comes through from Martha. The rundown on Richard's behavior, attitude and alleged plans takes only a minute or two. Betty is plainly in no mood to talk about her son and knows she has no ally in her daughter. Martha feels her brother should go.

"How are things with Mark?" Betty asks innocently and holds her breath.

Martha has little to say on that subject, and Betty immediately launches into a story Martha has heard before: at a plush wedding Betty catered, the bride was pregnant but everything was carried off as if she were the Blessed Virgin. As the guests were eating and drinking, the bride was in the kitchen with prenatal sickness, ready to throw up, asking for some hot soup.

"Don't ever do that to us, Martha," Betty pleads. "I'm not telling you about sex or not to get pregnant. Just let's not do it that way. I cried all the way home from the wedding."

"Good God, Mother, if I have to hear that one again, I'll croak," Martha replies irately. "If I have sex with Mark, you'll be the first to know."

To Betty, the rest of the conversation is strangely consoling; it shows her daughter is changing, adjusting. Martha used to bristle at even the hint of a slur against minority or ethnic groups, against any down and out people. Now she tells "sick" jokes, poking fun at paraplegics or the mentally retarded. Also, Martha would never put on a good front and be nice to anyone she didn't like. Now she has learned to brown-nose, to use Betty's term. Martha has always hated Miss Tard, the old-maid faculty adviser for her sorority. When Miss Tard voted to blackball Bo Weaver, a sorority sister who had to get an abortion, Martha's hate for her mounted. But Miss Tard also teaches a course in which Martha needed at least a B for her major. Martha began acting more civilly toward Miss Tard, even nominating her for "Woman of the Year" at Hillcrest, and received an A for the course. And Martha, who was so violently antiwar, is talking about enlisting in the Army for two years. "Going more establishment," Betty says with a smile as she hangs up.

The new week brings an uneasy peace to the Neumeyer house. Richard has announced he's leaving, but Betty and Art know that he hasn't found anyone to go with and he doesn't want to go alone. It has been quiet at 97 Birchwood, and physically the house looks no different—neat, everything in place—except for the small room in the basement. On Wednesday night as Art stands at the doorway to Richard's room, his eyes squint in anger. The bed is unmade; empty Marlboro packs litter the floor; clothes are strewn about. A navy-blue knapsack rests amid the clutter with a goosedown-filled sleeping bag and some flannel shirts carelessly tossed on top.

"That's it, Betty." Art turns to his wife, who is standing just behind him. "He cleans it up or he goes. Tonight!"

"I'm not touching it," Betty says, with a measure of anger in her own voice. "I'm not the maid around here." Her eyes move from the room to her husband. "But Artie, it's been calm the last couple of days. Maybe he won't go."

"It's calm because we're making all the concessions. All he does is live here. Like a pig!"

The front door flies open. From the look on their son's face Art and Betty know something has happened. The sullenness is gone from his blotchy cheeks; they are wrinkled in a huge smile. Art is about to say something when Betty takes his arm and whispers, "Shush."

"You remember Hank Leifson," Richard begins as he chews his wad of gum.

"Yes," Betty says disapprovingly.

"Saw him over at Morry's tonight. I was like asking if anybody wanted to hitch to California with me, and here Hank said he was leaving in a Cadillac for the Coast in two days."

"Slow down, Richard," Art says, hesitating between words.

"Hank's got an agency Cadillac to deliver to Los Angeles. Wants people along to share the gas and oil. Beautiful. I can see the land and get into it. Get out anyplace I want to. Better than hitching. A Caddy, too!"

"When?" Betty says, her eyes downcast.

"Two days."

There is a moment's hesitation, then Art says, "Well, until you—"

"Let's go eat." Betty cuts him off and starts up the stairs.

The two days stretch into four, and then a week goes by. Hank is having difficulty convincing the car-transporting agency to let him have the car. As the days wear on, poignant scenes abound at the Neumeyer house. No member of the household is immune. One morning before she goes to school, Joan tiptoes into Richard's room and kisses him lightly on the cheek for fear he'll be gone before she comes home. That afternoon Richard leaves his mother in tears after asking if he can take along a bottle of the family's multiple vitamins. Art bowls a season's low, 119, and tells Betty he couldn't concentrate.

Randy Short calls Richard and mocks him for not leaving after all his boasts: Richard, the college dropout, has talked of "crashing pads and making the scene at Berkeley"; Richard, who was a poor Boy Scout and dreaded overnights, has talked about sleeping out under the stars. After hanging up, Richard disgustedly throws himself on his unmade bed just as John Lennon sings over the stereo, "One thing you can't hide is when you're crippled inside."

On Thursday, March 16, Betty and Art lie in bed at midnight. They are awake, as they have been many nights this week at this hour. The same questions come up.

"Is he going, Artie?" Betty says.

"God knows, I don't," her husband replies.

"He's so strange. Like he's not even our son."

"Roll over, honey, and let's sleep."

The Neumeyers reposition themselves in their double bed and are quiet. But neither is asleep at one o'clock.

ART: Right now, I think he's putting off the trip. If a kid wants to bum around the country, he doesn't make all these preparations. He won't admit it to himself, but he's going to have a hard time out there. OK, he's got a sleeping bag. Where in this country are you going to put down a sleeping bag and go to sleep with peace of mind? The thing that really set him off, I think, is that we insisted he keep his room clean. It doesn't take much to set off a teenager; nobody should tell them what to do. Right now we're saying, "Go, have fun, and when you're tired, come back." I think that takes the fun out of it for him.

The biggest thing that's getting me about Richie is that he believes anybody but us. He never was the leader type, but I hate to see him just following the latest jerk. If somebody said they were giving out gold in California, he'd believe it. If we said the sun was out, he'd say it was night. Sure he's a disappointment to us; I think even more to Betty. She wanted a lot for him, even from the time he was in sports. She wanted him to do well, and he was always short and dumpy and not very good. I know; I coached two years of Little League. We used to talk, Richie and I, but it's not easy any more. He's not interested in my bowling and I'm not interested in his fabulous tales about a six-pack of beer. What would our conversation be?

BETTY: It's not good for Joan to have all this coming and going; it's a good thing she has a stable home life. And Richie's attitude! What he is saying is "Screw you, I'm not coming in, I'm not cleaning my room." I love him, I don't want to be fresh back to him and I don't want him to go away. But I end up the one that fights with Richie, and Art stays calm. In the early days of our marriage that was humiliating because I wanted to fight and there was nobody to fight with. I threw a pot of corned beef hash at Artie once because he said it didn't taste like his mother's. He just looked at me.

I really don't think he's going to go. Buying all that stuff is babyish. He always wanted possessions whether he used them or not. He had to have skis one Christmas and everybody gave him money and he still hasn't used them. He's fifteen, not eighteen.

If he has to go I want to make it fun for him, make it an adventure and make a map of where he's going. I want to have the pastor come over and have a service before he leaves. All Richie can say is that we cramp his style. But it's really better that he goes even though we are going to cry because we don't know where he'll be at night.

Richie is so easily influenced by all the big talk around the gas station; that was a big factor. But those kids are so full of bull. They don't realize that a lot of life is like mine—humdrum, routine, nothing to brag about, nothing to lie about. Of course we have this complex that our kids have to have more than we did, but there's a good side to that. They'll be more relaxed about money. They'll be happier. I have a real hang-up about money because we had a hand-to-mouth existence. I'm much too intense about money.

And I'm also too self-analytical. I'm always looking to see where I went wrong. Other parents aren't like that. They think whatever they're doing is perfectly fine. At least they want you to believe that. Well, nobody knows what really goes on in a family.

On Friday, Joan comes home from school to find her mother standing at the top of the stairs in silence. Betty does not even make a move to kiss her daughter but merely says, "Your brother wants to see you."

"Leave your stuff on, Joanie, we're going out this afternoon," Richard calls from his room.

The little girl, in her midi-length coat, pink knee socks and patent leather shoes, looks questioningly at her mother.

"Hank called. He got the car. Richard's leaving Sunday," Betty says tonelessly.

Richard and Joan go to Strike and Spare Lanes and, lost in an afternoon of gutter balls, Cokes with crushed ice and potato chips, they laugh together and hug each other often.

As Joan takes off her bowling shoes she looks up at her brother. "You know I love you, Richie."

Richard, who has been tapping his hand against his side and watching the four high school girls on lane three, is still. "Baby, I love you, too. You know that."

"Are you going because Mommy was fresh to you? Because Daddy always hollers?"

"Naw," he says, brushing the hair out of his eyes and breaking into a smile. "Just want to see what there is outside of Mariposa. I want to see the world."

"We go on vacations, Richie; we see all kinds of things. You don't have to go by yourself."

Richard looks down at his sister. At eleven, she is already a beautiful little girl with a finely chiseled nose, long, straight brown hair and warm brown eyes. Some people have said she looks like a miniature Ali McGraw. Often people are surprised this lovely creature is the sister of Richard and Martha Neumeyer. Richard puts his arm loosely around her shoulder. "I . . . you know for sure, Joanie, I'm going to miss you the most." He tightens his grip. "OK?"

"OK," Joan says, her bottom lip quivering the way it does when she is ready to cry.

Richard is gone most of the day Saturday, returning home around dinnertime to shower and to finish his packing. Betty has made spaghetti and meatballs, and when Richard tells her he is hungry, she is pleased.

"Be eating in a few minutes," she says. "It'll be nice. Your last meal home and everything."

"No time," Richard says. "Got a lot of stuff to do tonight."

"Meatball sandwich?"

"Yeah, but quick."

As Richard stuffs the sandwich into his mouth, the other members of the family gather in the kitchen. Art breaks the silence.

"Guess you'll be leaving early tomorrow."

"Crack of dawn. You people won't be up."

"Well, keep in touch," his father says, extending a hand.

Richard wipes the sauce off his hand on his jeans and shakes hands.

"You want your camera; I'll get it," Joan says.

"God bless you," Betty says, as her son gets up from the table. She throws her arms around him, almost knocking Richard off balance. He puts his arms around her, then releases quickly. His mother hangs on for a few more seconds, her tears streaming onto his flannel shirt.

Richard picks Joan up and squeezes her until she wheezes. "You be a good girl and I'll send you some cool postcards, OK?"

"Every day?"

"Almost."

At four thirty the next morning Richard Neumeyer leaves 97 Birchwood, bound for California in the Cadillac. But the trip isn't actually started until almost eight o'clock. Hank has some dirty clothes to do at the laundromat before leaving Mariposa.

4

Home Movies

THREE DAYS LATER, March 22, Richard Neumeyer is many
hundreds of miles away from his parents. He sits down at a table in
a trucker's stop in New Mexico with his friends, and Marybeth
begins in her squeaky voice, "I was so scared; you must have been
going two hundred miles an hour; I just didn't even want to look
where . . ."

Richard gets up and goes to the card rack. He picks out a postcard, writes a short message, addresses it to Joan and comes back
to the table only long enough to pick up his hamburger. He eats it
in silence, standing by the front window, watching the lights of
passing cars and trucks.

For Richard, the seventy-two hours have seemed like one long
day as he, Hank, Marybeth, the girl Hank brought along, and
Peter, another Mohawk County boy, have made their way west.
Richard's clothes show the cycle of riding, sleeping and eating in
the car: a mustard stain on his wrinkled jeans, a continuous moist
feeling in the front of his shoes from three-day-old socks, a stale
taste in his mouth from unbrushed teeth. After the first few hundred miles, most conversation—except for Marybeth's incessant
monologues—stopped. Only an extraordinary sight like the rising sun or the speedometer reaching 105 miles an hour brought
comment.

In Mariposa this evening his mother climbs out of Lillian's car in front of the Neumeyer house and scurries across the grass, which crackles under her feet from the hard freeze. The frost is already thickening on the red Chevrolet parked in the driveway. Her husband is not in sight as she comes in the door, so she calls out, "Art. Artie." She walks back to the bedroom, still calling his name. But there is no answer. Opening Joan's door, she finds her daughter asleep. "Artie, Artie!" she calls louder, walking back toward the living room. The house is silent.

Betty's hand goes to her mouth and her eyes scan the house quickly as if she could have somehow missed seeing her husband. She hurries down the stairs. The workshop door is closed, but she can smell a pungent odor coming from within. She throws open the door and flicks on the light. A freshly painted table glistens under the bare bulb. The bathroom is dark, as is the recreation room. Then Betty sees the dim light coming from Richard's room. She is about to call out her husband's name again as she looks into the room, but the word is lost in a rush of air she expels from her lungs.

The room is clean and tidy once more, the product of Betty's work less than twelve hours after Richard left. The new brown and orange shag carpeting is bright and fluffy. Books, models, records are all in place and dusted. And, on the neatly made bed, Art Neumeyer is asleep. Spread out around him are pictures of Richard, from the time he was a toddler to the retouched high school graduation photograph, showing a boy with perfect complexion and smile.

Betty kneels down beside the bed and gently kisses her husband on the cheek. Art's eyes flash open. "Come on, honey," she says, "let's go to bed."

As husband and wife walk up the stairs, Betty says, "Don't make it harder on yourself, honey. Don't punish yourself over him."

"Just fell asleep, Betty," he says, yawning. "Everybody dozes off, don't they?"

Betty looks at two bananas, sitting in a wicker basket on the kitchen counter. Both have gone past ripeness, and now inside the brown skin they are beginning to rot. "If Richie was here, I'd make him a banana cake," she says. "He loved banana cake."

"Throw them away already, Betty. I can't stand to see them like that," he says, reaching for the bananas.

"Not tonight, Artie. I'll . . . I'll throw them out tomorrow."

With Easter approaching and Martha on her way home today, March 24, Betty has spent a busy day in her house cleaning, cooking and thinking. It is not the first holiday that the children have given her concern. But it is the first holiday they will not at least be physically present. Early in the afternoon, she shares her mixed thoughts with Pam Brown over the telephone. "Richie just had us up in the air. You know kids. I'd say one thing, Artie would say another, Richie would huff off and we'd just be looking at each other. Me and Artie are getting along so much better."

Pam Brown says nothing and there is a pause.

"But you know me, Pam, I like all the cows in the barn at night," Betty says. "I remember when he went on his first overnight with the scouts; I almost died. I have this vision of him in his sleeping bag in a field and a tractor running over him. Damn kid. Left without the decency to have one last meal with his family."

"Heard from him at all?" Pam asks.

"If you call it a card," Betty says, her plump hand going to her hip. "I don't even want to explain it over the phone; you've got to see it. Came today. He's just being a smart-ass about the whole thing."

Other calls from friends interrupt Betty throughout the afternoon, and she worries about not having her housework done by four o'clock when Art is due to come home and the three remaining Neumeyers will go to the airport for Martha. So, when the phone rings in midafternoon, she answers with a brusque "Hello."

It is a collect call from Richard.

"Yeah, right, just cool it." There is a giggle on the other end of the line.

"Rich. Richie, is that you?" she asks anxiously.

"Right, yeah; listen, I'm on the phone long distance; I'll catch up with you," he says, his voice strained with a nervous exhilaration.

71

"Richard!"

"Mom, right, yeah, wow! Hey, I made it to California. Blew two tires on the way out and almost got thrown in jail, but I made it."

"Just calm down, Richard; you're babbling like an idiot," she says angrily. "Now, are you going to talk to me or—"

"Mom, don't hassle me." Richard covers the receiver but his muffled voice comes through. "Let me talk, OK?"

"Richard, is everything OK?"

"Yeah."

"Must be hot out there."

"Like summer. Got to get rid of my coat."

"Don't sell—"

"Don't worry."

"Try to get up to San Francisco; I hear it's nice up there."

"Yeah, yeah. We had to wait twenty-four hours in New Mexico to get a caravan license. So we really had to move after that."

"Everything's OK? Allergies?"

"Right. How's Joanie and Black Beauty?"

"Fine, fine. Got your card today."

There is silence on both ends of the line. Betty bites her lower lip. "We better not talk too long," she finally says. "Daytime rates."

"That's your problem, not mine. You told me to call collect every week. You're paying for it."

Betty stares into the telephone, ready to snap back. She hesitates, then says calmly, "Next time, call at night when your father is home so he can talk too."

"Yeah, right. Well, good-bye."

"Good-bye, Richard."

It is noon as Richard hangs up in the phone booth on Hollywood's Sunset Boulevard and looks toward the Arby's Roast Beef stand where Hank said he was going for breakfast. Hank, who had taunted Richard for "calling up Mommy," is nowhere in sight. Richard walks slowly down the street, blinking often in the bright sun.

RICHARD: I've got to blow these guys off—and that flaky bitch we brought out. She's driving me crazy. Just like my mother. If I tell her the sun is shining, she'll say it's the moon. These people are ripping me off anyhow. Gone through a hundred bucks and I'm paying for too much stuff.

Shit, I had to pay for the ticket in New Mexico. And they were driving like maniacs. Topped out over a hundred, and with bald tires. I'm glad we got the hell out of Mariposa. But it's freaky out here. As many guys dressed up as girls as girls dressed up like girls. Wow, the queers! I don't know what I'm going to do definitely. Maybe work in a car wash this weekend and get some bread. Eating tacos every meal. Love them. Gaining weight. It's good out here, I guess. We dropped off that car yesterday and started walking, and then I realized where I was. All of a sudden I was scared shitless.

When Art arrives home at four, Betty glumly relates the short, jerky conversation but does not say Richard didn't ask about his father. Art nods and says nothing. Joan hurriedly puts up the "Welcome Home Martha" sign she made on the aluminum storm door. As the family starts the drive to the airport, Betty quickly shifts from her subdued state and makes the talk light: she jokes about Joan's first date tomorrow with Billy, the boy down the block, how much fun it will be on Easter with lilies perfuming the church, how good the chocolate chip cookies are this year that Joan and she made for Martha.

For the most part Art and Betty have been putting up a good front for Joan and for their friends since Richard left. Julia, one of their best friends from the old city neighborhood—she carried Richard home from the hospital after he was born—called the other day and asked how he was liking his job. "Fine, just fine," Betty lied and then moved on to other subjects.

It is rush hour in Mohawk County, slowing Art to stop-and-start driving. He looks impatient as he strains his neck to look ahead. Betty has expended her burst of happy occurrences, and when she does talk it is of her concern they will not meet the flight. Otherwise she is another absentminded traveler, staring out the window

73

at passing cars. Joan is in the back, giving a peace sign to drivers she thinks are friendly and a wave to the rest.

A few minutes before the scheduled arrival time, the Neumeyers reach the airport only to find the ramps jammed with cars. A news broadcast tells them the airport police are demonstrating for higher pay by snarling traffic with their own cars.

"Come on, come on," Art says softly, pounding the steering wheel with his palms. "What's this world coming to, even the cops on strike!"

"They're no better than anybody else," Betty says, suddenly perking up. "Myrtle said a boy on her street got stopped by the police and they were really ugly with him. Just 'cause he had long hair."

"Look like bums, most of them; how do the cops know?"

"Bums! The police could shoot somebody by accident, just searching them. I'm as conservative as they come, Artie, but you should be able to have your hair as long as you want it."

"I see them every day in the city. Bums."

"Look at your son; he doesn't look that different from—" Betty stops, the conviction gone from her voice. "Let's get out here, Joan, and walk. Daddy can meet us inside."

The plane is late, and by the time Martha comes into the terminal her family has gathered. Her father gives her a rough squeeze, causing her to gasp and bulge out her eyes. Joan leaps into her arms for a hug. "Let me have mine," Betty says, pressing her cheek firmly to Martha's and hugging her tightly. Her eyes closed, Betty hugs her daughter again.

"Mom, you got your hair frosted; it looks cool," Martha says.

"Do any girls at school wear shorter dresses than you?" her father says.

"Daddy! This is nothing."

In the slow-moving stream of college students making their way through the terminal, Martha Neumeyer looks almost straitlaced. Kansas University coeds shuffle alongside the Neumeyer family in dirty jeans, sandals and long, stringy hair. Martha is one of very few girls wearing a dress, a patchwork print which stops halfway up her generous thighs. She is slightly taller than her mother and full-breasted, with features that, while not particularly unattractive, do not seem to work together: a fold in her cheeks, from the nose to the corner of her mouth, an upper lip that protrudes the slightest bit, understated eyebrows and lashes. She wears round-rimmed glasses that seem wrong for her face.

As she walks toward the car with her parents and talks more, her slight lisp becomes more noticeable. Somehow her tongue holds on too long to her upper palate and teeth so that her *s*'s whistle outward; words like "embarrass" and "predicaments" have wet sounds to them. Her parents and her sister listen attentively to the latest happenings at Hillcrest, hanging on intonations, plainly pleased that the college girl is back. But she is careful not to show the impatience, the restlessness she felt as soon as the plane touched ground fifteen minutes ago.

"That's from Mark, isn't it?" Betty says, touching the dog-collar necklace Martha is wearing.

"Let's not talk about it right now. Heard from Richie yet?"

"Yeah, we got this super card with drunken cowboys and drunken women on it and everything," Joan excitedly blurts out.

"Shut up," Betty snaps at her. "Your brother wrote from New Mexico, and the only thing he said that made sense was that the desert was beautiful. I wish he would send a card with some scenery so we could know what it's like where he's at."

"Well, I thought it was a super card." Joan pouts.

"How's everything with the big college girl?" her father asks. No one answers.

"How are your fingernails?" Joan says, sticking her hand in front of Martha's face. "Look, haven't been biting."

"Not so good," she says, tucking her own hands beneath her arms.

"Joan, sit back there and be quiet!" Betty shouts. "You can't be the center of attention all the time."

"I never am," she whines. "I just want to talk to Martha."

As the Neumeyers drive back to Mariposa the conversation bounces from Martha's pregnant roommate who was married last

75

week, to the WACs, and then to Martha's dissatisfaction with, among other things, men and the narrow range of courses at Hillcrest.

Art turns off the expressway and the red Chevrolet makes its way along Main Line Drive, whose neon signs lean out, beckoning with flashes and splashes of color, with slow, tempting rotations. Soon the signs are replaced by a tunnel of uniformly aged trees as the family turns off Main Line and Art drives past the brick pillars with the sea horses on top that mark the entrance to The Knolls.

Supper tonight is strictly Martha's. Betty prepares her favorite foods: pork chops, turnips, a tossed salad with blue cheese dressing. The meal is later than usual, so Joan is in bed soon afterward and Art, feeling the strain of the week's work, goes to bed at ten. With both of them gone, mother and daughter sit at the kitchen table and, almost as if they had been censoring their words before, waiting for this opportunity to be alone, their conversation reaches more personal problems.

"Richie always felt like nothing; you know that, Mom," Martha says. "We could have gotten along better if I didn't get A's and he got C's and you wouldn't have kept reminding us of it. He's not a dummy, but that's what he was treated like. You should have held him back a year instead of pushing him into school. He was always the runt of the class or the team."

"You did so many things when you were at Parkside Methodist, Martha," is Betty's reply. "I wish Rich had been more active. Would it make any difference now? Does it make any difference to you?"

It is near midnight as the two women sitting at the kitchen table stare in silence at the tea stains on the bottoms of their mugs.

"Mark sounds like such a decent guy, Martha, why can't you just relax and let yourself like him?" Betty says without looking up.

"Mother, you know absolutely nothing about him, so don't meddle."

"He's not like that guy, what's his name, that travels all over the state without his wife. . . ."

"Barry."

"Yes. Don't you get involved in anything like that."

"You really want to choose my husband, don't you?" Martha says with a brassy note to her voice.

"You haven't always been so wise."

"Len Morris another good example of my unwiseness?"

"Well, yes," Betty says haltingly.

"Let's see. He wasn't married but he sure was black. That couldn't have had anything to do with it in this unbigoted, unprejudiced, churchgoing family?"

"It had everything to do with it," Betty says dryly.

"Mother, let's go to bed before we get into it the first night. I'm tired."

"I'm sick and tired, Martha, more than you'll ever know."

Martha walks slowly back to her bedroom and sits down between the cloth dachshund that bears autographs of high school friends and the fading green serpent—two of the stuffed animals that inhabit her bed. Her eyes slowly scan this room, which saw her through her high school years. The dressing table with its three-sided mirror and ruffled skirt and bottles of perfume might hint that Martha used it often to prepare herself for dates. But there were few dates. On the corkboard above the desk are party favors, losing their color with age, and a yellowed clipping of a voluptuous teenager in a bathing suit, cutting a ribbon to mark a store's opening. In Richard's room is Brigitte Bardot, the girl he will never date. Martha has posted the girl she can never be.

From birth, Martha was taught "ladylike" manners. Even as a preschooler, she could go to a party in a spotless starched cotton dress and return home in the same mint condition. Martha was a happy child, content to play with paper dolls when there was little money to spare in the Neumeyer household, entranced by the organ grinder and his monkey who would play in the courtyard behind the apartment building. Martha did well in school from the start. She would come home to sit on her mother's knee and tell her what she did, who had what for lunch, and what was planned for tomorrow. So when the first black children attended classes, she came home excitedly to tell her mother. Betty and Art were hardly that happy. They had heard rumors that still more blacks were going to be bused to Martha's school, so as soon as a down payment could be scraped together, the family moved to Mariposa.

Martha often played with her little brother, Richard, in the city but once the family moved to the suburbs she found that girls her age considered younger brothers an annoyance. Also, she found that her pretty dresses and polite ways were not the standard. Girls with mud on their faces and hands would laugh at Martha as she stood on the sidewalk with her doll buggy. It was lonely at first on Tulip Lane until Martha discovered that she needed to change if she was to have friends. So she became a tomboy, a girl other girls liked and a girl other boys considered "one of the boys."

In high school Martha became an outstanding gymnast and softball player. But when she saw that the girls with the bleached hair and C averages were the ones boys were interested in, she wanted desperately to be like them. She planned what she would say to a certain boy at a dance, how she would flirt with him, but her attempts never got further than a blush-red face and a few stammering words. She would often dance with girls or play Ping-Pong, anything to get through the night. Martha sounded as enthusiastic as her friends when they talked about dating, about being "swept off my feet," but when her senior prom date tried to kiss Martha, she was almost revolted. Companionship of boys, she yearned for; their touch frightened her.

There was one exception. Len Morris, virtually the only black boy of Martha's age within the small black population in Mariposa, was different. He and Martha exchanged poetry, talked about song lyrics, played tennis together—and didn't touch each other for months. By the time Martha was ready for college, she was seeing Len regularly and her parents told her if she didn't stop they wouldn't help her through school. Martha still wrote to Len, saw him on vacations and suffered her parents' wrath. At school her dating, as with Len, was platonic, often with boys other girls called effeminate or queer. It wasn't until Martha met Mark Hard this school year that she had ever felt strongly, physically attracted to a member of the opposite sex. As she told her friends, "I fell so hard for Hard it hurt."

It is now Sunday, Betty's forty-third birthday. She was up early this morning to make her own birthday pie—chocolate with Dream Whip topping. The family has been to church, and Grandma Santangelo is at the Neumeyer house. Grandma is a bubbly, ever-smiling woman of seventy who sells handbags at a local discount department store. Although she has never taken a lesson, she plays the piano by ear, banging out such tunes as "Hello, Dolly!" "Red Sails in the Sunset" and "Raindrops Keep Falling on My Head" and then, as Martha and Joan bring out the pie with a single candle on it, "Happy Birthday to You."

Betty looks into the flickering flame. "I make a wish that Richie calls tonight."

"It won't come true now that you told us," Art says.

"Yes it will," Joan says, popping out of her chair.

Betty's presents this year are: money from her mother to buy clothes, stationery and a pink candle from Joan, a pink nightgown from Art. From Martha there is a small box that she leaves for last, almost sure what it will be and savoring it like the cherry on a sundae. Betty carefully unwraps the package, unfolds the tissue paper within and then gives a girlish squeal of delight. She hugs Martha tightly and again closes her eyes.

Martha says without emotion, "I thought you'd like it, Mom."

It is a mother's pin from Martha's sorority. Vicariously, Betty has lived out Martha's college life. Now she has a symbol of this other life, and she immediately pins it on.

"This mood is too good to pass up," Art says, getting up from the table. "Time for home movies." He goes into the closet to get projector and screen and several boxes of film. The family takes up positions on sofa, chair and floor, and soon a Christmas tree flashes onto the screen.

An electric train faithfully makes its rounds about a huge stack of presents under the tree. Martha appears as a four-year-old, a pretty, dark-haired girl with pigtails and a prim, long, starched dress. Richard appears and it is summer. Sitting in a horse and buggy at an amusement park, he is bawling. Next he is digging in the sand, much happier.

Christmases come and go, and the same shots reappear. A bottom-to-top view of the lush tree, which touches the ceiling in the Neumeyers' city apartment. "Grandpa always gave you the best one," Grandma says. "In our business we took the best and sold the rest." Martha daintily opens a Christmas package and smiles broadly over a set of play cooking pans. Richard rips open a package to find boxing gloves, which he puts on and begins sparring with his grandfather.

"Grandpa looked so good there," Betty says softly, "and Richie was so darned cute." The next shot is a tiny apartment bedroom with Betty still asleep and two children's beds sandwiching her in. "I wish we were still there," she says. "Those were such good days."

The children grow older. Richard looks about four, Martha about seven, as they walk toward the camera, hand in hand. In the background is the Memorial Day parade, one of the neighborhood spectacles in the North End. The parade shots wear on, so Art speeds up the film and smart-marching bands are now goose-stepping. The family howls with laughter.

It's hula-hoop time. The family has moved to Tulip Lane and, in a large back yard that has a collapsible swimming pool, the family takes turns. Martha and Richard keep the hoop spinning around their hips while Art and Betty have less success. Betty starts the hoop with a good spin but it quickly falls to the ground.

Laughter fills the living room at 97 Birchwood Street. "Go ahead, make fun of your mother," Art says, "but who can do this?" He runs the film backward, and the hoop leaps up from the ground to Betty's hips and begins its turns. Joan squeals with enjoyment and Martha grabs her and they hug each other, laughing, as the film goes forward and the hoop falls to the ground.

"Where am I, Mommy?" Joan says above the laughter. "Are you thinking about me yet?"

Betty is laughing so hard she has trouble answering. "Not yet, honey. Soon. Soon."

80

Neumeyer family life continues to unfold. Richard graduates from nursery school wearing a homemade paper mortarboard. Richard digs again in the sand at the beach. In the kitchen in the North End, Betty stands over a huge pot of spaghetti sauce. Martha in front of the Apache house at YWCA camp. Betty mimicking Betty Furness, opening her refrigerator and taking out a package of frozen food. Grandpa, puffing on the ever-present cigar in the back yard on Tulip Lane. Betty's brother, George, thin as Art, talking to his British-born wife, Bridget. A New Year's Eve party with many of the women in silver and gold lamé dresses. Betty and a man talking and laughing.

"See how broad-minded I am," Art says. "I'll even show Betty's old boyfriend."

"Oh, Artie, forget it," she says. "He only propositioned me once after we were married. Look, look, Joan, we're thinking of you now!" Betty is on the screen in a flower-printed maternity dress.

Martha appears once more, this time playing a violin. She is still prim, but the cute features of childhood are not making the transition well. Her forehead is becoming too high. Her once well-proportioned face is more round. There is a smiling baby, hips and legs in an oversized cast. It is Joan, who was born with a dislocated hip and who wore casts for nearly a year.

"There you are, baby," Betty says. "She always smiled, didn't she? No matter what."

"Where are the pictures when I'm in your tummy?"

"You saw those, honey, at the New Year's Eve party."

"I hope you're telling Joanie more about babies than I knew," Martha says. "Daddy used to tell me if you want a baby you have to get married and ask God, and that's what I went away to college believing."

The howls of laughter drown out the last few words. "I know, I know where babies come from!" Joan shouts. "And you don't even have to be married!"

The next reel shows a bedroom in the Tulip Lane home with a bunk bed, plaid blanket, bookcase, bureau and the initial R worked into the linoleum pattern. "He wasn't too proud of his son," says Betty quietly. There is a rocking horse for Joan that Betty thought at first was too expensive, and a boy Martha had a crush on for five years before he acknowledged that she was alive. Martha's first pair of high-heeled shoes and her wobbly walk. Martha's confirmation party in the back yard on Tulip Lane. Richard, Martha and tiny Joan at the zoo.

"I've got to have a camera at school and get some pictures before I graduate," Martha says.

"Take the old one," Betty says.

"I still use it," Art says. "It's better than the new one for some shots."

Betty whispers something into his ear, and he begins to smile.

"Like your mother said, take it, take it," he says emphatically.

"What did you have to do for that?" Martha asks.

"Never you mind." Her mother winks knowingly. Betty and Art Neumeyer have just negotiated sex for tonight. It is a consoling ending for this birthday, although the hoped-for call from Richard did not come through.

"Get out of here; I can smell you a mile away," Martha says. Art Neumeyer is stalking his daughter around the dining room table. It is now two days after Betty's birthday, Art has just come home from work and dinner is already on the table. "I don't trust him any more," she calls to her mother in the kitchen. "Yesterday he came up behind me and undid my bra."

"Honey, don't you want to kiss your daddy after a hard day's work?" Art says, finally grabbing her arm. "Who do you think I am, anyhow?"

"Ouch, oh, ouch, I know who you are; you're a dirty old man."

"Hear that, Betty?" Art says with mock indignation. "She called me old."

"C'mon, supper's getting cold," Betty says, "and I have to make a whole bunch of calls for church."

"Kiss your daddy, Martha," Art says, twisting her arm and bending her backward.

"Ouch! God, I'll kiss you, I'll kiss you."

Art puckers his lips and holds them just out of Martha's reach. She has to force against the pressure he's exerting to reach him.

The kiss obtained, Art releases his daughter and she heads for the kitchen to help bring in the food. Art reaches out to unsnap her bra but she moves quickly away.

After supper, Betty is on the phone and she is agitated. "Lil, about that chorus bunch. We have an extra student, and two others turn out to be a married couple so they have to stay together. Now where are we going to put them? These kids! They think we're Holiday Inn or something. Working would be better. I tell you, Lil, by the end of the summer this mommy is going to be working."

"Did you wash those jeans today?" Martha calls in from the bedroom.

Betty hears but continues her conversation with Lillian.

"Mom," Martha says, coming out of her room, "did you—"

"Hold on, Lil," Betty says, cupping her hand over the phone. "You selfish bitch," she goes on in a low, hostile voice. "I'm sweating out a concert, and you have the nerve to ask me if your pants are clean."

"God, I'm sorry I'm alive. I just asked. If they're not, I'll wear something else. Forget it."

"It just so happens they are clean."

"Forget it. I'll wear something else."

Martha is going out tonight with two high school friends, Carol and Theresa. Carol is a junior at a state college in the northern part of the state, and Theresa works at the telephone company, microfilming bills. Carol arrives at the house first, and as she, Betty and Martha wait for Theresa, they sit around the kitchen table. Carol looks over her shoulder to the refrigerator door where Martha's grades and a newspaper clipping are hanging. "Oh, is that Mark?" she asks, getting up from the table.

"Yes," Martha says softly, "he was elected president of our teachers' association."

"Nice."

Martha is quiet.

"Any girl'd be proud to have him, don't you think, Carol?" Betty says.

"Yes, they would," Martha answers. "Maybe we could take that down now, Mom. Just put it in my dresser, OK?"

Betty looks at her daughter. "OK."

Theresa arrives shortly after and the girls are soon riding in her car toward Land's End, a bar a few miles away. All three wear color-coordinated pants outfits, Martha's being red pants with blue patch pockets and a red knit top that is slit far enough down to expose the soft rounding of the tops of her breasts. The talk at first is about their classmates who have married. Then Martha asks, "How about you and Peter?"

"Same old stuff," Theresa answers in a bored tone. "I write him three times a week and he writes twice a month. He's home on vacation now but he's out with the boys someplace. To me, nineteen seventy-four can't come soon enough so he graduates and we can get married and end this foolishness. Five years of going steady," she says with resignation in her voice as they pull up in front of the bar.

Land's End, in one of the smaller shopping centers, has a long, narrow bar with stools in the front and a few tables in the rear. It is like many other bars that cater to Mohawk County's young people. The jukebox is loud, the beer is cold and cheap and the rest rooms smell of stale urine. As the three girls pass the bar, they run a gauntlet of inspecting eyes. A half-dozen young men are leaning against the wall, laughing and making comments as the girls pass. At the bar, other girls sit, nervously chain smoking cigarettes, trying to look relaxed until one of the men strikes up a conversation.

"Ohhhh, I hate that," Martha says, reaching a table that is still sticky from the last customers' beer.

"Over at the Penguin if you don't get a pinch when you walk in, you feel pretty bad about it," Theresa says.

"I can do without the pinches," Martha says.

The girls order screwdrivers and Martha, the only smoker of the three, lights up a Salem. "Remember senior prom?" she says.

"I went with Smittie and I couldn't stand him and I wanted O'Brien and he didn't even know I was alive."

"Didn't Smittie get you that big stuffed animal?" Carol asks.

"Yeah, and he wanted to kiss me good night after the prom Ugh! A guy tried to kiss me good night the freshman year at Hillcrest, and I cried and screamed and told him to leave me alone."

"But now with Mark, you like it, huh?" Theresa says, rolling her eyes.

"I did."

The two girls say nothing as Martha takes a sip from her screwdriver. "Men. Why do they have to be like that?"

"What are they like anyhow?" Theresa says. "Tell me so I'll know."

"Well, with Mark it was really good at first. He's twenty-five, mature—at least I thought he was mature—sure of himself. I was really getting used to the idea of marriage. For the first time I really had these vibrations, and he said he had them too. So he sent me his fraternity pin by mail and it got there on a Wednesday."

"You must have been jumping, huh?" Theresa says, smiling warmly.

"Well"—Martha hesitates—"yes, I really was happy."

"Big-time college girl gets pinned," Carol says.

"In our sorority we have a tradition of passing a candle when a girl gets a pin. So I went out and bought this gorgeous—God, it was gorgeous!—candle. So it's Monday and I'm all ready for sorority meeting on Tuesday night. I've passed enough candles for other people. On Monday I meet this friend of Mark's but I don't say anything about the pin. She tells me she saw Mark out with one girl Friday night and another on Saturday. And on Saturday it was at the local place where they park and neck. Hey, anybody else want a drink?"

"Wait a minute, kid, finish the story," Theresa says, reaching over to touch Martha's arm.

"I called Mark that night and asked him how his weekend went, and of course he said it was quiet and nothing about his two dates. The lie hurt more than anything. I told him I knew and hung up.

I'm just thankful I never passed that candle. What a fool I would have been!"

"What happened since then?" Carol says.

"We see each other at teachers' meetings, and either he's as cold as a fish or he gives me that 'Let's go out once in a while and see if we can put things together again' line. It's all shit. Honest to God, how the hell can men be so heartless?"

"I know," Theresa says. "So many of my girl friends at work feel unless they put out for their guys they'll lose them. This women's lib stuff about equality and bra-burning and everything stinks—I still want there to be a difference—but if I got to screw just to keep a guy, the hell with it! Let's have one more and then I got to go. Working girls get up early."

Only the porch light and one light in the living room are on when Martha comes home. It is nearly midnight but she is not sleepy. She takes out a well-worn set of cards and plays solitaire on the kitchen table.

MARTHA: When I go out to a place like I did tonight I really don't go to meet anybody. I just have never felt comfortable; it's like I was a piece of beef or something. If you can dance, that's better, but this way it's awful for a girl. Especially a girl like me.

I think I come off looking very straight, too intellectual-looking, and guys might avoid that. They'd go for somebody like Theresa, somebody good-looking and warm. Anyway, I really wonder how people see me. I don't really think I dress really, really cool and eye-catching. I try—I mean, I like to get new clothes and I sometimes convince myself I look just great—but I don't think I radiate. Maybe it's just the way I feel about myself inside.

When I go to a teachers' meeting full of men I'm comfortable. I feel people think I'm really great there. I just don't do so good boy-girl-wise. Who knows where it comes from? Am I afraid of boys? Probably. My father drilled into me that boys will try to get as much as they can from a girl right from the first date. Rape, at least. I was scared to death when I went to the prom with Smittie, and he wouldn't have done a thing.

Marriage has never been one of my priorities and especially now; I'm really down on it. I enjoy being with girls a lot more. They won't hurt you like guys always do. The old saying about you don't know about love until it hits you is true. Marriage sounded better and better with Mark. Before him I never gave in an inch to a guy, and there I was wearing everything purple because that was his favorite color. I hate purple.

Why shouldn't I be afraid of marriage? I haven't seen that many great marriages around. My parents have had really bad troubles, a lot of screaming and yelling. My mother walked out more than once. She was always threatening she was going to divorce my father. And when the divorce talk came up, Richard and I had to choose who we were going to live with. I said I'd live with Daddy and Richard said her. My parents talk about marriage like it was the perfect state. Living with them is a totally different picture.

5

Easter in Mariposa

"I HAVE A COLLECT CALL for anyone from Richard Neumeyer. Will you accept the charges?"

"Yes, yes, I will," Betty says, motioning to Art, who is reading the paper in the living room. "Get in there, it's Richie," she says under her breath. Betty self-consciously smooths her tunic top over her slacks and stands erect in the kitchen.

By the time Art reaches the extension in Martha's room the conversation has begun.

". . . pretty good life, really. Like in the mornings I just sit out in front of my cottage and sip tea and get some sun. Think I'm gaining some weight too. Eating like a hound."

"What, junk food or good food?" Betty says in a voice half motherly and half hostile.

"Some tacos and some other good stuff too, like TV dinners. Climbed this mountain yesterday over in Glendale Park. Far out. Observatory up there and everything."

"How are you feeling? Taking your vitamins? Any trouble with the allergies?"

"No, I'm clean. Martha get home yet?"

"Yes, Julie came out from the city and Joan went bowling with them."

"How's the work situation out there, Rich? Think you'll be able to find something good?" Art says, talking quickly to get his words in.

"I don't know, not looking too hard," Richard says casually. "Did a gig at a party where we were the bouncers—dressed in Santa Claus outfits. And then I worked one day at a car wash. Not spending that much that I have to work."

Art's eyes narrow as he reaches into his pocket for cigarettes; he has left them on the coffee table. A few minutes later the two phones in Mariposa are hung up and another phone in a booth on Sunset Boulevard in Hollywood is slammed into its receiver.

"Man, let's get something to eat," Richard says to Hank.

"Richie, you got to call them every week?"

"Listen, man, they pay for it, so what the hell?"

"What kind of shit do you tell them?"

"I told them we climbed the mountain, but I didn't say we were smoking grass all the way up. I told them about the show, but I didn't tell them it was "The Dirtiest Show in Town" and we were bumming joints all over the place. Told them we were in Vegas, but I didn't say this queer was hustling us. Told them there are queens all over the place, and all they said was that it was just like back in the city. Like I said, let's get some chow."

"Let's see if anybody else wants to go."

Richard and Hank walk a few blocks to Featherstone Lane, a quiet street with a mixture of houses, low apartment buildings and cottages assembled in courts.

The court where Richard and his companions have rented a cottage at 512½ Featherstone was built in Hollywood's heyday and from a distance has a certain kind of elegance. There is a pagoda look about it; the eaves of the stucco buildings gently turn up, and tall palms line the walk that separates the cottages. A closer look shows the stucco is crumbling, green paint peels from the window and door frames, and hunks of roofing are missing.

As Richard and his friend walk up to Featherstone Court, some of the other residents are sitting on the grass near the curb. One says he is a photographer but is now on unemployment after inhaling fumes from a solvent he was using on a job, cleaning airplanes at Los Angeles International Airport. His eyes are bloodshot and his breath reeks of bourbon. His wife, a skinny, braless girl who looks to be in her mid-teens, says she is a dancer but is now working as a secretary. Another man wearing a cowboy hat, boots and leather chaps has a gold earring in his left ear. He says he is a stunt rider in the movies but is between jobs now and is working as a projectionist in a local theater.

"Oh, man, let's forget the chow," Richard says to Hank. "You got any stuff left?"

"No. . . . You?"

"I've been supplying us forever."

On Easter Sunday morning, three days after Richard's call, Martha stands in front of the bathroom mirror with an anguished look on her face. Nothing is going right. The damp weather has turned her naturally curly hair into a frizzy ball. After attempting other styles, Martha finally yanks her hair into a severe bun on top of her head. She runs her hands over her cheeks where a mass of blemishes have flared up overnight. Two layers of orangish makeup later, their contours are still visible but Martha's face is at least a uniform color. After putting on her glasses and looking again into the mirror, she decides to leave them at home.

An hour later, Martha is seated with her parents and grand-mother in Parkside United Methodist Church as the choir proceeds toward the chancel, where potted lilies have been formed into a cross. Most of the lilies are given in memory of a deceased relative, but one of the cards reads:

> *Given by Martha and Joan Neumeyer in honor of*
> *their grandmother, Joan Santangelo*

For the first Easter since he was born, Richard has not been included. Also, this is the first Easter the Neumeyers have worshiped without all their children. Throughout their youth and into their teenage years, Martha and Richard were very involved at Park-side, but each viewed church and its activities very differently. For Martha, who was always a "good girl," church was an exciting place to see her friends, to probe the mysteries of the Christian faith, to learn about Bible figures. For Richard, formal services were so much punishment inflicted by his parents, so much time he had to be still. Never impressed by Sunday school, he often was a behavior problem. As Martha and Richard got older, Martha going to college and Richard finishing high school, they both turned cool on what they called "organized religion" and balked at going to church with their family. Martha still would attend when home on vacation; Richard often would sleep in or be out of the house when the family would leave for church. Others of the congregation are turning away from "organized religion" also. Last year there were nearly 500 for the Easter service; today there are no more than 400.

Martha has been staring off to the side of the altar. A gentle nudge from her mother brings her attention to a small group of children standing just outside the communion railing in their silky blue and white robes and to their leader, who is raising his hands to begin the hymn. Martha squints to bring Benjamin Morris into focus. He gently sways back and forth as he leads Joan Neumeyer and other members of the Gospel Choir in a Negro spiritual, "Keep Trusting in Jesus." It is an incongruous scene, this tall black man, a huge smile on his face, almost like a Pied Piper for a small band of followers in the midst of a staid, still all-white church. Martha squints again and sees a dark-skinned boy about her own age, wearing wire-rimmed glasses, who is playing the organ for his father.

MARTHA: Len was the ideal boyfriend. He wrote poetry; he wasn't physical; we could talk for hours about Simon and Garfunkel songs, like "Bridge Over Troubled Water" and "El Condor Pasa." He went to church, and at church we all learned that color didn't make a difference. But when little Martha dated Lennie, I got a different picture of that at home. I don't think my parents are terrible people or that different from others here at the church. It's just that they are all hypocrites. Blacks are fine as long as they keep their distance.

I had never gone out with anybody before, and my parents let me know that no white boy was going to date me if I was seen with Len. I'd get these strange looks when we'd stand in line at a movie, and one day a

91

little boy at the beach looked at Len as if he was from another planet. The kid had never seen that much black skin before.

When Len wanted to hold my hand, at first I thought something wasn't right, but then I knew I cared for him and it was good to have him hold my hand. For my birthday one year he sent me a six-foot roll of paper with all kinds of neat things on it. Even from the Bible: "Strip yourself naked before my eyes and I will not take what is yours . . ." And I made a hanging with *"Plus que hier, moins que demain"*—"More than yesterday, less than tomorrow."

On vacations in the summer, I'd come back from college and sit in the church and my parents would smile at the Morrises and say hello to Len. But when he came over to the house, they always had something for me to do so he'd have to leave. Or when we'd sit in front of the house and talk, they'd be knocking at the window, turning the lights on and off. And they'd check on me at night when I said I was going to a girl friend's, just so I wouldn't be with Len. "Next thing you'll be sleeping with him," my mother screamed at me. I never dreamed of that, and Len was as prudish as they come.

They won. It just wasn't worth the hassle after a while. My father said if I wanted their money for college, I had to live like they wanted me to. Well, they were the ones always preaching Christianity and equality to me! They wore me down and I compromised. And I hate myself and dislike them immensely for forcing me. Funny thing, I'm sure the relationship would have died a natural death. But they couldn't wait.

The reason Joan joined the Gospel Choir was that she had a crush on Len's little brother, Jerome. I don't think she told my parents, because it was confusing to her when they were saying one thing about blacks and doing another. I just told her not to tell them and to forget about Jerome. It's not worth getting involved with my parents at such an early age.

They're sitting here wondering why Richard had to get away from home. They really tried to be good parents, gave us everything and all that. They *are* good parents, but they aren't saying with their lives what they say with their lips.

92

At a coffee hour between services, Martha sees a few of the young people she knew from Methodist Youth Fellowship or high school. It is a series of excited, animated greetings—"Molly, how are you doing? I haven't seen you for ages!"—followed by uncomfortable pauses where there is little more to say. After church the family goes home for a light snack before starting the drive to Betty's brother's home in Ashville, some sixty miles away.

A light rain turns into a downpour as the Neumeyers and Grandma Santangelo get into the car to go to Ashville. Art can usually make the trip in a little more than an hour, but with the traffic today he knows it will take two hours. Conversation is sporadic and light as various members of the family doze off. Betty laughs as she tells about being too cold at night with their electric blanket while Art was too hot. Betty kept turning up the control on her side of the bed and Art turned his down. After another uncomfortable night Betty discovered that in making the bed she had reversed the controls.

"If I had to drive into the city every day, I would go crazy," Art says, pulling off the turnpike a few miles from George and Bridget's home. Ashville is an old industrial city which has retained its heavily ethnic flavor. There are Kosher delicatessens and shops and stores with Italian and Slavic names. As the car passes one of these small grocery stores, there is a hand-lettered sign in the window: "Lottery Tickets for Sale."

"George will sell anything, won't he?" Art says dryly.

"Don't criticize my brother," Betty says defensively. "He'll be retired with a bankroll and we're still going to be schlepping away."

"So what has he got besides work?"

"Shush, Ma's waking up."

Art, because he had so little feeling for his own family, readily adopted Betty's, but he has never gotten along with her brother. George, who had lived downstairs from his parents, grandly promised on the day his father was buried that his mother could continue to live with him until she died. After the funeral, Betty, Art, George, Bridget and Grandmother Santangelo spent many Sundays together, and Betty often boasted of the warm family feeling they had over hamburgers in the back yard or cannolis and coffee after a meal. At that time George was working as a routeman for a tool company, and as his area in Mohawk County was oversold and not especially lucrative he was dissatisfied. His company offered him the Ashville area, considered undeveloped territory, and George eagerly accepted. His decision and move were wrenching, especially for Betty, who always felt she had been more a mother than a sister to George. In Betty's eyes it was foolish, dividing the family for no good reason. At first she was angry with her brother for moving to a three-bedroom apartment and leaving Art and her responsible for looking after Mrs. Santangelo. It seemed that suddenly her brother was only thinking about himself.

Art roundly criticized George for leaving his mother. Betty initially agreed, but then she defended her brother—something that has always angered Art, who thinks of George as a "spoiled kid to this day"—saying, "His making a promise and breaking it is no worse than us not making one at all."

George's enthusiasm for his new district was short-lived and declined rapidly as his wife's interest in a neighborhood store increased. She found that the owner was retiring and convinced her husband that it was a "gold mine." It was crowded each time she stopped there. Her parents, who had worked as domestic help and then houseparents in a children's home since emigrating from England, were able to lend them the money for a down payment. It was not long after their move to Ashville that George and Bridget were the owners of the small jammed store and George was putting in 82-hour work weeks, taking off only four days a year: Christmas, New Year's, Easter and Thanksgiving.

The red Chevrolet reaches Princess Lane on the outskirts of Ashville and turns into a cul-de-sac of similar styleless, box-shaped houses. At the end of the street is a culvert, its sides littered with old tires and other debris. The brownish water in the creek foams as it nudges milk cartons and broken bottles. When Princess Lane was developed three years ago, the builder promised that the stream would be cleaned and beautified. George and Bridget have stopped telling Art and Betty, "Work will start any day now."

Their house was prefabricated at a factory several hundred miles away and hauled to this location in two pieces. A foundation was poured as the two tractor-trailers were en route to the site, and once they arrived the pieces were set in place and bolted together. Because the prefabrication was so complete—including a fuse box, a water heater, all plumbing fixtures, a fully appointed kitchen and bath and paneled walls—the house was virtually ready to be moved into. George marvels at this instantaneous construction. To Art, the house is two mobile homes tacked together and nothing more and typifies George's lack of interest in everything other than himself or his business.

As the family gets out of the car onto George's muddy driveway, Betty hesitates a moment. "Seems funny not to have Richie with us."

"He was no addition these last years," Art says. "Too windy for him so we'd roll up the window. Too much traffic; he wanted us to hurry up and get there."

"I'd still rather have that tension."

The front door opens and George, a man in his late thirties with a babyish face, Betty's pale complexion and a noticeable paunch, comes out to meet the relatives. There is a rattling sound at the door and then Road Runner, their Irish setter, bursts through.

"Get out of here, you!" Art says, turning away from the dog.

It is too late. Road Runner jumps up on Art and leaves a paw print on his coat sleeve.

"Brij, keep him in there, can't you?" George says. "Get in there with Mommy."

"You know this baby; he wants to say hello to everybody," says Bridget. As she gives Betty a hug, the contrast between the two women is striking: Betty stout, with a simple hairstyle in a neat, plain blue dress; Bridget thin, a matched hairpiece finishing off her dyed silvery-blond hairdo, dressed in a mini-length dress and fashionable boots.

"Martha, Martha, it's so good to see you," Bridget says.

"You too, Auntie Brij," Martha responds, beaming.

Everyone is soon inside catching up on what has happened since they last saw each other. Richard's trip to the West Coast and reports of his new life there weave in and out of people's conversations. Martha tells about snowball fights at school, Joan about how she decorated the Easter eggs she brought, Betty about the beautiful service that morning, Art about the traffic, Grandma about the nice young manager in her store who was caught stealing, George about the hot-selling line of lunch meats that he can no longer get because the company went bankrupt, Bridget about how cute Road Runner is when he puts his paws and head on the table and begs for food.

"OK, Brij, I'm hungry; how about that antipasto?" George says, rubbing his stomach.

"You're the last one to be worrying about food," his wife says. "Artie, don't you think he's getting too fat?"

"We were watching some home movies, George, and if you looked at them you would cry," Art says, a wry smile coming over his face.

"Betty, they're picking on me. Like I said, Brij, how about the food?"

Bridget has gone into the kitchen and George and Grandma are on one side of the living room when Betty whispers over one of the potted plastic plants to Art, "They're at each other, don't you think? Especially Bridget."

"No more than usual. And don't think your brother is perfect."

Art and Betty are less than pleased about coming up to see George and Bridget this Easter. Betty always prepares mammoth meals when her brother and his wife come to Mariposa, but today Bridget is only having Sangria and an antipasto—peppers, anchovies, sliced meats, artichoke hearts—and an Italian bread with cheese and meat in it, all of which requires no preparation except opening jars and bakery boxes. Everyone is to go to a restaurant for a Dutch-treat Easter meal.

As Bridget arranges the antipasto, Art stretches out on the couch to rest after the trip. His eyes move slowly around the room, then close. Martha and Joan are talking to their uncle in front of a smoky gray mirror that covers one wall. Gilded Greek statues stand mutely by, shoulder to shoulder with Joan. The rest of the furniture is not unlike Betty's and Art's Italian provincial, but the living room has the appearance of a showroom display of medium-priced but thoroughly unlived-in merchandise.

Just as Art is dozing off, a huge wet tongue swishes along his cheek. "Get that thing out of here!" he shouts, jumping up. Art's loud outcry brings silence to the house.

"Now you went and hurt Baby's feelings," Bridget says, coming out from the kitchen. "You big meanie; he wants to kiss you. Come on in and eat."

"Artie, don't mind Baby," George says at the table, talking through the piece of Italian bread he has stuffed into his mouth. "He's just welcoming you to his house."

"His house," Art says with no emphasis. "This thing going to hold up anyhow?"

"Sure, Artie, sure. Listen, instead of a two-by-four in the hall-way I got two two-by-fours because that's where the house was joined. What lasts today? It's as good as anything you can buy now. We just have to get a few things done."

"Yeah, if I could get you out of that store a little bit, we could."

"Brij, don't bug me, we're knocking them dead."

"*You're* going to be dead. Look at this, Art. Thumbtacks holding up pictures. He doesn't have time to put a nail in the wall."

"About time for eats." George cuts her off. "Everybody ready?"

George has made a reservation at Ye Olde Ale House, one of the area's better restaurants, which is on a hillside outside of town and commands a view of the industrial valley and a huge aircraft plant.

"You asked me, Brij, so I talked to a priest out at our Saint Edwards," Betty says, "and he said you have to arrange for adoption in your own area. They're pretty sticky about religion, too. Want both parents to be Catholic."

"I know," Bridget says. "We're not getting any younger. I want something else besides that store in our lives. But I just don't know how much time George could give to a child."

"Don't worry. When kids come into your life, they take over. Stuff you thought was so important just isn't."

"But we do have a baby." Bridget laughs uncomfortably.

"Road Runner will never graduate from college. He'll never bring you grandchildren," Betty says somberly.

At the restaurant, everyone orders a turkey dinner except Martha, who has lamb. As the relish dish and bread basket are placed on the table, Betty and her brother both reach for the basket. The restaurant specializes in a honey biscuit with nuts in it, and Betty holds one up and looks at the faces of the people around her. They stop their conversations and look back at her. Solemnly she says, "In memory—no, in honor of Richie, who loves these."

First there is silence. Then George says, "I'll eat to that."

"George, can't you eat like a civilized person?" his wife says. "Nobody's going to take it away. Look at him, Mum, isn't he fat?"

"Oh, Brij, don't worry, his father always thanked God for a good appetite," says Grandma Santangelo.

"He'll die from a heart attack."

"And your smoking is going to make you live longer," George says, puffing on a breadstick.

"I know that it's not good, Georgie. But too much food isn't either. Every time you cut a pound of meat, you have to taste a slice."

"Just to make sure it's not spoiled." He winks at his mother.

"Let him eat, Brij," Grandma Santangelo says with her warm smile.

The rest of Easter afternoon is spent back at George and Bridget's home, where Bridget gets out a shopping bag of pictures going back to her childhood in England. There are pictures of her as a young girl standing in front of a B-29 with the thin young airman whom she met at a base dance. Other pictures show George and Bridget's wedding in England and their early married life. The collection thins out as their married years go on. There is just a scattering of pictures taken during the past five years. They have owned the store that long.

It is early evening as the Neumeyers start their trip back to Mariposa. Again the roads are crowded. Joan is staying overnight with George and Bridget, and Grandma Santangelo soon dozes off, so Betty, Art and Martha are left alone to digest the day's happenings.

"There is definitely something wrong," Betty begins. "I feel so bad for George."

"He's doing OK for himself," Art answers back quickly. "He's been talking about closing a day a week for a long time now. He better do it so he can spend some time at the house. Spend some time having fun with his wife."

"She's always picking on him. Who can stand that?"

"Look who's talking," Martha says, a small smile creeping onto her face.

"Shut up." Betty jerks around toward her. "I never pick on your father for eating."

"Look at him, thin as a rail," Martha says.

"When I meddle, it's for people's good, so don't be a smart-mouth about it."

"Telling Aunt Brij to adopt a baby. That's their business."

"I just want them to be happy," Betty says, turning toward the front of the car. "And they won't be until they have something to love."

"Besides the dog," Art adds.

Grandmother is taken home and, as the Neumeyers near their house, Betty breaks the silence with a soft, "I just wish Rich would be there when we got home. What a surprise. I wonder if he knows it's Easter today?" Turning onto Birchwood Street, Betty sits up straight. "Isn't that Rich down there?" Three sets of eyes look down the street, but there is no movement except for shifting shadows caused by the locust trees moving in front of the street lamps.

MARTHA: My mother keeps on talking about how good it would be to have Richie home. Doesn't she realize they'd be hacking away at him if he were here? Many people think it's always my father picking on him, but she's behind so much of it. "Artie, don't let him do that!" or "Artie, he can't talk to me like that!" She used to do it when we were kids: "Wait till your father gets home and you're really going to get it for being bad!" He'd come home from a rough day and then have to punish us first thing. And they never made Richard feel worthwhile. He loved mechanical things and he bought this motorcycle that was all in pieces and he said he'd fix it up. They were so damned smug the day he sold it, never having gotten it to run.

ART: This Easter was no different than any other. Except Rich wasn't here. He was a crab and we all know it. He didn't add, he only subtracted. But when you love somebody, you overlook their faults.

BETTY: This morning we didn't have to worry what side of bed Rich would get up on, but still I would rather have him here, tension and all. Art doesn't say much; he downplays the change this Easter. But this is the pattern of the future. This Christmas, there might be only us and Joanie. Our family is falling apart. Only when the children get married and settle down and have their own children can it come back together.

So I'm possessive of my kids, so what? Twenty years ago, whoever had any training about kids leaving home? My Aunt Vivian's children never left; they just took an apartment in the same building or down the block. She went grocery shopping and she'd buy a three-pound can of coffee and give each of her daughters a pound. I never realized my children would leave someday, although I always wanted them to be independent. And yet if Martha would have been willing to go to a local college, I would have done anything to keep her here. I would have bought her a new car somehow.

ART: We've had eighteen years of having three children to take care of in this family, then all of a sudden it's cut to two, and all of a sudden you find yourself with only one. It's not an easy transition.

MARTHA: I just worry about Joan now that Rich is gone. I'm worried they are going to smother her, to hold on as long as they can. My mother knows that Joan spends too much time with her; she looks at my mother as her friend. That's good to a point, but she's got to get out with kids her own age, live her own life. My parents

100

love us a lot, they have sacrificed all their lives, but they have to realize that we have to be our own people.

Wherever Richie is tonight, I'm sure he misses the family somewhat, but probably not all that much. I cry when I go back to school each time, but I still am ready to go. This year it was hard for me to come home at Easter. My life is out there; this is an interruption. I'm just wasting time here, talking with people I haven't seen for three years who don't care that much about me and I don't care about them. Rich was smart to just go. He could have never done it gently; there is no such way. He probably misses us but I'll bet he's happy too. This is the first Easter he wasn't forced to go to church.

ART: I love these family affairs, but it's good we don't see George and Bridget all the time. Betty will say that it's great to have family all around, but she forgets how many arguments we all had when George and Bridget lived nearby. Betty always enjoys an affair after it happens. She enjoys in her memories. Because, beforehand, she'll usually be uptight, worried that something is going to go wrong.

Easter Monday dawns sunny and warm. Martha has packed the night before and is ready for the drive into the airport to catch her eight o'clock flight. By late morning, with Joan at her uncle and aunt's, Art at work and Richard and Martha away, Betty Neumeyer has done a couple of loads of wash. Before noon she goes to bed and stays there for the rest of the day, complaining of having one of her "sick headaches." She spends most of the next day in bed also—until Joan is brought home.

6

A Girl's Girl

THE WEEK AFTER EASTER brings unseasonably warm weather to Mariposa and to a wide belt of the country, including Kansas. On the campus of Hillcrest College the grass is still brown and matted from a bitter winter, but the temperature is already above 60 degrees on this Thursday morning. It is seven forty-five, and the campus is beginning to come alive. Groups of girls with miniskirts, pressed jeans or slacks, most of them with long clean hair—a few with the currently popular shag haircut—walk among the buildings. The boys are similarly neat in appearance, wearing jeans and flannel shirts for the most part; a few of them have shoulder-length hair, and there is a smattering of beards, mustaches and bushy sideburns distinguishing a few faces. For the most part, the scene this morning is one that many parents would like to envision for the college they send their child to.

On the top floor of the two-story shingle house on the edge of the campus that is home for Delta Zeta sorority, Martha Neumeyer has just been awakened by her alarm clock. She climbs out of her bunk bed, careful not to step on the girl sleeping below her. The room is no more than twelve by twelve feet and in it are jammed the bunk beds, a separate bed, desks, chairs and Martha's collection of stuffed animals. A pair of pantyhose hangs from one corner of a chair, books are strewn over the desks, curds of dust peek from under the furniture. Martha's posters dot the walls proclaiming "Love is everything" and "Let us discover the love in each other." Art made Martha a small shelf to fit into her corner of the room, and she has covered it with candles, most of which have never been burned.

Martha stretches and then walks down the short hallway to the bathroom. She washes quickly, brushes her teeth and returns to her room to put on a plaid lavender miniskirt. She then pulls a lavender turtleneck over her head. She looks at her breasts, amply pushing out the tight-fitting sweater, and smooths the material down toward the skirt. Then her eyes move to her face and a slight look of pain—as if she had just felt the twinge of a hypodermic needle—crosses her face. Martha quickly applies some makeup over the bumps on her chin and cheeks and blends the color onto the rest of her face.

A few minutes before eight o'clock, Martha Neumeyer runs down the stairs into the empty living room of the sorority house and out the front door. Her heel catches on the second step and she stumbles down to the sidewalk, just barely keeping herself from falling.

"Fuck," she says huskily, her throat still not clear from the night. She looks sheepishly around her, but no one is in sight. Martha starts on her way across the sunny campus, toward Old Main and her class, Methods of Secondary Education.

Hillcrest is on the outskirts of the city and could easily be passed by, for there is little to distinguish the school. The buildings are a collection of whatever was architecturally popular at the time over the past hundred years when there was money to build them, from stone fortress Old Main to the rectangular red brick and glass Arts and Music Building. Perhaps Hillcrest's best-known landmark is a paint-encrusted stone bench in front of Old Main. The bench is Hillcrest's billboard; whenever a group wants to publicize an activity, the bench is repainted during the night. An anthropologist studying Hillcrest would find, by peeling off layers of paint, that there was an Afro-American week, a memorial service for the students killed by the National Guard at Kent State, but mostly a yearly cycle of fraternity and sorority functions. This week, the

103

theater group is putting on Ionesco's *Rhinoceros,* and the title is displayed in stark white letters on a gray background.

Hillcrest, like many private schools, has had a hard time staying solvent in recent years. Once a proud bastion of Methodism—although never considered more than a mediocre school academically—it has severed its church ties in order to get more federal and private funds. It used to be a campus where the sight of a cigarette or a liquor bottle were rarities. There still are rules in Martha's sorority that a girl must not smoke or drink with her Delta Zeta pin on, but such rules are ignored. Beer cans make up a good portion of the trash that the cleaning crews remove from the dormitories.

Teetering on the verge of insolvency a few years ago, Hillcrest brought Osgood Haskins in as president. Students are often critical of him, citing high bookstore prices and low-quality food that they are required to purchase—but Haskins says he has had to impose rigid controls to keep the school going on its $3.5 million budget. However, students were pleased when he scrapped the old core curriculum of 63 credit hours, including religion, foreign language, philosophy and seven other required subjects, and brought in a 15-hour core curriculum in which students do not have to take courses they are not interested in. Haskins also encouraged old professors and told new ones that their courses should address themselves to current problems and interests and should use currently popular books. Soon *The Greening of America, Human Sexual Inadequacy* and hundreds of paperback books became course texts. Speakers like Jerry Rubin have been allowed on campus. "We can keep guys like Rubin in a controlled setting here," President Haskins told his board of trustees when they questioned him, "and let the kids see how invalid they are. And then the students can make up their own minds. Rubin called for them to overthrow the administration, and he didn't even get a rise."

Campus activism never made much of an impact on Hillcrest even through the tumultuous late 1960s. This week, an Indochina teach-in is planned, but the turnout will probably be small. With the renewed bombing this week of Hanoi and Haiphong, Harvard students stoned and vandalized their Center for International Study, and at the University of Minnesota students burned a flag and occupied the office of the Air Force recruiter. At Hillcrest, a Navy recruiter making a campus visit has handed out dozens of leaflets, answered questions about the service, and generally has been treated with respect.

Hillcrest does not have anything resembling a women's liberation group, and perhaps the girl from Mariposa pulling open the heavy door of Old Main is typical of the reason why it doesn't. Martha Neumeyer feels the women's libbers to be bra-burners and rabble-rousers who are protesting vehemently for insignificant points. Martha directs her energies elsewhere.

She is one of the better known students among the 1,300 people who attend Hillcrest, as is evident from the series of greetings she receives as she trudges up the stairs. Martha has been elected to the Student Senate; she was a member of the committee that evaluated faculty performance. She is active in the state student-teacher organization and is regional vice-president this year. She was a freshman orientation leader, has written for the Hillcrest newspaper and annual and was activity chairman of her sorority. Many of Martha's other activities on campus—like those of her mother at home—are service-oriented. Martha Neumeyer helped get oil drums onto the grounds when littering became a campus problem; she served Thanksgiving dinner at the Salvation Army and helped with an Olympics for retarded children and an Easter egg hunt for faculty children.

Hillcrest, for Martha Neumeyer, has a clear-cut set of advantages and disadvantages. The smallness of the school has allowed Martha, an above-average but not brilliant student, to participate and excel in many activities. But Hillcrest's smallness and lack of academic stature has resulted in a narrow choice of courses and a largely undistinguished faculty. This morning she is faced by a gangly young man who came off a Kansas farm, went through state university to receive his Ph.D., then was teacher, principal and superintendent in a tiny town called Blattyville. This afternoon

105

in English Literature the professor will be a man students call "tired and tenured"; in French History, an earnest young man who lectures in both French and English with a boring, plodding outline driving him on.

By this, her junior year, Martha has grown tired of Hillcrest and regrets having come here. She has had the same professors over and over and has had to change her major from French to Spanish to History to English as she ran out of courses that she thought might be interesting. In French and Spanish she found that the entire department consisted of a single professor. From the vantage point of Mariposa, Hillcrest is an ideal college for Martha, a place where she can be involved and not lost in the shuffle, as her parents warned her would happen if she went to a place like American University, her first choice. For Betty and Art, Hillcrest is a safe school, moderate to conservative in orientation, tangentially church-related, and buried in America's heartland, away from the excesses of both coasts. Like President Haskins, the Neumeyers see the college as a "controlled setting."

Hillcrest is the place where Martha really learned to research term papers and to read a book in a single day before a test. Here she also learned to smoke, swear, and "give the finger." Here she joined a sorority and as a vestal virgin was initiated with tears and candlelight. Here she had her first crushes, something most girls experience in high school. Here, this year, she experienced love, sensed passion for the first time and was two-timed. Also this year Martha found out that married men, not only in soap operas but in real life, cheat on their wives. She herself was attracted to a married man—Barry Lancer, the adviser to the student-teacher association.

Martha takes her seat in a room with a high acoustical-tile ceiling and drop fluorescent lights. Dr. Laker pulls out what looks like a long silver pencil, but then, with a flick of his finger, a piece of chalk is revealed.

"Individual differences, class, that's what I'd like to talk about today," begins Dr. Laker. He is a tall, rawboned man with closely cropped hair and a smile that verges on a grin. "There are many ways to deal with them," he says, putting a transparency on the projector. Dr. Laker goes down the list: A, fail and the student repeats; B, acceleration; C, electives; D, homogeneous grouping, E, heterogeneous grouping; F, enrichment; G, bonus system, H, contract. As he goes down the list, explaining each briefly, pointing to them with the chalk, Martha dutifully records his words in her notebook.

Dr. Laker again mentions the term "homogeneous grouping," and for the first time there are some stirrings of a class discussion. A black girl from Kansas City says groupings of students by intelligence is a caste system. Martha shows a flicker of interest—her slit eyes open wider—and raises her hand. "It's just another word for the tracking system," she begins, "and we had it at Mariposa High. OK, I was in the A track and A-track people ran the school, but then I had a br— Well, I knew a lot of people in B track and they knew the school thought they were dummies and out of it, and here all they did was score a few points lower on some stupid test in elementary school."

"Good point, Martha," Dr. Laker says. "We could go on all period about the good and bad aspects of homogeneous groupings. Now on this next transparency we see some other approaches used to cope with individual differences."

Twenty minutes later Martha is sitting in the Student Union, having her usual breakfast: a Coke and a doughnut. Across from her is her roommate, Pat, a stocky girl with short brown hair and somewhat mannish features. "Goddamn Laker," Martha says, tightening her bottom lip and chin. "Got to get the material out. Forget about the discussions. God forbid the spoon-feeding would be interrupted."

"You stayed awake the whole period, Martha?" Pat smiles and then drops her head on the table as if she had been drugged.

"No small effort."

"The lord and master cometh," Pat whispers as she looks across the Student Union.

Martha looks up to see Steve Brighton walking toward the table where the boys from Tau Kappa Epsilon always sit. He holds himself erect, his six feet giving the impression of at least four inches more, his blond hair cascading down his head, gently turning upward before it comes to rest on his shoulders. Steve asked Martha out in her freshman year—once. He has dated many girls at Hillcrest, and a call from Steve Brighton is something girls brag about for weeks.

"Arrogant bastard," Martha says. "Comes in like he should have a retinue with him. Tell me, Delta Zeta sister, why do men have to be the eternal pains they are?"

"Elementary, my dear Neumeyer," Pat says in a British accent.

"Let's run away together," Martha says, and she and Pat laugh heartily.

MARTHA: I vowed I never would join a sorority, but when I was a freshman, Delta Zeta had a bunch of fun girls. All the beauty queens went to Alpha Omega Pi. The DZ girls were warm, and I was lonely so I joined. But now the sorority is different. Everybody's worried about how many dates they have. Man-crazy.

I think a lot of the girls trust me. Like Bo came to me first when she was pregnant and wanted to get an abortion. I'm everybody's sister. But a girl like Darlene Stritch! She plays the big virgin role, and I'll bet she thinks I'm a whore. She knows I spent nights with Mark at conventions, but she doesn't know I never went all the way with him. I'll bet her fiancé is screwing her up one side and down the other, and yet she looks down on me. One really bad mistake was when Pat confided to Darlene I had a little tête-à-tête with Barry. He's married and I felt cheap after it happened, but it was really nothing. But Darlene told her fiancé, who used to be Delta Sig, and soon it was all over campus. A reputation I got. But I'm still the virgin. If they only knew.

I came to school so innocent. Now I'm this marked woman in some people's eyes. In freshman year I dated a black guy from Alabama. Never told my folks about that one, and it never amounted to much except to kill my reputation. It drove everybody crazy to see us together—whites and blacks both. A black girl from here in Kansas was in my history class, and she used every

108

opportunity to get off on some hostile tangent when we talked about blacks. One day she got into a whole big thing about the myths about blacks being so superior in sex, and she kept looking directly at me. And white guys let it be known they didn't want to date a girl soiled by black hands. I was so naïve. But after reading *Autobiography of Malcolm X* and *The Care and Feeding of White Liberals* it sunk in that white guys really felt inferior to blacks in sex and they were jealous. Sex! If that's what guys base their evaluation on, then to hell with them. They really can be bastards. Pat has been so crushed by guys—she hates herself anyhow—that her self-confidence is shot. I've been bruised too. They pick you up and then they drop you without a word.

Girls never treat each other like that. When somebody in the house is hurting, other girls really try to help them out. Girls will send a card or a rose when another girl is down. The guys just move on. They don't give a shit. That movie *The Fox* made me think a lot about lesbian relationships. At first I thought it would make me sick when I saw the two women kiss, but it didn't. It was beautiful. They really cared about each other. I could really see how two sensitive women could love and live with each other. I'm so damned confused about my own sexuality anyhow.

There's no place to talk out something like that. I sure can't do it at home. In fact my parents really get pissed at me when I tell them things aren't so rosy. I'm getting the college education they wanted, so how can I be complaining? So I tell them basically what they want to hear. I don't think they want to make me feel guilty—at least not consciously so. They just want me to enjoy these years, but they don't realize so damn many things are up in the air. I was a sheltered child, the original late bloomer. I never really dated until college. I didn't have my first menstrual period until I was a senior in high school.

By midafternoon, Martha has put in an hour's study plus two hours of work in the audio-visual lab, today learning how to thread a film projector and make a transparency. The sun has continued

109

to shine throughout the day, bringing people out onto the grass and bringing down class attendance in the overheated rooms in Old Main, but Martha has resisted the urge to leave her work behind. At three o'clock Martha and three of her sorority sisters take seats at the back of the class on the third floor.

"You know, Viv, that house meeting went on forever and ever Tuesday night," Martha says to Vivica Hanson, the sorority president. "We should use *Robert's Rules of Order* or something."

Vivica, a tall, Nordic-looking girl with curly brown hair framing her face, looks up from her notebook. "It goes on and on sometimes. Say, you weren't so perky at song time."

"They say you get senioritis in sorority; I got a bad case of junioritis," Martha says, as she puts the knuckle of her right thumb against her lips. "How many times has Rosalee been pinned anyhow?" she goes on, looking at Professor Frichly, who is talking to a student at the front of the class. "My arms get tired passing candles for her."

"Just about a dozen."

"Last time, class," the teacher begins, "I felt that the three hours were interminable. Getting longer every week, don't you think?" Members of the class, including Martha and her sorority sisters, nod yes. "Aha, just as I thought."

Professor Frichly exhales in a loud wheeze and begins in a bored tone to talk about Antony and Cleopatra. In his rumpled tweed jacket, he is almost a caricature of an English professor. His receding gray hair is scrambled and tumbles over his ears; his black turtleneck sags; his front teeth are so widely spaced that when he smiles it looks as though a tooth is missing.

"Now we have the Egyptians, who are subject to the Romans, and we have Cleopatra," he says, as he sits on his desk. "Hmm, now what could Cleopatra use to take care of her nation?" He smiles. "What was *uniquely* hers that she could use?"

"Sex," a married woman in her late twenties answers.

"Very good. Now without getting into Masters and Johnson"—he interrupts to laugh at his own commentary—"how can she use her sex?"

110

"Play off one man against the other." "Use her beauty and lure the men to her and then get what she wants from them." "Well, you know," come the answers.

"We must take into account what the Elizabethan audience was, shall we say, up for, when Shakespeare was writing," the teacher continues. "Queen Elizabeth herself was shameless in flaunting her sex and—I hate to repeat myself more than once a semester, so stop me if I told you this—Elizabeth wore dresses cut down to her navel and was given to—"

"Yes, yes, we heard it," come a number of voices.

Martha doodles on the margins of her notebook and looks over at Susy, another sorority sister. "The dirty old man in him never gives up, does it?" Martha whispers.

At the end of the class, Professor Frichly hands out test papers. Martha at first turns her face down, then eases up one corner. Her frown turns to a surprised smile as she sees an A-minus in the upper right-hand corner. She had picked the first of three questions: "Shakespearean tragedy reflects the intense interest of the Elizabethans and Jacobeans in psychology. Explain and illustrate. What dramatic functions are performed by psychological phenomena?"

Her answer reads, in part:

> Several of the plays we read depend considerably on psychology for dramatic effect. What is going on within the minds of the characters may be more important than the external action. One such play is *Othello*. Iago is a character whose mind we carefully scrutinize. Some critics go so far as to say that he was psychotic, and indeed his name does appear in the pages of several books on abnormal psychology. Psychotic tendencies come through in his cowardice. He stands back safely, watches others become tangled in deadly schemes. He cannot face reality and in times of stress he crawls into a protective shell. While Shakespeare in his time was not familiar with the scientific knowledge about the psychotic, there was still deep interest in the workings of man's mind and how such evil could destroy the innocence around it.

"Do OK, Martha?" It is a gentle voice, but it startles Martha; she didn't think anyone was watching her. She looks up into a pair of eyes which look all the more deep-set and sad because of the dark circles around them. Parker Blackwood has a thin face, thin body and thin arms that protrude from the bulge where he's pushed up his sweater. His mustache droops over thin lips—and, like Martha, when he talks there is a slight lisp.

"Yeah, A-minus, Parker," Martha says. "How about you?"

"Well, OK. B-minus. And I thought it was pretty good."

"You and Frich don't hit it off too good. What was that whole thing in literature yesterday? About Tennyson and Hallam having a . . . well, really caring about each other. Frich wasn't buying."

"Sexuality, Martha." Parker looks down and then directly at her as if a revelation has come to him. "Like Tennyson writes, 'There lives more faith in honest doubt than in half the creeds.' Hemingway was a real he-man, and now everybody wonders what he was trying to do. Late for class. See ya."

"Hope it gets better," Martha says. Then a questioning look comes over her face as she wonders what she meant, if anything at all.

MARTHA: We never talked about current events or culture or anything at home, so when I came to school I was a babe in the woods. I'm not really the activist; I attended the Kent memorial and I fasted for a couple of days for Bangladesh, but I'm more of a service-oriented person. This school has helped me come out, but still we're in the backwoods. Sure, we have good speakers like John Ciardi, Jules Feiffer and Hosea Williams, but compared to the state universities we're zero on campus movements and politics.

Maybe that's best for me. I'm not an exceptional person. I'll never discover a great medicine or write a book that will enlighten people, but maybe I can be the kind of teacher who makes Shakespeare or Richard Wright or the "Rime of the Ancient Mariner" come alive for kids. A lot of kids wonder if they shouldn't isolate themselves; maybe they are killing the albatross in their own lives, the really good things. "Rime" might point that out.

When I look at the teachers here they're not much inspiration. For the most part they're dead, out of touch. Insensitive, indifferent. Even I see that high school kids are much different today from what I was just five years ago. More independent. I want to be sensitive to their individual differences. If I had a homosexual boy in my class I'd want to be nice to him and not treat him like he had a disease like they do to the queer boys here. Like Parker. He's been kicked out of all kinds of campus things because he's a homosexual. His thoughts are put down by teachers. He's a very intelligent person, and I just hope that when I'm a teacher I'll remember what I'm saying now and not be a stodgy ass about it.

Although it is March, the warm breeze that flutters the wrappers outside the McDonald's stand on the edge of the campus and swirls the American flag around the pole in front of Old Main makes the early evening on the Hillcrest campus seem like the end of an Indian summer day. In the Delta Sigma fraternity house there is talk of a water fight with Delta Zeta sorority later in the week. A dozen freshmen boys outside the dormitory are packing ice around a keg of beer they are taking outside of town where the black ribbons of rich earth are already overturned in readiness for planting. On the porch of the Delta Zeta house, two girls sit on the wooden railing, their silhouettes profiled against a blazing sunset. One girl sits serenely, hands in her lap. The other nibbles at the knuckle of her right thumb.

"Mark called up Pat on some association business yesterday," Martha says, looking over Jessica Land's shoulder to see who is pulling up in the driveway.

"Yes, and what did the darling boy want?" Jessica asks. She is a thin girl who would be more attractive if her face were not so long, her features drawn out. She graduated last year but still spends much of her free time at the sorority house.

"I answered and we talked for a while. He asked if I was trying to forget him, and I said yes."

"You must be more careful of his ego."

"I was kind of mean on the phone . . ."

"He's been so considerate of you."

113

". . . so I wrote him one of those 'Hi-how-are-you' letters. I tore it up. I didn't want him to think I was crawling back."

Jessica smiles warmly at Martha.

"Men," Martha says, nibbling on her thumb and looking down at the peeling gray deck paint on the porch.

"A little more specific than just 'men,' please," Jessica says, putting her arm around Martha's shoulder.

Martha eases away from her touch. "Like those male chauvinist Delta Sig pigs. That card file with how far all the girls will go. Bet they don't even have me on file. Bet I didn't live up to their expectations as the hot chick from the big city."

"Just study and forget about men; you'll be OK, Martha," Jessica says. "You're too good for most of them anyhow. Say, what did the doctor say about your cyst?"

"Says I should have it operated on," Martha says, self-consciously touching herself low in her groin. "And says it'll be six hundred bucks."

"Hurt?"

"Right where I sit." Martha smiles. "Like a lot of men we know. See ya tomorrow."

The sorority house is empty and quiet as Martha curls up on the living room sofa with a British Literature anthology and turns to "In Memoriam to H.M.H." An hour later Martha looks up and realizes she has read only half a page. She looks around the room—at the grand piano, the beamed ceiling, the various trophies on the mantel, the songbooks on a neat stack near the window. She goes to the telephone.

"I know it isn't Sunday, Mother," she says a few moments later. "I just felt like calling. Do you mind?"

"Your father went out for milk," Betty answers impatiently. "Call later; you know we're always doing something after dinner."

"Mu—ther." Martha draws out the word. "I'm sorry the selfish bitch is again imposing on your life."

"Only think about yourself," Betty says. Then she pauses and sits down at her kitchen table and rests her cheek on her closed hand. "It's just that everything is messed up. Aunt Bridget called today and she's telling me all the things wrong with my brother and that she's considering a divorce."

"Divorce! We just saw them last week. Everything was fine."

"She says she's sick of George working in the store all the time. She forgets that she came over from England with nothing and now she's living in a new house and has fancy clothes. I think she's forty years old and tired of slicing salami for a living. Did you see that fur-trimmed coat she had on? Well, Martha, I got mine on sale at Penney's for thirty-nine bucks. That coat of hers didn't cost any thirty-nine bucks. And she looks down on my brother like he came from some crude, ignorant family."

"The store, God, that store."

"So they're going to see a marriage counselor or something. That's a lot of hooey. I just want to see what kind of marriage a marriage counselor has that he can be giving out all kinds of advice."

"They don't tell people what to do, Mom, they just get people to talk to each other."

"So Brij and Georgie talk already. And then your brother!"

"Yeah, how's he doin'?"

"Calls up last night and gives us hell from thousands of miles away that we're not writing him. 'Write to Martha every week,' he says. What does he think he's doing, going away to college? Artie said if last night would have been Richie's first night home, it would have been his last."

"You better go easy on him or he'll never come back."

"That would suit me just fine," Betty says, raising her voice.

"Mean that?" Martha says quietly.

"No," Betty says, matching her daughter's tone. "He said he was reading that education loans might be harder to get and right away he starts another argument: What if he wants to go back to school? The kid's a real grouch. But Artie says it's all talk."

"How's Joanie and everybody else?"

"He could have done the same things here that he's doing in California. He says he's close to the beach but never goes. He's not working, just laying around. He thought he was going to run

115

into action people, but they're all duds. Even had the nerve to ask for some roll-your-own tobacco."

"Going to send it?"

"Of course. He just wants to argue and Artie argues right back."

"Not you, of course?"

"Martha, of course me. I don't want to tell him not to call. I want to know he's alive."

"I don't want to run this up any more so I'll sign off. By the way"—and Martha hesitates—"the national convention is going to be over at Seaside Beach. And a couple kids from out here are going to come out. All right for them to stay over?"

"We'll juggle somehow," Betty says, taking on the martyr's voice that often angers her daughter.

"If you don't want to, tell me."

"No, no, we will. How many?"

"Four or five."

"Four or five! I've got to borrow Francine's folding bed!"

"Mom, it's not till June."

"Who's coming?"

"A couple of girls and Barry, the fellow who's our adviser."

"He's the married one that never takes his wife?" Betty says after a pause.

"She doesn't like to travel—don't start the wheels spinning. And, Mother dear, you will get the chance to meet your almost son-in-law."

"Mark!"

"Mr. Mark J. Hard himself. OK, I'm going. Don't get any hopes up. This is strictly a business meeting."

"Just let your mother work on this for a while. I'll have some grandchildren yet."

"You better talk to Joanie about that. She's your best hope right now."

Later that evening, with the table cleared and the dishwasher sloshing in the background, a wave of nostalgia sweeps over Betty. She plays a Guy Lombardo record and then goes into the closet to

116

fondle her father's threadbare sweater, which has hung there since his death. She asks Art to get out a short reel of film for them to see before Joan goes to bed.

"Martha's bringing some of her friends here in June for their convention," Betty says to her husband as he threads the projector. "Including Mark."

"My competition, huh?" he says, smiling.

"Don't laugh. Martha noticed you grew the same kind of sideburns he has. Oh, Artie!"

"Does he have these too?" he says, feigning ignorance. "Anything more from Brij and George?"

"Just that she's complaining and I can't see it. He's good to her."

"He's also the guy who falls asleep in front of the TV and the guy who puts his fist through the wall when he gets mad."

"She never had it so good. Come on, honey, we're ready."

Joan comes into the room carrying a board on which she's assembling a puzzle of a Norman Rockwell painting. It shows the rear of an apartment building with clotheslines strung across back yards.

"Looks good, honey," Betty says. "You'll be done soon." Betty has always been impressed with Joan's ability to play by herself and be interested in games and arts and crafts. But she is concerned the girl isn't "analytical enough," as Betty puts it. So Betty often asks her to explain what she sees in pictures. She asks about the Rockwell painting.

"It's a tenement and that boy has just come back from the navy and they're talking about it."

"What kind of people are they?" Betty asks.

"Oh, they're poor people, but they're still nice."

"Why do you say they're poor?"

"They live in the city, in a slum. In a tenement house in a slum. Look at the paper on the ground and stuff."

"Honey, we lived in a building just like that," Betty says, giving her daughter a gentle smile.

"Oh, but you were different."

"No, Joanie, no, we weren't. A lot of people lived like that."

Art turns off the lights and starts the projector. Short sequences flash onto the screen: Joan in a christening dress that has been in the family for decades; Martha playing with wicker doll furniture that was Betty's when she was a little girl; Betty's father sitting and talking, the ever-present cigar in his hand; Joan as a baby, giggling at a mobile over her crib.

"Why do they have to grow up?" Betty says to no one in particular. No one answers her.

She looks down at Joan, who is trying to wedge a piece into the puzzle that won't quite fit.

"I'd just like to pickle you sometime, just keep you like this," Betty says.

7

Yankee Doodles
and Dill Pickles

IT IS LATE APRIL, and the steel-gray clouds that have covered the
Los Angeles area for the past few days have yielded neither the
pleasure of sun nor the relief of rain. Richard Neumeyer, wearing
lavender-tinted granny-style sunglasses, eyes the sky and then the
surrounding cottages at Featherstone Court. It is eleven thirty.
Those few residents who work have left; the others are in bed or
getting their first food of the day. The other people living with
Richard left a half hour ago, and he did not ask them where they
were going.

Richard has just finished a cup of tea. With a bored yawn, he
smooths out a wrinkled piece of paper on a magazine and begins a
letter.

Dear People,

Things are coming together really good. I worked this
crazy gig in a discotheque where we were supposed to be
like security police except we were dressed up in Santa Claus
outfits. What a wild bunch of people. Everybody dresses
up like somebody else so you don't know if you're talking
to a guy or a girl. Ran into a really cool guy who is starting
a studio and I'm working with him. There are a lot of actors
out here who aren't stars or anything. They need these port-
folios and the going rate is $100 and this guy is only charg-
ing $40. Been putting up signs for him and everything.

"Who you writing, Richie?"

He looks up to see a short, frail-looking Polynesian girl standing in front of him in jeans and a flimsy T-shirt. His gaze moves from the nipples on her tiny breasts, which show through the shirt, to her face. "My old lady. What the hell, she sent me some pumpkin bread and a whole bunch of shit."

"But I thought you were mad at Mommy," she says in a little-girl voice.

"Listen, she wanted me to call every week. I showed her. I waited a week and a half."

"And what?"

"And she still hassled me. Got a letter and the first sentence was, 'This is the notepaper I got from your sister for my birthday,' and she put the date on it and underlined it like I didn't know her birthday. Then some shit about something coming from the florist, and 'I thought it was from you but I was wrong again.' The same shit I got when I was living there. She fucks up my head with that."

"Downer," she says, smiling sweetly. "Parents can bring you down."

"What's going on anyhow?"

"Nothing. I feel kind of draggy this morning."

"Man, me too. All I do is sleep."

"Thought maybe you'd have something that could help," she says, biting her bottom lip.

"Hey, I ain't no Santa Claus around here."

"I got the bread. Just don't know where to get something."

"What do you need?"

"Well, you know. . . . What's around?"

"I got a lid of pot. I could do you some of that."

"Yeah, but I really want to get off better today. Something to open my eyes."

"I was on speed the last time I called home. Parents said they couldn't understand me, I was talking so fast. They asked if I was drinking. I said we had a bad connection."

"You got any connections now?"

"OK, but you got to take care of me too."

"Right, right," she says excitedly.

A half hour later, Richard walks back into Featherstone Court whistling and bouncing a rubber ball he found in the gutter on the way. The girl has been watching through the screen door and comes out to meet him.

"Just cool it now, I'm not going to lay them on you right here." He motions for her to follow him into his cottage. Inside, Richard pushes aside dirty clothes on the sagging couch and plops down. In the kitchen, flies buzz around dirty dishes and pans. A quarter pound of butter sags forlornly over the edges of a plate too small for it.

From the back pocket of his jeans he brings out a smudged white envelope. He opens it and lets tiny pills run into his hand, then back into the envelope. "They're OK, mini-whites, but take at least two or nothing happens."

"Richie, thanks a lot," she says, reaching for the envelope.

"Hey, what about me?"

She sprinkles three of the pills into his palm. "OK?"

"Yeah, I guess," he says, looking down at them. "Why don't you hang around for a little while and we'll pop together? See what happens." He reaches to put his arm around her.

"Monte gets crazy jealous, Rich. If he gets back, catches me here, he'll go nuts. Maybe later, OK?"

"OK," Richard says with little hope in his voice.

"Really, Rich, I appreciate this. Man, I was down."

"Same way," he says, rolling the pills around in his hand. "My old man and old lady think when I come back it's going to be like before. No way. If I go back, I ain't cutting my hair, and if I want to light up a joint in my room I'll do it. And I ain't paying them rent either. And when I want to leave, I'm splitting."

"Yeah, right," the girl says. "I better get back."

The screen door slams behind her and Richard looks again at the three pills in his palm. He rinses out a glass in the sink, tosses the pills into his mouth and gulps down the water.

After a few minutes Richard feels tingling sensations in his arms and legs. He begins to smile. The tingling spreads, and he is soon up and walking about the small cottage. He looks at the dirty

121

kitchen, and the messy living room that also serves as a bedroom for him, Hank and Marybeth, plus a young couple Hank met and their baby. (Peter left soon after they took the apartment, saying it was too crowded and it depressed him.) He opens the closet where a mop, pail, rags and a hand sweeper are jammed into a corner, covered with a fine coat of dust.

Two hours later Richard is in the shower, whistling to himself. Dishes are draining in the sink, the carpet has been swept, clothes have been picked up and the beds made. Even the front porch is clean.

A few days later, a call goes over the PA system at Rabinowitz Diecutting: "Art, pick up five-one." Art Neumeyer grinds a half-smoked cigarette into the factory floor and reaches for the phone. After listening for thirty seconds he says, "He has, huh? Well what else did he say? A studio? What does he know about photography? Sounds like a deadbeat outfit to me."

Betty Neumeyer, the phone cradled beneath her chin, is wiping the glistening tile counter around her sink as she talks. "It's like the other week on the phone. His head is in the clouds. Everything is wonderful. He's living like a bum, and he thinks that's just great."

"He's so used to making things up now, it's going to be a long time before he tells the truth."

"Why us, Artie, why us? We did everything right by those kids."

"Yeah, we can talk about it tonight."

"What's your big hurry?" Betty says. "He's your son too, you know."

"Don't remind me. Right now I'm trying to get the strength to go back in the office. And not kill Mort Stern."

"What today?" Betty says in a tone of impending doom.

"Nothing out of the ordinary. Just all the time. The talking, talking, talking about things he doesn't know about. We had this job where they needed a double-fold and I told him what it would cost and he said I was out of my mind, that we could do it for half. So I said, 'You quote them then!' We lost money on the job and he's bitching at me that I didn't warn him. It's not even quitting time and he's sitting in there with a mixed drink in his hand ready to go after me."

"Quit, Artie, quit. Get a job out here. Go back to the machines."

"Back to the machines, she says! Try and live on a hundred and fifty a week. Go back to the machines!" A frown wrinkles Art's brow.

"I don't want you to get an ulcer working with those Jew bastards, Artie."

"We'd starve if I went back to the machines."

"You don't have all the problems either," Betty says, again in her doomsday tone. "Grandma has to move. Landlord's daughter's husband died from cancer of the testicles, and the daughter wants to move in with her mom. Do you think George is going to find Grandma a place? Hell, no! It's us again. George and Brij will probably get a divorce on top of everything. Nobody thinks about us. We're supposed to worry about everybody. I'm sick of it, Artie."

Art Neumeyer looks at the four extension buttons on the phone. Only the one he is talking on is lit. "They're flashing me for another call. I got to go, Betty."

"Well, go!" Betty explodes as she presses down on the phone lever. She gets a tone and dials Lillian Rose. Busy signal. She dials Pam Brown. Busy. She begins to dial Patsy MacIntosh, the pastor's wife, but stops after the first three digits. There are a lot of things swimming around in Betty Neumeyer's head. She is angry, confused and disheartened with what is happening in the family—both the one she came from and the one she created.

Finding her mother a new place to live is no mean chore in Mohawk County. Single-family zoning has kept apartments to a minimum and hostile reaction to proposed senior citizens' housing on a number of sites has successfully postponed that kind of construction. "Property values will drop," is the ringing cry when it appears that there might be some divergence from single-family occupancy. Mohawk County people are fearful that any variance in building codes—such as that which would allow for sorely needed senior citizens' housing—will automatically lead to subsidized low-income apartments, which will in turn bring the very people they escaped from in the city.

Grandmother Santangelo now lives in what is called an "illegal two," a one-family house whose attic has been converted into an apartment. It is just down the street from George's old house, where she also lived in this space. Betty and Art will have to find her a similar place because legal apartments are both scarce and expensive. It will be just another on a long list of services that the Neumeyers provide for her. Betty buys her mother's groceries—and Art delivers them—although Grandmother works in a shopping center where there is a supermarket. And Betty does her mother's Christmas shopping, although she works in a discount store where most of the gifts could be purchased. Betty is the first to acknowledge that there was a strange dependency pervasive in the Santangelo family and that she bore and still bears the brunt of it.

Betty's mother never had spending money of her own. When she needed to buy anything, she asked her husband for the money and gave him the change. Betty's brother never sent his parents birthday or anniversary cards, so Betty got in the habit of buying them for him. Even when he was stationed overseas, Betty would dutifully buy cards a month before a birthday or anniversary, and send them across the Atlantic, so George could send them back.

Her parents, especially her father, always said they didn't have to plan for their old age because their children would take care of them. Betty recalled that last night to Art and said with hostility, "I just don't see how we owe everything to my mother, who never took any responsibility for her own life. I'll go to the old-age home before I burden my children." The pressure of a dependent mother, coupled with anxiety over Richard and her brother's marriage crisis, drives Betty deeper into depression as the morning wears on. It is only because Betty has a commitment this afternoon that she does not go to bed, for one of her sick headaches is coming on. She has promised Patsy MacIntosh she'd go with her to the crafts program at the Mariposa Public Library.

The crafts program draws from the cross section of women who are home during the day either because they cannot work, choose not to, or don't need to. By one thirty Betty, in a simple wash-and-wear dress that she bought for $5 on sale, is sitting between Patsy MacIntosh, in a light woolen skirt and white blouse, and Patsy's neighbor, an overweight but elegantly dressed woman who is wearing an oversized diamond ring. The craft that the women will learn today is a style of New England painting where aluminum foil is crinkled, then applied to a backing, followed by a paper doily. A painting is then made on a frame of glass, and the white-and-silver pattern provides a backdrop. Betty outlines a heart on her piece of glass and plans to insert "Betty loves Art."

As the class ends a light rain turns into a downpour and Patsy says she'll get the car and bring it around for Betty and for her neighbor, who came in a cab. Betty pulls a plastic foldout rain bonnet from her purse as she stands on the library steps. Patsy's neighbor pulls on a raincoat and Betty notices the label as it flashes by: Bonwit Teller.

"This weather," the other woman says. "And my husband has to drive in every day."

"Into the city?" Betty says.

"Not only the city," she says, giving Betty a warm smile that shows the crow's-feet masterfully applied makeup had concealed. "Way up in the North End. Just started a new job."

"North End," Betty says excitedly, returning the smile. "Whereabouts? I used to live there."

"Way up around One hundred sixty-eighth Street." Then what Betty has said registers. "I used to live there too. Where were you?"

"My father had produce stores. First around One hundred fiftieth and then One hundred sixtieth."

"Oh, Betty, no!" she says, her hands going to her cheeks. "My father had a fruit stand too. Right on the corner of One hundred fifty-fifth. Solomon's. You remember it? Right next to—"

"Of course. Next to the newstand. Oh, my God, you can't be serious?"

"Ladies, la-a-a-dies, please!" Patsy is calling from the car as the two women go on.

Once inside the car, they continue. "Jennings High School, right?" says the woman, whose name is Ruth.

"I graduated in nineteen forty-seven," Betty says animatedly.

"Nineteen forty-nine. Remember Miss Busby, the typing teacher who always—"

"Stuck the pencil under her wig to scratch her head. What a small world."

"Ladies," Patsy says gently. "Can I please be informed as to what is going on?"

"Patsy, we lived in the same neighborhood, our fathers were in the same business," Betty says, and the flow of words slows, "and we're both out here now."

The women part, promising they will get together soon and talk more about the old neighborhood. Betty and Patsy are alone in the car. The smile is still on Betty's face. "Things were so great back there," she says. "Kids didn't go running off all over the place. Everybody was in the same boat; nobody was stuck-up. Nobody acted like they had anything more than anybody else." She stops for a moment, and the only sound in the car is the rhythmic beat of the windshield wipers.

"Her father didn't make any more money than mine," Betty says, the smile suddenly gone and her voice tinged with bitterness. "Look at the start he gave her in life. Probably helped them out with a down payment, got them on their feet."

"Hard to tell," Patsy says.

"I know. I know what other parents did for their kids. Patsy, I loved my father but how could he have done it to us? It all went, Patsy." Betty takes out a Kleenex and dabs at her eyes. "He gambled every day, and he dreamed of dying at the track. He was twelve hours away the day he died. All he left my mother were his clothes and unpaid notes at the bank."

BETTY: In terms of where I came from, I'm a millionaire. But in terms of where everybody else is out here, I'm just as poor as I was back in the North End. I'll always be a step below the people out here. I'm still the immigrant's daughter. Coming out to the suburbs instills grand ideas in you. You definitely always want more when you see what other people have. Things become obsolete. You finally get every appliance you want and the next year they come out with turquoise. Your white ones are obsolete. It's so easy to fall into the trap of buy-now-pay-later. The day we paid off our last Seaboard Finance loan was a big day in our lives.

But so what? Artie tells me we have as much money as we're ever going to have. What about that cruise we always wanted to take? Forget it. I'll never be happy out here because I'm like a fish out of water. One friend goes to Russia, one to the Holy Land. I can't stand it. I cultivate poor friends when I can find them. I should have stayed back in the North End, and I would have never known the difference. The way I talk about money, I probably need a psychiatrist. Sure, I'm possessed with it; I wonder if we're going to have enough for now, for retirement, in case of illness. My parents never worried about anything but the next meal. I can't recall the word "future" ever being used at home.

Anthony Santangelo, Betty's father, was born in Positano, a small coastal town near Naples, Italy, to a landed and financially comfortable Catholic family. For reasons that Betty does not know, the family migrated member by member to the United States. Anthony arrived in 1899 at the age of nine. His future wife, Joan Bataglia, was born in the North End in 1902, her family having arrived around 1880. The Bataglias left Italy as Catholics, but soon after they arrived in the United States they changed to Methodism. Methodists greeted the Bataglias when they arrived at Ellis Island and arranged for their first night's lodging, where they slept on mattresses made of dried banana leaves. They didn't forget this first kindness and rewarded the solicitous Methodists by attending their church and converting to their faith.

Anthony Santangelo remained a nominal Catholic until he died, but he wanted his two children brought up Protestant. Before the first Santangelo child, Betty, was born in 1929, the newly married couple lived a good life. Anthony had part interest in two fruit stands with his brother Gennaro and was able to buy stocks in the heady 1920s. Anthony's brother William was the most prosperous Santangelo during that decade, dabbling in many businesses but specializing in bathtub gin. Anthony also sold the homemade product, but when the federal agents cracked down, they knew which brother to raid. Thousands of dollars were drained off from the produce business to keep William out of jail. Anthony and Joan Santangelo, who had fine furniture and sculptured carpets for their five-room apartment in one of the North End's newest buildings, had to put their household goods in storage and move in with a relative soon after Betty was born. The stocks Anthony owned were worthless, debts were being called in that he could not pay, and he eventually lost both stores.

In adversity, Anthony Santangelo was not one to bemoan his state. He still placed his numbers bets with the old man who delivered papers and either went to the track or bet on the horses through a man well known on the block as a "walking bookie." He bought into other fruit and vegetable stands, holding them or losing them with equal good humor. Even in the toughest days of the Depression, any market run by Anthony Santangelo was a place where credit would be extended. He would always give a head of lettuce or an extra apple or two to the poorer families and would sometimes send up a box of produce free of charge.

When he was "between businesses" during the Depression he would work at other markets, where his pay might be a hunk of cheese or slices of Italian ham. A proud man, even in poorer times, he refused to go on relief. Betty was born into that good-humored poverty, and it wasn't until she was well into grade school that she knew there was another way of life. Her first pair of glasses were ugly wire-rims, supplied free by some agency, and her underclothes were often ribbed lisle, which she hated. She remembers shivering through one winter in a blue spring coat because it was the warmest one she had.

When she was nine, Betty began to feel a strange achiness in her body that wouldn't go away. It worsened one day and she woke up feverish and so stiff the visiting nurse had to cut her pajamas off to examine her. An immediate transfusion was needed, so Anthony Santangelo lay down beside his daughter and talked gently to her as the blood flowed from his arm into her buttock. Betty was then taken by ambulance to the hospital, where her illness was diagnosed as rheumatic fever and she was given little chance to live.

When she did recover a year later she was assigned to a school for handicapped children, along with the mentally retarded, those who were crippled with polio and shuffled along in braces, and with boys like Mortimer who had cerebral palsy and drooled constantly. To help with their nutrition, all the children were allotted milk, which was poured into tin cups early in the day. By lunchtime the milk would have a thin layer of hardened cream and a sprinkling of dust on it, but Betty was forced to drink it, even though she often threw up on the school bus on the way home.

Although she was left with a heart murmur and a shortness of breath that would stay with her, Betty was reasonably well recovered by the time she reached high school. Still, her mother kept her back from the normal activities of a teenage girl, saying she shouldn't exert herself. Betty couldn't jump rope, Betty couldn't roller-skate. When the children played ring-a-levio, Betty always minded the flag.

However, Betty was deemed strong enough to work in her parents' store, where she began to realize that the family's low state in life was because her father was gambling profits away as fast as he made them. But Betty loved being in the store with her parents. At least then she had their companionship. She yearned for more time alone with her mother, but Joan Santangelo seemed always too busy at the store or too tired from it. On free days from school Betty used to dream that she and her mother would go to the park or the zoo or go window shopping. Instead, her father used those days as opportunities to go to the track, leaving his wife and daughter to mind the store.

Betty saw what was going on and to her it was clear: her mother was at fault. Betty blamed her mother for the cover-ups—like rumpling her husband's bed so no one would know he'd spent the night in jail after a card game in the back of the fruit market had been raided. Betty blamed her mother for smiling blithely as the family lived their roller-coaster existence.

Though all the years and disappointments, Betty retained a deep love for her father, the person directly responsible for the family's

129

poor fortunes. She or George would always greet their father at the door, take his coat, take off his shoes and, kneeling, put on his slippers. When Anthony Santangelo won the daily double for $99 a few days before Christmas one year, took back a cheap coat that was to be Betty's Christmas present and purchased a better one, Betty was brought to tears. His failings could be washed away with a single act of generosity.

As a teenager, Betty was an innocent girl, like most of her friends, whose crushes were lived out on the screen of the Ritz Theater in the North End. She munched on crackers spread with peanut butter and jelly and sighed over Van Johnson. On the day Tyrone Power was arrested for attacking two girls, Betty ran down the block to Myra Walter's building and breathlessly told her the movie star had been accused of "rap." Rape was surely outside her vocabulary and understanding.

Her life was simple, her desires few. She was happy to wear a wartime corsage to her junior prom made of red, white and blue ribbon and defense stamps. She wanted little more out of life except a husband rich enough to buy her all the Yankee Doodle cupcakes and dill pickles she could eat. As high school graduation approached and she was accepted into the honor society after rising to the top 10 percent of her class, she looked ahead to going into nurses' training, which was almost free at one of the city's charity hospitals. Her mother kept telling her she wasn't strong enough, but Betty kept on dreaming. She made application to St. Vincent's Charity Hospital and was deliriously happy when she was accepted. She would be a nurse, one of the highest jobs North End girls ever aspired to. Her mother maintained Betty was not strong enough, so she got one of her relatives who was a doctor to tell St. Vincent's about Betty's bout with rheumatic fever and to say that the illness had left her permanently weakened. The acceptance for nurses' training was withdrawn and Betty was crushed.

The road to a profession closed to her, Betty was all the more determined to pursue another career: motherhood. Doctors told her that childbirth would kill her—as indeed it did some of her friends at North End Elementary who had had rheumatic fever—but Betty was willing to risk death for this crowning achievement. She would marry; she would have children.

Betty saw her friends marrying and their parents giving them furniture and down payments for houses, large sums of money to start their life together. Her father was always a generous man: he peddled black market butter, sugar and eggs during the war but gave away as much as he sold. The refugee Jewish family with concentration camp numbers tattooed on their hands, pregnant mothers—they could get free what others paid premium prices for. Yet there was never any money for luxuries, and sometimes not even for necessities. The Santangelos never had a savings account, never had a phone. It was a bitter realization for Betty that whatever she got in life would have to be through her own efforts. So when she met the slim young man in the glen plaid suit at a New Year's Eve party in 1949 and married him in August of the next year, she was determined to build a secure life with him and the children she would try to bear. She would make sure then they didn't want for material objects or for attention—as she had.

In the evening, Art sits down on the sofa and lights his after-dinner cigarette. Betty pulls a turquoise and yellow afghan over her legs as she lays her head on his lap. "Met a lady from the North End today, Art; folks in the same business as my father."

"Really?"

"You could tell just by looking at her that her folks gave them plenty for their wedding. Plenty," Betty adds with emphasis.

"Baby, you got everything you need." Art looks down at her. "You got me, first of all. Kids. A great house. All kinds of machines to do your work. I would love being in your shoes right now. A little cleaning each day and then just do what you want to. You couldn't pay me to go to work." Art gently rubs his wife's generous midsection with his maimed hand.

"How can you say that, Artie?" she says as she shuts her eyes. "We got more problems than ever."

"Passing stuff. These are the best years of our life."

131

"You sound like a soap opera."

"I mean—" Art is cut off by the ring of the telephone. Betty jumps up to answer.

"Now don't get excited or anything because this doesn't mean I'll make it or anything," Martha says after greetings are exchanged. Art, on the bedroom extension, looks puzzled. Betty somehow seems to know what her daughter is alluding to, and her eyes roll back in a look of ecstasy.

"*Who's Who.*" Betty makes a statement.

"Who's what?" Art says. "What is it?"

"Now don't go planning on it or anything," Martha says.

"Artie, Martha's been nominated for *Who's Who in American Colleges.* Oh, Martha!"

The conversation goes on for another fifteen minutes. At last, when Martha hangs up and Betty and Art are back in the living room together, Art looks at his wife. "You're out there with her, aren't you?"

"You're damned right I am. I've just been nominated too."

The ring of the telephone interrupts them. "I don't need another call for a week," Betty says as she goes to answer it. "Artie, I should just believe you that things are going to be fine."

"I have a collect call for anyone from Mr. Richard Neumeyer. Will you accept the charges?"

"Hello, Richie?" Betty says tentatively.

"Just don't go sending any more stuff because I'm leaving here in a day or two, going to stop in Kansas and see Martha, and then I got to get back to Mariposa because I got a lot of shit to get together—"

"Have to call us collect for all the cursing?" Art interrupts his son's torrent of words.

"Christ, why the hassles right off?"

"I thought everything was going so wonderful," Betty says sarcastically. "You just wrote us."

"I just got a lot of sh—stuff I want to get done back there," Richard answers defensively.

"What's here you can't do out there?" Art says.

"Oh, man, you people don't understand anything."

132

"Did you tell Martha? Maybe she won't even be there," Betty says.

"I thought I'd call her from the airport when I got there."

"Rich, you don't think about anybody," his father says. "She has a lot of plans, so you call her now. You hear?"

"This booth is hot as hell; I gotta go," Richard says.

"We didn't call," Betty says.

"Yeah, well, I got to split."

"Call us from Kansas so we know when you're coming home," Betty says.

"Yeah, if I remember."

"You call," his father says tersely.

The short, jerky conversation over, Art and Betty again sit down in the living room. Betty is the first to talk.

"Aren't you proud of me?"

"For what?"

"You didn't see me begging him to come home. Like my mother begged us to come back from Florida. He went away to be a big shot and nothing happened, so he's coming home with his tail between his legs."

"He'll never admit it."

"But I know it. He didn't do anything in California he couldn't have done here."

"He's not so adventuresome either. All that sleeping bag and knapsack stuff, and here he is coming back on a plane."

"We won, Artie. We showed him. We didn't plead, and now he has to come back."

"And it's going to be on our terms this time."

"At least he could take a bus so he could see some of the country."

"I could wring his neck. Calls all that way and then he wants to hang up right away."

"We can't rub it in when he gets home, Artie; can't rub it in that he wasted his time and money and everything."

Black Beauty stands at the top of the stairs, wagging her tail and looking at Art and Betty. "OK, OK, let's take you out for a walk," Art says.

Inside the house, the Neumeyers have control over their dog. They have trained her to come no farther than the top step, and the dog is so indoctrinated that if she is carried into the living room she cries; if put down on the carpet, her legs turn to jelly and her kidneys become weak. But outside the house at 97 Birchwood, it is different. As Art takes the dog out the front door, Black Beauty strains at the leash, pulling so hard she cuts off her own wind and sounds as if she's choking. Inside the house, the Neumeyers have always tried to have control over their children. Betty and Art know, as they walk through the night, saying nothing to one another, that once outside the front door, it is quite different.

8

Coming Home

ON THE MORNING OF MAY 9, Betty sits at the kitchen table looking over the postcard that arrived the day before from Kansas. The day after he called, Richard left California and flew to Kansas, where he considered, then rejected, spending the summer working on a farm there. He is again on his way home. From the date on the card, Richard should by this time be somewhere in the Great Lakes region, hitchhiking toward Mariposa.

"Fix this for me, Mommy," Joan says, backing up so her mother can get at the top button on the high-necked frilly blouse she's wearing today.

"What a wonderful Mother's Day present if he gets home before Sunday," Betty says, hunching her shoulders forward the way she does when she wants to accentuate a smile.

"Yeah, I hope so too," Joan says. "We can go to the beach and do all kinds of fun things this summer."

"Hurry up so you won't miss the bus, honey."

"Joseph Mangano is just going to be smoking at the bus stop anyhow."

"Why don't you tell Mrs. Durgin?"

"I did." Joan's eyes get bigger. "And she just told me I was a tattletale."

"That teacher! What kind of example is that?"

"What do you think Richie will look like, Mommy? Will he be different?"

"He'll be beautiful," Betty says wistfully.

"What if his hair is long and Daddy hollers at him?"

"Let me take care of the details. Once he gets home, everything will work out fine. Go get that white ribbon, honey; it'll look nice after all with that outfit."

Joan goes back to her room and picks up the ribbon from between the bottle of Dura Gloss tropical-pink frosted nail polish and the Sugar Pink lipstick on her dresser. Joan's is a small room but colorful, with pink walls and green objects, the colors being those of her sister's sorority, Delta Zeta. There are green curtains and a green bedspread, a green rug and a matching wastebasket. About sixty stuffed animals and tiny ceramic figures—mostly birds —sit on the bed, dresser and shelves. A huge poster of Donny Osmond, another poster stating "Love Is the Key to Happiness" and pictures of birds look down from the walls. With the ribbon gone, Joan moves her identical framed pictures of Jesus and her 1940s-era brush and mirror set to fill in the gap.

After her mother fixes the ribbon in her hair, Joan looks up at the clock. "Wow, am I going to be late! Don't let Daddy holler at Richie so he leaves again. OK?"

"Everything will be fine."

A few minutes later Joan is at the corner of Birchwood, waiting for the District 32 school bus that will take her to Pawnee Elementary School. She nods or says "Hi" to a few of the twenty children standing on the grassy traffic island. Most of the children are talking in groups or with a friend, but Joan seems to have no one to talk with so she goes over to a pine tree and intently studies the needles. Two trees away is Joseph Mangano, but he is not smoking.

Soon the yellow bus speeds up to the corner and comes to a jerky stop. Joan is one of the last children to board, and she takes a seat near the front. As conversations and wads of paper fly about her, Joan sits quietly, a vague smile on her face.

She was always a smiling, happy child, even in adversity, even with pounds of plaster and gauze surrounding her midsection like a huge diaper. Her good-natured ways assured Art and Betty they had done right to have another child; the child, they agreed, would symbolize to them that their marriage would go on, that Art was still a man after his hand was mutilated.

Joan was born with a dislocated hip, and the cast that she had to wear most of her first year of life was medically necessary, but it also served as an invitation into the adult world that she would grow to enjoy. Betty had to take her everywhere, and even when the cast was off Joan remained her companion at meetings and activities of the Women's Society at the church. Joan was never a disturbance. In fact, she seemed entranced by the endless discussions and the work, and so she was readily accepted by the other women. Martha had also been a good companion to her mother, but Betty knew Joan was her last baby, her last opportunity to form what she began to call "the ideal child." As Betty often tells Art, "We made our mistakes on the others; now there's Joan."

When Joan started school and was not as vivacious and responsive in a classroom, Martha told Betty, "She's saying 'ugh' to this school business; she knows there's a better world outside." Betty only smiled, allowing Joan to take "sick days" from school so they could shop together, go to lunch, do things Betty's mother never had time for.

As Joan grew older, she never had problems relating to adults; she was the adorable, attentive child. In school, it was different; the audience was not so captivated. To Betty, it was a phase, and she showed little concern; the Joan she saw was turning out exactly as she had planned. Joan benefited more by the Neumeyers' increased affluence: she had the wardrobe, the knickknacks, the colored sheets which the other children didn't. Martha had showed signs of being a good pianist, but it wasn't until Joan was taking lessons—and Martha was at college—that the family could afford a piano. As Joan grew older, Betty continued, without apology, to mold her daughter. When the Sunday school class was going to hear and discuss the record "Jesus Christ, Superstar," Betty removed Joan until that phase was completed, saying she wanted her daughter to hear Handel's *Messiah* first. When Joan talked about becoming a baby-sitter, and even took a Camp

137

Fire course in child care, Betty showed little enthusiasm. She wanted Joan to gear herself toward volunteer work, such as being a candy striper in the hospital. Betty told her daughter that volunteer work brought maturity and responsibility. Baby-sitting brought only money and inconvenience, as Art and Betty would have to take their daughter to her work or at least wait up for her.

Along with trying to impress responsibility on Joan, Betty always wanted her to be "social," to be comfortable with all groups and then choose the one she wanted, a comfort Betty had never felt. This year she has allowed Joan to date a boy named Michael, who has taken her for walks to the park to feed the fish and birds. The half-dozen times Joan has asked her mother if she could wear Betty's blue eye shadow, Betty has happily applied a smudge to her daughter's waiting lids. Martha hated makeup, and Betty never pushed it on her. Joan has been more willing to learn about how to act with boys: why they should be allowed to open doors, how the right clothes enhance appearance. Betty feels she somehow didn't impress such things on Martha. With Joan, it will be different. "She'll be just like me, demanding," Betty has told Art.

The bus jerks to its last stop, in front of Pawnee Elementary School. Betty and Art, formulating the "ideal child," were careful to make sure they were in what is considered an ideal school district, both on Tulip Lane and now on Birchwood Street. District 32, as its ragged boundaries show, was tailored to exclude the children of Union Heights, which is on the border of the county and 40 percent black. Betty and Art are probably typical of District 32 parents; they wanted to be assured they were buying good and, as importantly, all-white education.

Joan's school is set back from Pawnee Road by a lawn, a parking area for teachers and a scattering of flowers and shrubs, the most noticeable of which this morning is the forsythia, in full bloom. The school was built to house thirty-one classrooms in 1964, but a few years later the soaring population forced the construction of a wing with sixteen more classrooms. Eventually, there was room for 1,300 students. If anything distinguishes Pawnee, it is the contrast between the original building, a handsome, low, brick structure accented with white trim, and the annex, an austere, utilitarian two-story box. The first was built with some forethought; the second almost in a panic.

Behind the buildings are several acres, mostly worn through to the sand, where the Pawnee children have their athletic activities. Inside, the school hallways and classroom walls are faced with painted cement block or tiled, all surfaces a clean, bright, lime-green color. Each room has its own sink, water fountain, paper-towel dispenser, and huge blond-wood cupboards for supplies, and smoky tan chalkboards, supposedly easier on the eyes.

As children stream into Pawnee this morning, it is a noisy but happy scene. At nine o'clock, the doors slam shut and all visitors or late students funnel through one corridor which is barricaded with a long table. There was an incident a few years ago in a neighboring state where a child was taken out of class and molested, and Mariposa parents immediately tightened up on their own children's security.

The school, like other Mariposa structures, was built for the boom. But, like the Neumeyer house on Birchwood and the Park-side United Methodist Church, the school does not adapt easily to these less generous times, less than ten years after it opened. The student population is shrinking—next year three teaching positions will be eliminated—and the projections are for Pawnee to lose students for the next ten years.

Some parents criticize Pawnee as an experimental, progressive school. There are cassette recordings of children's classics in the "learning center" formerly called the library, and there are reading machines to help students increase their speed. But apart from the modern conveniences—some, ironically, paid for with federal funds earmarked for "educationally disadvantaged students"— most of the classrooms at Pawnee are run as they were a generation ago. Students sit in alphabetical order, in rows, and quiet is a crowning virtue.

Many parents, especially the most recent arrivals in Mariposa, back traditional methods. Benjamin Caruso, the sturdily built crew-cut principal, has seen a hardening of attitudes over the past five or six years. Mariposa used to be the first step out of the city for the upwardly mobile salesman or junior executive, and they and their wives seemed open to experimentation. Now Caruso talks about the "terminal families" that have bought homes, people who struggled to get out of the city, people to whom change itself is a threat. Buying in Mariposa is like buying an insurance policy; they want to see the status quo preserved, as they have no intention of ever moving again. These same parents fought the building of benches and shelters at bus stops, fearing they would become gathering places for undesirables or, in fact, for their own children.

Joan Neumeyer meets Bunny, one of the girls from her class, and the two girls walk into the classroom on the second floor of the Pawnee annex where their teacher, Mrs. Merleen Durgin, is busy putting up the bulletin board, which is headed MAYTIME MAGIC. Above it is one slogan she keeps posted: "The world owes you a living, but you have to work hard to collect it." Some of the boys are pitching baseball cards against the back wall, and as Mrs. Durgin turns toward the class she says, "OK, fellows, you know the rules. Bring them up here. Joseph, you too. Come on, turn in all the cards."

Mrs. Durgin is a widow in her early fifties with whitish-gray hair. She has been teaching at Pawnee for fourteen years and has raised a family on her salary, which is now $16,000. She is a motherly, even affectionate woman who is not afraid to hug a child when he or she is in need of support or encouragement. She is also a strict disciplinarian whose daily litany of "No's" keep her children in order. "No talking in line." "Don't go beyond the end of the corridor." "There will be no lunch until these rows are straightened." She begins her class each morning with the traditional salute to the flag and then the singing of "This Land Is Your Land," a song written by Woody Guthrie, who was accused of Communist affiliations in the early 1950s and whose music was once banned from the radio.

The first period calls for a half-dozen members of the class to be in band or orchestra practice, so the remainder work on covers for their autobiographies. "The trend is toward the individual,"

Mrs. Durgin says in her nasal voice, "yet you are a member of this class; isn't that right, Josephine?"

"Yes, Mrs. Durgin," answers the girl, who was caught giggling at the boy next to her.

"But you are an individual, and I want your covers to show that individuality. OK, begin, and please keep quiet. We'll be much better friends and have a lot of fun today if everybody is quiet."

Students take out construction paper of various colors, place them on blond Formica-topped desks and go to work. Most of the titles have already been traced with stencils. For Josephine, a gregarious little girl who already dyes her hair a bright red, it is "My Life and Me." Josephine, popular among the boys and a fashion plate—today she is wearing all blue: a stylish crepe blouse and matching miniskirt, panty hose and shoes—giggles once more and sets to work. Next to her is Beth, a thin girl with stringy blond hair and bags under her eyes. Beth's parents are separated, and she lives with an aunt. Her cover reads simply "My Life." Roger, a short, hyperactive boy who often has to be disciplined by being kept back from activities, has titled his "ME!" Berry, a tall, dignified girl with curly brown hair who is one of the best students in the class, and Patty, an awkward girl with a lumpy padded bra and food-stained clothes, sit side by side and both have "My Autobiography." In the fourth row, third seat back, Joan Neumeyer carefully completes her hand lettering: "All About Me." Her classmates are satisfied with merely a title, but Joan goes on to draw and color a large striped vase full of tulips and zinnias. When Mrs. Durgin is ready to move on to reading, Joan has to be told twice to put away the artwork.

Mrs. Durgin hands back the comprehension sheets from the last books the children have read. They are allowed to choose from dozens of books, and those on adventure, animals, science and history are dog-eared from use. Books on interesting women and their contributions stand straight and unused. *The Texas Rangers*, *The Abraham Lincoln Joke Book* and *The Story of Submarines* are especially popular. Joan's scores, as usual, are below the class average. For instance, in the vocabulary section on her book,

Pagan the Black, she got 50 percent where most of the class got between 70 and 90. As Mrs. Durgin hands back the results she looks at Joan straight on. "Joan, all we have to do is look the words up in the dictionary. We can't be lazy and expect to get good marks."

"Yes, Mrs. Durgin," she says mechanically, not looking up at the teacher.

After thirty minutes of reading it is time for American History. Berry, who is wearing a Brownie uniform, slowly raises her hand as the class takes out a text, *The Changing New World, North and South America.*

"Mrs. Durgin, doing the homework last night, I found that the encyclopedia gave fifteen states in the Louisiana Purchase but the book had only thirteen."

"You'll often find conflicting information," Mrs. Durgin recites in a monotone, "and when we do, we need to do more . . ."

"Research," someone finally fills in the end of the sentence.

"Very good; we need to do more research. Raise your hand before talking next time, Rachel."

Mrs. Durgin has called herself an unorthodox teacher because she allows students to do macramé projects in their spare time and encourages them to expand on their classroom work by doing outside research papers. But in history, social studies and science classes, she is pleased when students answer in complete sentences, even though those complete sentences are taken right from the book.

In social studies, Mrs. Durgin asks, "Is food a big part of a family's budget?"

Answer: "Food takes a big bite out of the money United States families spend."

"Are food prices going up or down?"

"Food prices keep rising because of a number of reasons."

As the school day passes, Joan's interest rises and falls with her level of participation in the class. In music appreciation, which is taught by Mrs. Tifton, Joan has her hand up for most of the questions about Beethoven. Her eyes open wide, standing so she can be seen, she joins the chorus of children breathing "Oh, oh, oh," hoping she'll be called upon to tell about Beethoven's birthplace or what instrument he played. In math Joan stares blankly at fractions like $5\frac{1}{2}$ minus $\frac{3}{4}$ and has completed only ten of the twenty problems when most of the class has them all finished.

Betty says the school is stifling Joan's native creativity. Even the principal, Mr. Caruso, admits that the brand of teaching that goes on in most schools, including his own, dulls children and that by the third or fourth grade they have adjusted to the lock-step mentality of Obey and be rewarded, Be different at your own risk. Whatever the reasons, Joan's ratings in various subjects are below average: 46th percentile in word meaning, 18th in spelling, 4th in arithmetic, 66th in language, 24th in social studies and 20th in science. Teachers' comments in her school record, coupled with her mother's replies, paint a picture of unfulfilled promise and parental frustration:

"Joan understands the concepts but poor work habits account for the poor report card. . . . Works very quickly but much too careless; does not correct her work; when told, does not follow written or oral directions." Comment from mother: "Wants reading retested."

"She's too social and chatty. She's very impressed by clothes and teenagers. School should be her major concern." Comment from mother: "Wants an IQ test."

"Joan has not learned to follow written or oral directions. I mentioned that Joan did not use the scrap paper to complete the arithmetic computation in the achievement test. Mrs. Neumeyer said she did not have much faith in these tests."

"Joan is having a reading problem. She has the ability to do the work but prefers to relax and let the others read instead. . . . Joan often hands in incomplete work, and Mrs. Neumeyer feels she needs a very strong hand."

Mrs. Durgin knows Joan's record, she has seen her perform in class and she has had dealings with Mrs. Neumeyer.

MRS. In the parent-teacher conference, Mrs. Neumeyer said
DURGIN: she doesn't care about pushing Joan; she just wants her
         to proceed at her own pace and not be uptight about

school. Fine. But then the mother is incensed at Joan's low reading level and grades. She starts blaming everybody but Joan or herself. Joan doesn't have to produce because the blame is never laid at her feet. I think the child has learned to be a little manipulator, not in any horrible sense, but she just knows what will work. It works at home fine. At school it's a different story. She can't fool me and she doesn't fool the other kids.

She is hated by the boys; they even steal things just to get to her. In the fifth grade, girls usually have a best girl friend. Joan doesn't. She just drifts from girl to girl. When her mother had her in modeling class, Joan could dangle that in front of the girls and she was popular for a while, but it didn't last.

Her mother has standards that Joan can't live up to—Mrs. Neumeyer wants her to be a good student without the effort; she wants her to be popular; she wants her to be everything. She's one of these city mothers who vows that everything is going to be different for her children whether the children want it or not. And Joan just cops out.

Mrs. Neumeyer called the school one day and started screaming at the nurse that Joan had been hurt in gym class and the nurse wouldn't see her. It turned out she had twisted her leg, and when she went to the nurse's office another kid was there and he told her the nurse wasn't seeing anybody else that day. Joan took it at face value and went back to class, but when she got home she was injured all over again. I called Mrs. Neumeyer, told her the whole story and suggested she apologize to the nurse. She was indignant! Her girl can never be wrong. Joan must be a change-of-life baby that the mother can't decide how to raise: Is she a child or a companion? So the child is torn between the children's world and the adult world and she's not fit for either.

It is now 2:50 P.M. at Pawnee and the bell will ring in twenty-five minutes. Mrs. Durgin knows better than to start new material at his time, so she uses two things that have always produced results in the past. "Class, if you behave until the bell rings, everybody gets a Sugar Daddy. And if you pick up the papers around your desks and sit up straight, we'll play . . ."

"Word games!" comes the shout from the class.

Mrs. Durgin looks sternly at them. "No one raised their hands. Now, is that the way you're going to be?"

Soon the class members are sitting straight at their desks, their social studies books turned to page 98.

"Jagged countryside," says Mrs. Durgin.

Joan raises her hand. "Rugged," she calls out.

Just about the time the bus riders from Mrs. Durgin's class are forming up in sexually segregated single lines to march outside at the end of the school day, there is a sound at the front door of 97 Birchwood Street. Betty Neumeyer has been dozing on the couch for the past hour. It is shortly after three, and the newspaper boy doesn't deliver until four or later. She sits up as Black Beauty races up from the basement, barking and whining. The doorknob turns slowly and the door opens.

A familiar face looks through the iron railing alongside the stairs and says simply, "Hi, Mom."

Betty throws the afghan to the floor and rushes down the stairs to embrace her son. His hair is at least an inch longer than when he left and is matted and separated by the rain. His dirty flannel shirt and jeans give off a stale body smell accented by dampness.

"Richard, Richard, we just got your card this morning!" Betty beams. "I didn't think you'd be here already."

"Except for a while this morning when I got soaked, I got good rides. Man, the place still looks the same."

"It's only been seven weeks," Betty says, then repeats "only" softly.

"Hey, Beauty, how you doing?" he says, reaching down.

The dog backs away from him.

"C'mon, girl, it's me."

"Well, we didn't forget you, Richard. How was it? Did you have a good time and do a lot of interesting things and meet a lot of interesting people?" Betty's eyes scan her son, dancing from his face to his muddy boots and back again.

"Yeah, it was good. This dude gave me a ride and he said they need workers over in Pennsylvania where they had the floods.

145

Cleaning up the crap that's still there. Five bucks an hour. Said if I could round up some guys and chicks too—they've got to set up a field office—he could put us all on."

"Already you're going and you're not even in the door," Betty says angrily, her smile wiped from her face in that instant.

"We'll see. Man, I want to get cleaned up, get a shower."

Betty smiles once again. "I'll make your favorite food tonight. If I would have known, we'd have killed the fatted calf. Or had a turkey at least."

"What's my favorite food?"

"You'll find out."

By the time Joan gets home from school, her brother is already in the shower. She shouts through the bathroom door, "Hurry up, Richie, I want to give you a big kiss before I got to go to Camp Fire. Richie, come on!" Brother and sister meet a few minutes later, and Joan leaps into her brother's arms. "Wow, your hair is long," she says. "What is Daddy going to do?"

"Joanie, we'll have to see. If my hair goes, so do I. Hey, did you get all those cards I sent from the road?"

"Yeah, Richie, the first one was best. The one with all those drunken cowboys at the saloon." Then she says softly, "Mommy and Daddy didn't like it that much, but I thought it was neat."

"Richie, answer the phone," Betty calls from the back bedroom. "Hello."

"Hel— Rich?" The tone is one of guarded enthusiasm.

"Hi, Pop. Just got in a little while ago."

"How did everything go?"

"Good, yeah, good. You want to talk to Mom?"

Art Neumeyer hesitates. "Yes, I guess so."

Running a towel over his hair, Richard goes to his room and turns on his stereo. Hearing the music blasting out of the two speakers, Betty says to her husband, "He wouldn't have that set if we'd have let him sell everything like he wanted. He acted like he was never coming back. Seven weeks. Big deal."

"How's he doing anyhow?" Art says.

"Talking about a job in Pennsylvania working with floods or something. I don't know."

146

"We're not going to be a stopover between his jaunts, Betty."

"Let's just be glad he's home."

During the afternoon, Richard unpacks his knapsack and Betty eagerly puts the pile of sweat-stained, mud-caked clothing into the washer. Joan is off to Camp Fire, where the girls have to decide either to take teddy bears or Instamatic cameras as their reward for selling their quota of candy. In a lifeless meeting of seven girls of Joan's age, there are complaints about having to march on Memorial Day and further complaints about the colors of the construction paper they are to make the group's symbol out of. Ne Lua Ho Ki Hi is the group's name, which is Indian for song, outdoors, trust and accomplish. When Joan arrives home her mother questions her about her disappointed look and Joan answers, "None of those girls care about Camp Fire any more. They have too many activities. They just argue about everything."

"Honey, you don't have to be in it if you don't want to," Betty says.

"No, no, I do, Mommy," she says almost plaintively. "I just want to have fun."

"OK, so get dressed up now for tonight. We've got to be at church at seven thirty. And I don't want to rush through the first meal with Richie home."

Richard's friend, Ron Bronowski, arrives at the house just before five o'clock, says hello to Betty and goes to Richard's room. Meanwhile Betty hums under her breath as she prepares the evening meal.

By the time Betty begins to scrub the Idaho potatoes, Art Neumeyer is already on a train to Mariposa. He left work early and, because the 4:56 is more crowded than the train he usually takes, has to stand for most of the ride.

In Richard's bedroom, Ron sits on the edge of the bed and silently watches Richard comb his hair. "Going to hell at home. God what a mess," Ron finally says as he looks down, his eyes on the new shag rug. "It's OK to work at a mental hospital, but then when you get the same stuff at home! Hey, how did it go anyhow?"

"It was great," Richard says, patting the comb against his palm.

147

He is shirtless, and as he throws his shoulders back his ribs show noticeably through his pale skin. "All kinds of freaky people. And nobody works. Everybody's on welfare and food stamps. You learn a whole new way of life out there. Maybe I'll never work steady again. Fuck it! Who needs all the hassles?"

"Why come home then? You know you're going to get hassled here."

"I got a lot of shit to get together. We're going to Colombia, and I want to save up some bread."

"I don't know, Rich, with the way things are going at home."

"Anyway, if they don't like the way I look and the way I act, they can kick me out," he says defiantly. "I've lived away from home. I can make it anyplace now. Hey, let's see what's going on in this hole of a town."

"It's not even six o'clock. Nobody's around."

"Let's go."

Betty passes Richard on the stairs leading to the front door. "Going?" she says, looking surprised.

"Yep," Richard says with no note of apology in his voice.

She takes two packages of frozen food from the freezer and then suddenly something registers. She races up the stairs and hollers out the door, "Richard! Are you going to be home for supper?"

"Probably."

Betty's eyes roll back in her head. She slams the frozen packages onto the counter, puts her hands on her hips and stares out the kitchen window to the house next door, some twenty feet away. Then she looks up at the clock. There is at least a half hour until she expects her husband to get home.

Richard slouches in Ron's truck as they bump along over the covered trenches where new sewer mains have been laid. Richard lights a cigarette and throws the empty pack out the window. "Got it all figured out, Ron," he says. "I'm going to get me a trail bike and a truck, get it all together and head back for the Coast. It's cool as shit out there."

"Why couldn't you just work out there, Rich, and get all the stuff?" Ron says, his face, as usual, expressionless.

"Ron, it's just easier to get shit together here."

"You're going to be right back where you started. Making money to get wheels so you can get to work to make money to get— You know."

"This time it's different. I got it better in my head."

RICHARD: The plain and simple fact is that I got to where I felt out of place everywhere. Why come home? I don't know. No place else to go, I guess. I just wanted to get out of California because those people were ripping me off like crazy. I'd buy two bars of Ivory, and those dudes say they like Dial. That's cool, so I say, "Buy the Dial." They say, "Why buy it right now when we got plenty of soap?" I got sick of it. Bum joints off me, make me pay for food. Hank goes shopping with my money and buys butter every time. I always use margarine. Man, I got sick of it.

All of a sudden I had to get out of there. I was going to hitch but I heard that places like Flagstaff in Texas or New Mexico, they catch you with your thumb out and you don't see daylight for four months. Maybe you get to make a phone call. I just couldn't waste any time, so I flew most of the way.

I'm going to be hassled at home, I know it, but I don't give a shit any more. I'm eighteen years old and for the last three years I thought I had my own mind. I went to California and I found I didn't. I know a lot of stuff now, stuff I would never have learned if I didn't get away. I'm going to do what I want from now on. I don't want to hurt people. But when I see something I want— like a trail bike—I'm going to buy it without batting an eyelash.

Ten minutes after Richard leaves the house, Black Beauty barks and whines in the special way that she does only once a day. The red Chevrolet pulls into the driveway and Betty shoots an alarmed look the clock. It is only 6:10.

Art comes in the front door and, as is his custom, says nothing.

149

He scratches Black Beauty under the chin, then walks up the stairs, places his paperback book on the newel post and hangs his topcoat in the closet. He kisses his wife and asks casually, "Where's the boy wonder?"

Betty rolls her eyes again. "Ants in his pants, that kid. Got in, took a shower, dumped all his dirty clothes on me, and Ron Bronowski came over so they already went out."

Art looks at the clock. "We eat at the regular time."

Twenty minutes later, Art, who seldom smokes at home before dinner, has finished a second cigarette and is going through the paper. The house is still except for the rattle of Joan's hamster, engaged in a rare daytime sprint on his metal wheel. "Supper ready?" Art asks quietly.

"Maybe we should wait a minute, Artie."

"Put the food on, Betty," he says, getting up suddenly, "just like usual."

"He might be right back."

"Listen, if he's going to live here, he'll be here for meals like the rest of us."

"But Artie, the first day!"

"Put the food on."

Chicken roll with a teriyaki sauce, baked potatoes with dried onion soup mix combined with sour cream, asparagus spears with grated cheese sprinkled over the top, garlic bread and a crisp salad are placed on the table.

"OK, Joan, pass the chicken; what are you waiting for?" Art says, his forehead wrinkled into a frown.

"Nothing. Oh, nothing," she answers, looking at her mother as if she could and should stop the meal.

"Be easy on him Artie," Betty says.

"Not when he can't grow up and be here like a human being and treat us like equals, Betty," he snaps back.

The homecoming meal is taken mostly in silence. When the Neumeyers are finished, Betty says to Joan, "Take a mint, honey; after the garlic bread your breath will smell."

Joan goes to her bedroom, and Betty and Art Neumeyer stare at each other across the dining room table. "Just too big, this table," Betty says, pressing in on the sides as if she were trying to condense it.

"All the leaves are out."

"I know. Just too big for the three of us, Artie." She looks at the remnants of the meal on the serving dishes. "Stereo blasting, laundry—I love it."

"What was that?"

"Nothing. Let's put this food in the refrigerator."

"No." Art gets up from the table. "I'm going to teach you a lesson and him too. Make a plate for him and put it on the kitchen table. Either he eats it there or it spoils."

"Artie, what kind of sense does that make?"

"Daddy, you got to be nice to Richie or he's going to leave again," Joan says, running in from her bedroom.

"Not until he grows up. We had seven peaceful weeks, and we're not going from one crisis to another now that he's home. And you mind your own business!" Art angrily strikes a second match after the first goes out.

Art takes Betty and Joan to Parkside United Methodist for mother-daughter night, picking up one of Betty's friends, Nancy Tufts, along the way. Once Betty tells her that Richard has come home, Nancy turns to Art and says, "How does he look anyhow?"

"I don't know. I haven't seen him yet," Art says.

Art rides alone back toward his house. As he turns onto Birchwood, he stops suddenly as a dog runs out into the street. As he nears his house, Ron Bronowski's panel truck is backing out of the driveway at 97 Birchwood. The truck picks up speed as it comes toward Art, and as his lights shine into the truck's front seat he sees not only Ron's familiar blond hair but the dark hair of his son. Art waves and pulls over, expecting the truck to do likewise. It races by and disappears around the turn at the end of the street.

Art pulls into his driveway and slowly gets out of his car. He looks once more up the street. It is dark except for street and house lights. He walks into the house, up the stairs and for a moment stands transfixed, his eyes staring blankly at the kitchen stove. The increasingly louder noise of a running motor breaks Art's

151

gaze and he goes to the window. The sight of Ron's truck on the street in front of the house brings him to the front door.

Richard jumps out of the truck and, seeing his father standing behind the aluminum storm door, waves halfheartedly before walking toward the red Chevrolet.

Art walks slowly out of the house, also toward the car. He reaches in his shirt pocket for his cigarettes but they are not there. "How ya been?"

"OK."

"You still look alive."

"Gained ten pounds. Couldn't find my house key; that's why I was going this time."

"There's a lot of food left. Probably still warm. On the kitchen table."

"Yeah, I'll be in in a minute. Ron's got some cable trouble on his radio." Art says nothing and walks back into the house.

Art pulls the portable television set into the living room and turns on the basketball play-off. Ten minutes later Richard comes into the house with Ron and, standing in the kitchen, wolfs down huge hunks of chicken and garlic bread. "Want to get my car back," he calls into his father through a mouth filled with food.

"When you get time, we'll sit down and talk about the whole thing: insurance, the new muffler I had to put in, everything. And it's not your car. Remember, I bought it." Art turns up the volume on the television set.

"Man, I was the only Lakers' fan in this bar in Kansas. Man, that was rough!"

Art says nothing.

"I was going to stop in the city and see you today on my way in, but I was soaked and everything."

The play-off game has been a seesaw battle, seldom more than four points separating the teams. Art turns down the volume and meanders into the kitchen as if he had nothing else to do.

"Seeded the back yard already?" Richard says.

"Yeah, I think we stand a good chance this year."

"Bathroom looks good; new tile, huh?"

"Big Andy had a sale on linoleum. Just took me a Saturday afternoon."

"Well, me and Ron are going to split. See you later."

"Rich, just let me see you alone for a minute."

Ron walks out to his truck, leaving father and son facing each other in the kitchen but neither able to look the other in the eyes.

"I'm not going to make a big deal out of it, Rich, but if you want to live home, you know the house rules. Clean room, respect the other people who live here. OK?" His voice is calm; if Betty were to hear him, she might even describe it as compassionate.

"Yeah, right," Richard says airily. "Hey, somebody threw a cardboard box on my car in the garage."

"Whose car?"

"Yeah, OK, we'll talk about it right away because I've got to get wheels. I'm going."

Later that night Betty and Art are in bed and Betty has told her husband how beautiful the mother-daughter night was. Art tells her he has "laid down the law" for Richard.

"He going to leave again?" she asks. "Then he'll only come on Thanksgiving and by invitation. He has to know this is his house and he can run free, Artie."

"Baloney. He'll respect us for it some day, Betty."

"Did you find out if Blue Cross will cover Martha's operation?"

"No, she's over twenty-one now. How did we get on that?" Art says, turning his head quickly toward his wife.

"That cheap goddam company you work for."

"She better have the operation out there; it'll be cheaper. How much is it going to cost?"

"Artie, a cyst isn't just an ingrown toenail. Six hundred dollars! And where are we going to get it, Artie? Tell me, where?"

"We'll probably have to take out a loan. It won't be the first time, so calm down, Betty, and let's get some sleep."

153

9

Troublesome Ministers
and Lemon Meringue Pie

"EITHER BE HERE or don't."

Richard Neumeyer stands with his hands on the back of a chair at the dining room table. He looks at his father, who has just spoken and who is now placing a piece of meat loaf on his plate.

"So I'm five minutes late," Richard says, looking bored and shifting the weight from one leg to the other. "Can I eat or not?"

"Sit down," Betty says softly.

"Before you do, get a shirt on. We don't live like your friends in California," Art says.

"Say the prayer while I'm gone," Richard calls over his shoulder.

Richard has been home for three weeks, and many things are back to what they were before he left. He has his old jobs—at the factory, with a raise in pay, and at the hamburger stand—he is again driving the black Chevrolet; he is in almost constant squabbles with his parents. Martha, who finished her junior year at Hillcrest and had her operation, came home a few days ago. She is also at the table, looking down in silence at her empty plate.

"Grandma went to the broker, and everybody wants two hundred or more for an apartment," Betty says. "I don't know what she's going to do."

"Did you call the senior citizens' office to see if she can get a supplement?" Art says, spooning some broccoli onto his plate.

"Supplement? She would never take anything like that."

"She ought to do it," Richard says, as he pulls out his chair and sits down. "Martha, pass me the meat, huh? Lot of people out on the Coast on welfare, and they're doing great."

Art digs into a mound of mashed potatoes.

"This guy and his old lady that were living by us had a kid, and welfare paid for the whole thing."

"Martha could have been on welfare for her operation; Grandma could be on it right now," Art says, his eyes blazing. "But they have pride."

"Old lady meaning his mother?" Betty says, looking at her son.

"Naw."

"Old lady meaning his wife?"

"Naw."

"When they have children, then it's his wife. I don't care what anybody says."

Richard hurriedly eats his food. "Man, I don't understand all the hassles," he says. "I'd go on welfare or unemployment in a minute. Anything for free bread; I don't care."

Betty slams her fork onto her plate. "So your father can go into the city every day and work, to pay your welfare!" she yells at her son, her face becoming flushed. "Your grandmother can work to pay your welfare."

"I'll just take what I can get," he says cockily. "I'm not taking what isn't mine. It's the American way." He smiles.

"Your generation makes me sick," Art says.

Richard looks passively at his father and goes back to finishing his meal. There has been one change since the trip. The nervous boy of two months ago who couldn't eat at the family table has been replaced by a young man who has at least a veneer of sureness. And he has a lot of what Betty tells her friend Lillian Rose is "smart-ass talk."

The meal ends in silence. Betty, Martha and Joan clear away the dishes as Art sits on the sofa and reads the newspaper. Richard goes to his room for a short time and then leaves, bound for Ron Bronowski's house.

"Hey, Martha," Art calls in from the living room, "what did the WACs have to say today?"

"Those people. Because of the operation, they won't accept me until I have another physical, which is July first. Then, if they accept me, I'm supposed to be ready to go on July fifth. Which effectively shoots the hell out of my summer. Who's going to hire me for a month? I don't know if I want to go any more."

"Nobody here's forcing you," Art says. "When do those kids from Kansas come?"

"June twenty-first. And I don't want to work that week. This looks like the worst summer ever."

"Ah, but we get to see the fabulous man in your life, Martha."

"Don't expect too much. Anyhow, that's history."

"Our girl would pass over the best thing around, Artie, just give her the chance," Betty says.

"Now I know what Richie's been going through around here," she says angrily, biting her lower lip. Before her parents can reply, she hurries to her room and slams the door.

"Now what did I say so wrong, Art?" Betty says.

"Nothing, nothing. These kids are so touchy. If we did that when we were still home, we'd get our necks wrung."

"She could be a little more grateful. We're working our butts off to get her through college, and I'm going to get a job so we can go to her graduation without stopping at Seaboard Finance first."

"She's going to be six thousand dollars in debt when she's finished, Betty. Don't forget she's paying her share."

"Go ahead, side with them, Artie."

"Baby, I'm not siding with anybody," Art says in a voice laced both with anger and pleading.

Later in the evening, Martha grows restless reading, and after finding out through a series of calls that her old friends either aren't home or don't want to go out, she decides to go for a ride in the balmy June night.

As she stops for a traffic light along Main Line Drive, she recognizes the easy gait of the lean, dark-skinned boy in a red-white-and-blue striped T-shirt and bell-bottom jeans who has just come out of a liquor store. He is laughing to his friend, and both of them have bottles in brown paper bags in their hands. An elderly couple looks at the two boys; then they shake their heads.

Martha rolls down the window on the rider's side and calls out, "Going shopping for your momma, little boy?"

"Hey, Martha, how you doing?" Len Morris says, breaking into a wide smile that accentuates the whiteness of his teeth against his brown face.

Len introduces his friend to Martha after she gets out of the car, and the three of them lean against the fender. After telling Len a little about the last semester at school, Martha asks with mock innocence, "What you got in the bag?"

Len looks around to see if anyone is close enough to hear. "Party tonight, Martha, but this is for the other people. Me and Johnnie got some better things going." He pats his back pocket. "This grass is so beautiful. Man, on this stuff you can see things so clear. You listen to music and it comes through like you never heard it before. Come on over with us."

Martha pauses. "Supposed to be back with the car already. I didn't know you were burning incense to the god Pot, Lennie."

"Booze gives you hangovers and makes you dull. This stuff sharpens you up."

"Now what did you find out on pot that you couldn't otherwise?"

"Wow, I mean things like Camus, existentialism. Me and Johnnie were high last night, and the whole thing about insanity came through. You know, there's a very thin line between the sane and insane. It just came through in a flash. Dig it?"

"That's wonderful," Martha says. "Seems like something we talked about in high school."

"Martha, you're missing the point. I'm open to so many more things. Don't tell me you never turned on."

Martha lights a cigarette, feigns a smile and repeats in the same cadence, "Don't tell me I've never turned on."

"You know the old story; don't knock it till you've tried it."

Martha nibbles at her calloused knuckle. "Anything else going on, Len? Going back to school?"

"Not for now. I'll get back. But right now I got a group together and we're playing some jobs and I just want to see what I want to do. Not rush into things, you know. Hey, come on over, Martha. We'll have a good time tonight."

"The car."

"We'll pick you up. That is, if your parents aren't gunning for me."

"I'll take a pass this time. By the way, you sounded good on Easter. Joan really loves that gospel choir."

"The Morrises bring soul to Parkside Methodist."

The Morrises, the Neumeyers: two middle-class couples of about the same age, two family names on the rolls at church whose religious and social lives are intertwined. Martha Neumeyer met Len Morris in Methodist Youth Fellowship, a place where adolescents are allowed to come in social contact with the opposite sex under sanctioned, controlled circumstances. When the MYF did things as a group, Martha's pairing off with Len was acceptable, although certainly not encouraged by her family. Betty and Art knew Benjamin and Polly Morris from church and had convinced themselves it wasn't because the Morrises were black that they had reservations about them. To Betty and Art, Benjamin was "using his blackness" in the job he had at that time, a cutlery salesman. Benjamin called on all the members of the church, and the Neumeyers felt he was applying a subtle pressure: If parishioners didn't buy it would be construed as a racially motivated rejection. Betty and Art personally did not buy.

It was all the more painful for Art and Betty to face the fact of their daughter's attraction for Len because she had not dated any white boys before him. Betty repeatedly told Martha that Len avoided black girls and dated white girls like her to prove a point, not because he cared for her personally. For Martha, the years of church and parental teaching on racial equality began to look more and more like so much sham in the face of what church people said behind the Morrises' back and how bitterly her parents opposed her seeing Len. For Martha, the squabbles over Len marked the beginning of her estrangement from organized religion and to some extent a distancing from her mother and father.

A few nights after Martha saw Len on Main Line Drive, Betty and Art are getting dressed to go out for an evening that will include some contact with Len's parents. Tonight, the Couples Club of Parkside Methodist will have their progressive dinner where couples will have different courses at three houses before returning to the church for dessert. Betty tugs at the lime-green polyester knit slacks that cling to her legs and show the gentle ripples of her flesh as well as the outline of her panties.

Art pats her on the rump. "Solid, baby, don't lose an ounce. I love all of you."

"This stuff is like skin, Artie. I look like I'm poured in."

Betty and Art climb into their car, and soon they are on their way to the first of two homes they will visit tonight, one for appetizer and the other for salad, before returning to their own house to serve the main dish.

"Molly has the nerve to do that at the last minute," Betty huffs to Art as they turn onto Parkside Avenue. "When I work a dinner party for Mrs. Donahue, she has eight people in and she can't handle it alone. If I asked anybody else to take four at the last minute they'd kill me."

"Betty, we got a big roast beef; I put a leaf in the table. It's no big deal."

"Art, you don't know a thing about it. You don't know about place settings and chairs and everything! Responsible people just don't call you up at ten o'clock and tell you they're copping out. Especially a main-course person!"

"Betty, let's have a good time and forget about it. Do we have to stop for anything?" Art says as they approach Parkside United Methodist, whose white columns glow in the streetlights in contrast to the nearby houses which are shielded by trees.

Betty's slight frown turns into a soft smile. "Our second home. No. For once we don't."

The Neumeyers do not have a wide circle of friends in Mariposa, and most of the people that they know well and spend time with are members of Parkside. So the Couples Club and its monthly functions are the key to their social life. Art and Betty are considered faithful members of the club, seldom missing any function, whether it be a scavenger hunt, Hawaiian night or dinner dance. Even as the church's membership has declined, Betty and Art have been steadfast, giving of their "prayers, presence, gifts and service" as Methodist doctrine demands of its members. As have all churches—except some with fundamentalist orientation—Parkside has seen especially hard days in the past decade. More than a slackening of religious interest or fervor is to blame. The church has been racked by internal battles between factions of the congregation and has turned into, in the words of the Methodist district superintendent, "a church that eats up ministers."

Parkside was founded at its present location in 1947 when a seventy-five-year-old frame church was floated down the Pewaunee Canal and then trucked to a location in the midst of the burgeoning suburb of Mariposa. Members flocked to the new Methodist church, seeking both a religious and social base, and soon there were three Sunday morning services being held in the simple wooden sanctuary. Worshipers had to be there a half hour early if they expected to get a seat. The congregation was divided on whether or not a new sanctuary was needed, but the builders won out and a handsome new colonial-style church of red brick, white pillars and trim was constructed. Members continued to be added and, at its peak, Parkside had 1,100 members and a $110,000 budget. Today, the budget is only $60,000 and there are 600 members on the books, perhaps 400 are active, and only 150 make it to the two Sunday services. White paint turned gray in the sanctuary hints at the financial condition; roping off the last ten pews so the few worshipers will move forward attests to the scarcity of people at Parkside today.

On a balmy autumn Sunday in 1961, a new member was accepted into the congregation. Joan Neumeyer was baptized with water on the same day that the pastor, Roger Stanford, invited a baptism of fire by advocating open housing. Art and Betty had bought their house in Mariposa Park from a real estate broker who said, "There are no niggers out here. We pride ourselves on that." When they asked the broker how close they would be to a Methodist church, he brightened up and said, "I'm a Methodist too; you'll like it over at Parkside."

Art and Betty made it no secret they were escaping from blacks by moving out of the city, but when a petition was circulated to oust Pastor Stanford because he wanted Mariposa houses to be available to all races, Art refused to sign it. Art didn't want black neighbors and he was angered at "dragging civil rights into church," but still he would not sign the petition even after Dave Bismark, who would later become a bowling team member, tried to persuade him. Dave was one of a group called the "Unholy Seven" who worked hard to get rid of the minister.

The petition, with hundreds of names, was presented to the district superintendent but he would not remove Stanford. If he would not leave them, the more vehement protesters vowed, they would leave Stanford. They inquired of the various denominations until they found one that was willing to start a church in Mariposa. And so the Mariposa Reformed Church was begun with hundreds of Parkside's members, among them some of the heaviest contributors and most active members. Faced with continuing community criticism, a much smaller congregation and a new Mariposa church that was there only because of him, Pastor Stanford resigned less than a year later and left the ministry.

Still other members left Parkside Methodist in protest for a variety of reasons over the next eight years: when a black assistant minister was assigned; when Pastor Mark Warwick took an anti-Vietnam stand and offered to counsel conscientious objectors; when a young assistant minister was thought to be corrupting the minds of the young people with his thoughts about love, community, sharing and concern. Anonymous phone calls were made to the church office, threatening violence if the ministers didn't get back to their proper work.

When Firth MacIntosh was interviewed by the pastoral relations

161

committee, they made it clear that they had had enough of controversy and factionalism; they wanted a "Bible preacher" and not a social activist. Pastor MacIntosh has fulfilled most of their expectations. A Southerner by birth, he has brought a love and knowledge of Scripture to the Parkside pulpit, but occasionally he also has stepped on toes. He has obliquely criticized the war, the President and national priorities—too mildly for Martha but too forcefully for her parents—but he has been careful to combine enough of the "old-time religion" so that his already ravaged flock is not scattered any more.

Church is an integral part of the Neumeyers' lives, but to Betty and Art it evokes different thoughts.

BETTY: Church is my community; everybody in Mariposa has a group, and mine is the church. You can expand from a small group like a church, but you have to have that nucleus. Religiously, church is the place where I can be born again each week and be made over in God's image. I pray each day, many times, but church is special.

My criticisms of the church would be mostly about people, because, while most people are willing to write out a check for twenty dollars, they aren't willing to give of themselves, their time. And we spend everything on just keeping the church doors open and nothing on programs; our social concerns are whatever binge the one or two socially concerned people in the congregation are wild about at the moment. We should have a place for children of mothers who are stuck at home so they could get out once a week and shop or get their hair done and know their children are safe. Our day care center is all Jewish mothers who could afford the baby-sitters anyhow.

Church is where Martha learned to help other people; it's why she is involved in service projects at school. For the time being, it might look like she's lost her faith because she doesn't go to church, but there is something that's been planted inside her and Richie that no one can take away. It isn't just that the people going to church are good anyhow. Pam Brown never misses at the Catholic church, and she hates blacks.

162

ART: Church is the one place I should be able to go and just relax and, if I have any special thing on my mind, I should be able to point to one thing in the sermon and say, That's what I need to know; that was meant for me. But a church won't survive if all you do is sit around and read the Bible. It's got to be friendship.

It makes me sick that people use the church to force their views on you—whether it's the pastor or other people who happen to be riding some bandwagon that month. A pastor is supposed to serve his people and not shove integration or draft dodging down their throats. I'm selfish; I come to church to meet nice people and to get some insights whenever I have a problem. I don't want all this political stuff.

I think we do pretty well with the number of people and the budget we have. The impact of this church on the community is made by letting everybody in the community come in and use the building. We help support two missionaries, and we are one of the few churches in our district that has met its apportionments. When we had all the projects going on in the church we had more fights and bitterness. For churches nowadays, we're pretty good.

The red Chevrolet turns onto a street whose small trees and similar, gaily colored ranch homes tell of recent rapid construction. In the middle of the block stands the Pierce house, a large two-story in weathered Cape Cod siding, with a small cottage beside it. The Pierces are one of the church's most affluent couples, and their older, elegant house amid the limes, yellows and reds of their neighbors' homes classically understates their place in life. Soon, Betty and Art are inside with six other people, chatting about the difficulty of raising children, the horrible days ahead as streets are dug up for sewer lines, and the need for painting their sanctuary. Marta Pierce, a calm, warm woman in her mid-forties, and her husband, Gordon, who is wearing an expensive-looking tweed jacket and smoking his pipe, have filled their house with early American antiques. Rough pine tables and spindleback chairs —the style many Mariposans favor but are able to afford only in mass-produced imitations—are plentiful. It is a chilly evening, and

163

a fire burns on the hearth in a handsome brick and pine-paneled den.

Betty soon drifts into conversation with the other women, Art with the men, the topics reflecting the concern of each sex: food prices and baseball, day camps and gas mileage; dental costs and commuting fares. Unlike the other couples, who remain separated during the stay at the Pierce house, Art and Betty often come back together. They hold each other's hands or Art puts his arm around his wife's shoulder. The other six people avoid physical contact.

"Good-tasting tomato juice," Art says to Bart Rose, Lillian's husband, who is the group's traveling bartender.

"Had to put a little water in it; was a bit too thick." He winks at Art as he mixes himself another Bloody Mary with a double shot of vodka.

"Just go easy on the water," Lillian calls across the room. "Don't forget we're good Methodists."

"John Wesley would have approved," Bart returns. "This is top-notch tomato juice, Gordon."

Gordon Pierce puffs gently on his pipe and smiles. He and his wife are arranging the appetizers on their early nineteenth-century dining room table which has been covered with a simple lace tablecloth. There are Swedish meatballs, cold vegetables such as cauliflower, carrots and celery and a series of dips, hot tomato soup with sour cream, strawberries and sugar to roll them in, a cheddar cheese log and a variety of crackers.

As the Parkside members begin to fill their plates, comments are profuse. "Marta, you shouldn't have gone to all the bother— but it's fantastic." "This dip, I've got to have the recipe." "This is a meal in itself!"

Bart Rose is the last to eat. He finishes his fourth Bloody Mary before picking up the plate. Of those people who had an alcoholic drink, most stopped at one. Art had two Bloody Marys and Betty had two daiquiris.

Betty and Art suspect that the Pierces have family money to be able to live this well. Gordon is principal of an elementary school, but the house, its appointments and their life-style could not be supported on his salary of a little more than $20,000 a year. Betty likes the Pierces but feels inadequate, especially with Marta. As Betty has said to Lillian, "Marta never looks down her nose at me, but I don't feel right around her. I'm just the immigrant's daughter and she's from a family that practically came over on the Mayflower."

To the outsider, the Pierces have everything, including three lovely blond-haired daughters. An oil portrait of the three girls sits on an easel in the living room. But there is a slightly vacant look in the eyes of the youngest Pierce girl, Lisa, who is nine. She is mentally retarded and must attend a special Mariposa school. Her parents and the people at Parkside try to include her in church activities as if she were a normal child, but every so often there is evidence she is not. For example, a month ago she went up behind another little girl in Sunday school with a pair of scissors and snipped off a sizable lock of her long brown hair.

After an hour at the Pierces, it is time for the couples to divide up and go on to the next houses, where the salad course will be served. Bart takes Art aside as coats are being handed out. "Artie, I made up two more Bloody Marys. Never know if there'll be any at the next stop."

"I feel the ones you made already," Art says, pretending to stagger. "I can't handle it like you. Go ahead, have both. On me."

"Stuffed shirt. OK, I will."

The Shelly home, some ten blocks away, is the more typical Mariposa house, almost exactly like the one the Neumeyers moved to when they left the city. There are five rooms in the Shelly home, all on the same level, and as the eight people arrive and sit in the living room for a few minutes, it appears almost crowded after the spaciousness of the Pierce house. On the inexpensive, non-descript but neatly dusted furniture, there are a series of pictures of the Shelly children, including graduation pictures from high school and from college. The Shelly children are doing well, physically, mentally and academically.

Lydia Shelly's thinness is accentuated by her gaunt face. When the couples started arriving she apologized for the house number's being hard to see because of the forsythia bushes. As they talk in the living room, she apologizes because there are not enough upholstered chairs, and some must sit on kitchen chairs. Once the eight people are sandwiched around the table in the small kitchen, she apologizes for the lack of space.

"Lydia, honey, don't worry about it," Betty says with a wide grin. "With Bart's water in our drinks we couldn't care less."

"His water has the strangest effect on me," Art says, "almost like . . . no, he would never do that. A good Methodist like him."

"Wouldn't do what?" Lydia asks, batting her eyelashes nervously.

"Water," Art says. "Somehow it's almost like booze."

"Oh, oh, I get it," Lydia says. She follows with a nervous laugh that catches in her throat, and she has to rush to the sink for a drink of water. "Dear me, I hope this is enough," she says, placing on the table a mammoth salad of lettuce, pineapple, shrimp, onions and tomatoes.

"Lydia, it's beautiful," one of the women says.

"Mmmm, like that onion in there," Art says.

"Is it too strong, Artie? Too much onion?"

"Just right, Lydia. Really good."

The conversation around the small table starts and stops with the jerkiness of people who might have just met. Two women talk about bronchial asthma and how it always seems to crop up during the Sunday sermon. One man, who is a dentist, tells about the new high-speed drills and how anesthetics often are not needed.

Conrad Shelly, an insurance salesman, struggles to get the cork out of a bottle of wine as his guests eat their salad course. Conrad, a man with thin lips and slicked-back dark hair, says, "The guy in the liquor store said it was worth the extra twenty cents, better than the American wines. But I like those twist-off caps." By the time he has shredded the cork to the point that some wine will dribble through, it is time for the couples to move on.

Betty and Art leave early, to make the final preparations for the main course at their house. As they ride home in the car, Betty says, "She was more jittery than usual tonight."

"Maybe the tranquilizers wear off this time of night."

"She never has had any Couples Club thing in her house. It really got to her."

"How long has it been since her breakdown?"

"Which one?"

"Was there more than one?"

"So some people say."

By the time the couples begin arriving at the Neumeyer home, Betty is back in the happy mood in which she left the Pierce house. She and Art have had a glass of red wine as they warmed the gravy and took the roast and baked potatoes out of the oven. Standing at the top of the stairs, Betty greets each of her guests with a squeeze and kiss. The group that has been assigned to the Neumeyers are what Betty calls "the swingers" of the Couples Club.

Laughter flows easily, and the talk is loud, helped by the alcohol and by the basic chemistry between the couples: the Neumeyers, the Dupreys, the Roses, the Freeholds, the Devitos and the Dixons. There is a lot of conversation about the drinking that went on at various houses.

"You Methodists are like a bunch of teenagers," Betty says. "Just because we were dry five years ago."

"I haven't been dry for thirty years," Bart Rose says, and the room is filled with howls of laughter. "And why did you bring that stuffed shirt of a husband along, Betty? We could have had a better time without him." With that, Bart puts his arm around Betty and his hand hovers above her breasts.

Lillian Rose and Art Neumeyer smile weakly at one another.

Conversation moves from rentals being hard to find in single-family-oriented Mariposa to one of the more weighty subjects of the evening. A man who works in middle management at the telephone company says that, since the long strike, the pendulum has swung away from the workers and back toward management. He says that jobs are hard to find and workers "who don't work, won't have a job. We can finally get a day's work for a day's pay."

By ten o'clock, cars are parking in the back of the church and couples scurry across the windswept asphalt into the church basement. Once inside, Art and Betty stand by the door of lower fellowship hall talking with a group of people.

"Like to freeze to death out there," Polly Morris says, her voice barely tinged with a Southern accent. She is an attractive woman, set off from the others not only by the color of her skin but by her warm, infectious laugh and her clothes. In a sea of pastels and plaids and solid colors, Polly stands out in a wildly printed blouse.

"We're not cold any more," Art says, failing to meet either Polly's or Benjamin's eyes. "We got injected with enough antifreeze along the way."

"Not good Methodists. Mercy!" Polly says, her hand going to her mouth.

"Now let's not have the pot calling the kettle black," Art says, the last words almost uncontrollably spilling out. He looks sheepishly at the door. "Everybody act sober; here's the reverend," he blurts out.

Pastor MacIntosh, taking off his coat outside the door, sends a half-baked smile Art's way. A moment of silence follows, and then Art, with a nervous grin on his face, walks toward the kitchen to help bring out the lemon meringue pies.

Some of the pies are homemade and others are frozen or from the bakery. Methodism, which has always prided itself on the prowess of its women in the kitchen, is undergoing subtle changes at churches like Parkside, and where a frozen pie would have been a scandal five years ago, it is now an accepted sign of the busy times. For each table of eight people there are three pies, and, because most of the members are already stuffed from three large courses, the pies are hardly touched.

Art and Betty sip their coffee out of Styrofoam cups at a table and listen to Dave Bismark extolling the virtues of the Methodist-related college in the South his daughter is attending.

"Values, the school keeps drumming values into these kids," Dave says, his eyes moving from face to face to see who is still listening to him. "I would have broken her legs if she wanted to go to a state university. But she didn't. She wanted Purcell as much as we did."

168

"Drugs and free sex and no bras," Art says lazily. "You should have seen those Kansas University bums get off the plane. Ugh!"

"Values."

"I'm glad Martha went to Hillcrest. At least they stand up for right and wrong."

"Values, they really teach values."

"And church-related. Keeps the right stuff in front of them."

Betty Neumeyer has been staring blankly at her husband for the past few moments. Her eyes focus slowly. "Getting late, Artie; let's get the kitchen cleaned up and pick up Joan."

10

Take the Puppets Home

FIVE DAYS BEFORE MARTHA'S FRIENDS from Kansas are due to arrive for the teachers' convention, she pulls up and parks in front of her house. Before she gets out of her brother's black Chevrolet she takes the bottom of the baggy T-shirt she's wearing and wipes her forehead. The "I'm a Greek" shirt, which already had some paint spots on its back, now has a variegated pattern of factory grease and body oil on its front.

Martha trudges over the lawn, stubs her toe on a built-in sprinkler near the stairs—where it has been waylaying family member and visitor alike for years—and says "Damn!" Her shoulders sagging, she exhales audibly and trudges up the cement steps.

"Rosie the riveter," her mother calls down from the kitchen when she sees her daughter through the screen.

"Oh, don't start . . ." The words fade out and Martha begins again. "Yeah, Rosie the Riveter. The most educated bench worker at Ridge Electronics. Should have seen me spot-welding today."

Martha knows better than to return her mother's flip remark with one of her own. Since Richard came home, tension at the Neumeyer home has been heavy and family squabbles have been easy to come by. Last night, there was a major blowup at the dinner table because Richard again came without a shirt. The night before, Art and Betty bitterly chastised Martha for being irresponsible because her driver's license had lapsed. Just this morning

Martha stood by helpless as her mother lashed out at Richard for using a purple ribbon as a headband to keep his long hair out of his eyes. "That's it!" Betty screamed at her son. "Take your clothes and get out of here! That's the limit!"

Martha has known her mother to get on a subject and belabor it for days. For the last week it has been "cutting the ties." Betty has shouted, cried and said rationally that the time has come for the two older Neumeyer children to "be on their own." How that is to be done is never spelled out and Martha knows that if her brother attempted to live outside the house there would be even more friction. As Martha told a friend at a bar, "I think my parents are going through a phase. They'll grow out of it."

After the shower, Martha wraps a terrycloth robe around her, lights up a cigarette and curls up in a corner of the sofa. "Just thinking about Darlene's wedding," she says as she watches the smoke curl toward the ceiling.

"Marriage on your mind," her mother says, "and Mark's coming to town. We'll make this work yet."

"Mother stop that . . ." She clears her throat and starts again. "It was just so devoid of feeling; everything was organized."

"So that's bad on the biggest day of her life?"

"It was too much. In this room where we dressed, her mother had boxes of pins—straight, safety or hair."

"I wish my mother would have done that for me, Martha."

"They did the right things, had readings from Whitman and Lowell, but it was so bloodless."

"Too organized for you," her mother says icily.

"When you have a girl who's been planning all her twenty-one years for an event, it's not exactly going to be spontaneous."

"Keep talking yourself out of it, Martha."

"I'm not," she says defensively. "I just can't see spending your whole life waiting to get married, waiting to have children. There are a lot of other things to do. Darlene had her suitcase packed a week before the wedding."

Betty Neumeyer says nothing. She stands by the kitchen door and looks out at her daughter.

171

"How many of our summers were ruined because Daddy had to pick you up after work at night?" she says quietly. Then her voice builds. "What about the packages of food we send you? Go ahead, tell me none of it matters. Women's Lib, hooray. The hell with being a mother."

"You wanted to do all these things, Mommy. I could have walked home from Main Line Drive. You didn't want me to at ten o'clock."

"OK, Martha, that is it!" Betty says with finality. "We are making reservations for the cabin in August, and you and Richie can go to hell. We're going to live our own lives."

"That's fine; don't worry about us," Martha says weakly.

"You don't have to get the black paint out to paint me a darkie. I'm sick of it. *Sick*, do you hear?" Betty's face shakes so violently that ripples appear on her smooth cheeks. "Clean the toilets here, clean the kitchen at the church. AA leaves the mess behind and good old Betty cleans it up."

Martha looks stunned.

"So, I'm an outdated mommy, huh? Done my duty, had my children, now everybody can shit on me. My career was being a mother. Career! I'm going back to work by September, and then the whole bunch of you can shift for yourselves. When I was your age, I didn't have anybody to back me up." The tears are running down Betty's face. "I had kids, responsibility. Well, I'm not going to be tied down any more. So forget it."

"Oh, God, why do we have to argue all the time? I thank you, I thank you for giving birth to me. What more do you want?"

"You ungrateful bastard." Betty Neumeyer wipes her face with the sleeve of her dress. "You heard me," she says bitterly. "You are an ungrateful little bastard."

Martha Neumeyer looks at her mother, and she also begins to cry. She runs back to her bedroom and closes the door.

MARTHA: It hurts so bad when she uses that word "bastard." She knows what it does to me. She knows it can get me when nothing else does. Why blame me? I didn't force my parents to get married. They never tell anybody

172

about it, but you don't have to be a genius to figure out that I was born seven months after they were married. And I wasn't premature. I *am* an illegitimate bastard.

God, I remember the days when she'd say it over and over again: "bastard, bastard, bastard." She's out of control when she does it, but that doesn't diminish the hurt. She's a master at digs. When I dated Len she said, "Ready to give up lasagna at Christmas for chitterlings and collard greens?" Or the day she said, "Why were you ever born? If I didn't have you I could have been something." It hurts so bad I get numb after a while.

I remember one day when she was really after me I said, "You really hate me, don't you? Just because I'm illegitimate you shouldn't treat me any differently." She looked at me like I had three heads. And then as if nothing had happened, she laughed. "Oh, didn't you know? Your father and I were married in a civil ceremony four months before the wedding. You're not illegitimate, honey." And then not another word about the civil ceremony to this day. Am I supposed to believe that? But things begin to fall into place as I look at the way my father is toward boys. So suspicious. Like sex was the only thing on their minds. He knows how *he* was. Do you have to be suspicious of the whole world out of your own guilt?

By dinnertime there is an uneasy calm at the Neumeyer house. Betty checks the turkey roll to see if it is done while Joan fills glasses with water or milk. As the family gathers around the table, there is little conversation. Richard flops Joan's long hair into her face and she laughs. His father stares at him unapprovingly.

Halfway through the meal, Art picks up an envelope he had placed beside his plate. "Here's your insurance, Martha," he says. "They gave us the Kansas rates. That'll be a hundred and sixty-five dollars a year and you'll be paying it."

"I know, I know," Martha says.

"The title transfer will be going in soon."

Richard rubs his stomach beneath his shirt, which is unbuttoned. "This is wonderful," he says. "I work my—I work hard to get that

173

car, and now Martha gets it handed over just like that. Wonderful."

"We would have gotten you a car for graduation, Richard," Betty says. "All you had to do was go to college and you could have had everything."

"That's a good car. I paid four twenty-five for it and I got four new tires."

"I paid you four hundred cash—four crisp hundred-dollar bills—and now you're going to get the truck," Art says, putting a forkful of food in his mouth.

"Four hundred and Martha gets it free. Wonderful."

"Maybe you want to give me one of those beautiful crisp hundred-dollar bills, Richie," Martha says, smiling across the table at her brother.

"Listen, I earned that money; that's more than you can say," he snaps back.

"OK, big deal, I won't say anything to you any more," Martha says. And then quietly, "When are you going to get off your high horse, anyhow?"

"Mommy," Joan cuts in, "you still going out Friday?"

"Yes," Betty says, "and don't interrupt."

"She has a right to talk just like everybody else," Art says.

"That's my birthday and you're going to that bowling dinner. That's no fair."

"Joan, we'll still have a birthday party," her mother says. "We'll have it Saturday. I bought a new dress and I intend to wear it to the dinner."

"Well, what are the choices?" Joan says haughtily.

"You can have kids over for ice cream and cake. We can take them bowling and have ice cream and cake after. We can organize a scavenger hunt."

"But we did that last year," Joan whines.

Martha looks quickly around the table to see if anyone is watching, then thrusts her middle finger in Joan's direction.

"Mommy, Mommy, Martha did it!" Joan cries. "She put her finger out at me. Mommy!"

"Did you?" Art asks in a low voice.

"You can't do that, Martha, because when I do it you tell Daddy and I get bawled out," Joan says.

"What kind of a zoo are we running here?" Betty says, slamming her fork onto her plate.

"Martha, you treat your sister with respect, " Art says.

"Everybody just ease off," Martha says. "God, we're all so uptight."

"I just want you to know that your father and I do very well when both of you are away," Betty says. "So don't think either of you are doing us any favors. Joan, stop crying. Get a tissue and blow your nose."

"Wonderful," Richard says, rapping his fork against the rim of his plate.

"I just hope things settle down before your friends get here or they're going to walk right back out," Betty says.

"I wouldn't blame them," Martha says.

Martha's friends are supposed to arrive sometime today, Monday, and so she has stayed home from work. For the past two days, Betty has made great efforts to avoid friction in the Neumeyer household, and she has been largely successful. The only time she blew up was when Martha mentioned a boy at work who wanted to take her to lunch. Martha told him she had brought her lunch. "Joan would have thrown hers in the nearest wastebasket and gone with him," Betty said.

The hours pass, and with the sound of each car slowing down at the house, Betty goes to the window. It is a sunny but cool June day and all the windows are open, fluttering the curtains and sending breezes scented with cut grass through the house. Martha is silent, pensive. Betty tries to engage her in conversation. The church was broken into on a day the local schools had off and the vandals squirted the fire extinguishers all around the building and broke dozens of light bulbs. Wasn't it terrible? While parents were at the Pawnee school for Back to School night, Mohawk County police were ticketing their cars on Pawnee Drive. Didn't they have any sense? Topics like these would usually spur a healthy conversation between daughter and mother, conversations that Betty cherishes and, because of them, feels she is "growing." But not today. Martha is in her room watching old movies on television or in the living room reading.

At 10 P.M. a Ford station wagon with Kansas license plates pulls up in front of 97 Birchwood, and Betty, Art and Martha go to the front door to meet the six occupants. Betty and Art shake hands warmly with the three young men and three young women in rumpled jeans or Bermuda shorts and sweat shirts. Martha has a slight smile on her face as she hugs her roommate Pat and says hello to the others, meeting everyone's eyes except Mark Hard's.

Mark is over six feet tall, sturdily built, and wears long sideburns that grow down to meet his mustache. Martha has described him as "mature" to her mother, and his bearing does set him aside from the others. His smile is controlled, almost as if he must carefully ration his emotions. His movements are deliberate, and he seems to get tasks like unloading the car done with an economy of effort.

Barry Lancer, who at twenty-eight is three years older than Mark, looks and acts younger. He is the paid full-time consultant to the student-teacher group, and Martha has known him as long as she has Mark; in fact, she met both on the same day. Barry has dark-blond curly hair and a boyish face complete with a smattering of freckles. Tom, the third boy, Martha does not know well as she has seen him only at a few student-teacher gatherings. He is tall, thin, almost delicate, and goes to a small state college in the western part of the state.

Bert, whose real name is Beatrice, is an overweight girl with dyed blond hair, blue eye shadow and a bubbly disposition. It is Bert who initiates much of the conversation, jumping from the cost of tolls to the emergency stop they made so she could make a trip into the woods. Lacey, a sophomore at a Presbyterian college, is an attractive girl with large brown eyes and short brown hair. Compared to Martha, Pat and Bert, Lacey could easily be considered a beauty.

Martha takes her friends for a ride around Mariposa at midnight and returns to the house after two o'clock and shows them where they will sleep on couches and cots in the living room and recreation room. Pat is sleeping with Martha in her bedroom, and once they have washed and are in their pajamas, they have their first chance to talk privately.

"This must be one first class bitch to have both of them in your house," Pat begins.

"Haven't thought about it much," Martha says as she continues to brush her hair.

"Right. Of course. You see Lacey sucking up to Barry and you don't think about it. She's like a dog in heat."

"Well, every convention he has one, doesn't he?"

"Don't, Martha."

"I had my turn, now it's somebody else's. Anyhow, what the hell is the story with Mark? I keep on catching him looking over at me."

"He got me aside and said that he really wanted to patch things up. Said you were the greatest."

"Bastard. I *was* the greatest. Past tense for him too. At least Barry isn't a bullshitter."

"He's no angel either."

"He's even looking at me funny. Mark I can handle, but when Barry looks at me like that I just melt. Why does he have to do that? Is he just playing a game?"

"Who knows what evil lurks within the heart of the predatory male? So he's hot for you. He's hot for a lot of people."

"I know, I know. I just don't want to get involved with him again. I hope this week isn't a disaster. Both of them. God!"

Martha and her friends sleep late the next morning, and by the time they finish the sweet rolls and coffee Betty has ready for them, it is eleven o'clock. They have agreed they should have a strategy meeting, to see how the Kansas delegation will vote on the various issues that will come before the convention. Mark sits cross-legged and barefooted on the rug in the Neumeyer living room, proposals neatly lined up before him like a game of solitaire with oversized cards. Barry shuffles through his stack; Pat and Bert look at theirs with little interest. Lacey stares at Barry, and Martha has her eyes cast down.

"The first two days won't count, and then the action will start," Barry says in a flat Midwestern accent.

177

"OK, fine," Martha says. "But unless somebody has menthol cigarettes I'll have to run out for some. My lungs just aren't pumping right."

"Shouldn't smoke, Martha," Mark says, smiling gently at her. "Bad for your health."

Martha feigns a smile. "Now, who's got the cigs?"

"I'm out too," Pat says. "I'll go with you."

"No, I'll take her over," says Mark, who is already on his feet. "The wagon is parked right in front. Give me the keys, Barry."

As Mark follows Martha out the front door, Betty catches Pat's eye and they wink at one another.

Over lunch, convention topics are mixed with lighter subjects. Martha tells her friends about walking Black Beauty a few nights ago and being attacked by Butch, the dog owned by the Giordanos across the street.

"Those wonderful people." Betty huffs. "Artie called the police and Giordano finally came over, looked at Martha's leg and said, 'Don't look bad to me.' No apology or anything."

"It could only happen to me," Martha says. "This beast is attacking Black Beauty and I try to peel it off so it bites *me!*"

"You got to take better care of yourself, Martha," Mark says. "We can't lose a delegate on the eve of the big convention."

"See, Martha, Mark is concerned about you," Betty says hurriedly.

"Yeah, well, thanks." Martha says softly. "Only me it could happen to."

"Just look at her leg, Mark," Betty says.

Martha pulls up the leg of her jeans to reveal a swollen calf with a black and blue mark as wide as a baseball with two neat toothmarks at the center. Mark takes her heel and moves the leg closer to him. "You've seen a doctor, haven't you, Martha?"

"Yes, he gave me a tetanus shot." She eases her leg out of his hand. "OK, back to convention business."

As the students meet in the living room, Betty bustles in and out, at times talking to herself but loud enough so they can hear. "Have to give pastor a call. . . . Car pool still isn't organized. . . . Septic's backed up; dirty water in Richie's toilet."

When Pam Brown calls, Betty walks into the living room—as far as the extension cord will allow her—to carry on the conversation. When she can get the attention of one of the students, she rolls her eyes back as if Pam were holding her from doing some important things. But it is Betty who keeps the talk going, moving from dog bites to septic tanks. One of the few times Betty walks back into the kitchen is when she asks Pam what happened today on "Search for Tomorrow," the soap opera she missed because of her company.

One of the resolutions that will be voted on by the students asks for minority representation in all state delegations to the next convention, and Mark speaks out strongly against it. "If this is passed, qualified white kids are going to be forced out."

"What's this 'qualified' business?" Pat says. "What makes you think that some Indian kid isn't going to be just as qualified as any of us?"

"Great white father over here," Martha says sarcastically.

"He's right, Martha," says Betty, coming out from the kitchen. "Color shouldn't matter. Ability should count. Why have a whole bunch of different colors if nobody knows what they're doing?"

"And I suppose we do," Martha says. "Oh, crap, forget it. It's just like the Supreme Court on the private clubs. They still can keep blacks out. You and your wonderful President Nixon, Mark." Martha's right hand goes to her mouth, and her teeth run across the callus on her knuckle.

When Martha first met Mark, they agreed on most of the things they talked about—school, the teachers' association, educational philosophies, even man-woman relationships, giving and sharing. She told her mother he was "a thinking person," but she has lived to regret saying those words; her mother has haunted her with them. When Martha complained that Mark was anti-black, for capital punishment, for having a family immediately after getting married, against any kind of contraceptives, for a woman staying in the home and against her having a career, Betty merely responded with, "You always said you wanted a thinking person."

"But not thinking exactly the opposite," Martha said.

As the afternoon progresses, Martha chews more and more on

her already raw knuckle. She finishes the last of the pack of cigarettes before her father gets home from work.

There is time before dinner and, as they often do when there is company in the house, Art and Betty are going to have cocktails. Betty has changed into a revealing blouse, one that has a high neck but which is scooped out and shows her ample breasts. She reaches up and puts her arm around Mark's shoulder and says, "We have a bartender in the house; how about a couple whiskey sours and whatever you kids want?"

"Glad to make them, but nothing for—"

"She knows you don't drink, Mark," Martha says, biting hard on her knuckle.

Betty has directed most of her conversation today to Mark or to her daughter. She has been friendly to the rest of her daughter's guests, with the exception of Barry. So when she speaks to him just before dinner, it catches him off guard. Lacey is leaning against him, and when Betty suddenly speaks, Barry starts and Lacey, caught off balance, almost falls.

"Honey, you have to be careful," Betty says to the blushing young girl. "Art brought home some puppets from the shop. I want all of you to have one. And you, Barry"—she hesitates—"I want you to have three so you can give something to your children." Betty puts a heavy emphasis on the last word.

"Thanks, Mrs. Neumeyer," he says.

Betty moves toward him, her drink in hand and a wan smile on her face. "Must be tough for your wife with you traveling all the time. Must miss her, don't you?" When Barry doesn't answer immediately, she repeats, "Don't you?"

"Yeah, yes, of course," he answers haltingly.

Betty has prepared an Italian meal—spaghetti and meatballs, garlic bread and tossed salad—one of the few concessions to her ethnic origins. Her mother was never "heavy Italian," as Betty says, and preferred chops and steaks to lasagna or zitti. And Betty cooks even less ethnic food than her mother.

The guests dig in with gusto, each of them telling Betty how good the homemade sauce and meatballs are. Betty smiles in return

180

and then looks across the table. "Oh, Mark, where did you learn to eat spaghetti the right way?"

Mark calmly rolls another forkful of spaghetti into the soup spoon and says, "Just always done it that way."

The other guests look dumbly at the forks in their hands. "Mother, there is no right way," Martha says. "I live here and I chop it up and slurp it all over my chin. So what?"

"It's just nice to do the little right things," Betty says. "Just shows a gentleman at work."

"A gentleman at work," Martha repeats. Her gaze meets Mark's, and she quickly looks down at her plate.

Richard is at the table but has said little, and no one except Bert has tried to draw him out. She asked what he did at work and Richard answered tersely. "Same thing I've been doing for the last four days. Putting two holes in a piece of metal."

Before dinner, Joan played "Love Story" on the piano and drew the guests' applause. During dinner, when there is a break, she tells them about what has been going on the last week at school and mentions that there will be two open classrooms in the sixth grade next year and she could be in one of them.

"So what is this open classroom?" Art asks. "From what I hear, it's just everybody running around and doing their own thing."

"No, no, Daddy," Joan says, jumping out of her chair. "It's when they take away all the rows in the room and you do the fun stuff during the day and the rest for homework."

"That school is the most experimental thing going," Betty says in a disgusted tone. "Don't they see that some kids don't need less structure?"

"Mother, Joan hasn't even been selected for it yet," Martha says.

"Well, we're going down to school and make sure she isn't," Betty says with finality.

"Mother! Some kids do better with a less structured setting. Joan is bored silly in school."

"Yeah, I really am, Mommy. Mrs. Durgin just talks and talks, and we can't say anything."

"It's really a good thing, the coming thing, Mom," Martha

says. "If a couple kids like working on a science project, they go in a corner and do it. Other kids do spelling work together or help each other with math."

"Over my dead body; what are teachers for?" Betty says.

"Really, Mrs. Neumeyer, if I might say something about them," Mark says, "open classes really allow for much more individual expression, let kids come out."

"You really think so?" Betty says, suddenly changing her tone.

"Especially a bright girl like Joan; I'm sure she's an excellent student. If she isn't, the school isn't doing something right. Any child that can do something like this—"

Mark holds up Joan's eight-page handmade Father's Day card. A broken clothespin is pasted on a page with a line underneath: "He saves me again, he fixes things." A cigarette butt with an X through it has beneath it, "But I don't want him to smoke. Smoking kills. I want a dad."

Mark looks at Art and says, "You have a very, very bright daughter."

"Oh, God!" Martha says softly, looking over at Pat.

"Betty, did you see the tests she brought home today?" Art says, trying to get back into what has developed into a two-way conversation. "Terrible marks. That kind of class is going to help her? I doubt it."

"Art, listen to Mark," she snaps back. "He's studying this; he knows more about it than we do."

Art glares at her for an instant, then resumes eating.

Once dinner is over and Martha and her friends have gone out for the night, Art and Betty sit on the sofa. Betty has her head back, looking at the ceiling while Art is thumbing through the paper.

"Like a puppy dog," Betty says.

"What puppy dog?"

"Mark follows Martha around like a puppy dog. Can't she see he's crazy about her? And that creep of a Barry with that floozy all over him. I wonder what his wife thinks. If Martha . . ." Betty stops. Martha has confided to her that she and Mark have dated, even spent a night together, and Betty has passed that along, almost triumphantly, to her husband. Martha has also confided that she is attracted to Barry, that she has been out with him several times during teachers' meetings. Betty has not told her husband about their daughter's involvement with a married man. As Betty told Martha, "Your father could never look at you the same way if he knew."

"Yeah, he does seem to like her," Art says, picking up the conversation. "But she's not giving him the time of day. Say, is she going to wear that thing I saw on the bed?"

"The halter dress?"

"Yeah, the one they forgot to put a back on."

"Sure, so what?"

"With or without something underneath?" Art says, cupping his hands over his chest.

"She modeled it for me braless. Now don't look shocked; you always tell me how you love to watch the girls downtown with their boobs jiggling around."

"But not my daughter."

"Arthur Neumeyer, you sound like a jealous father."

"I am. And I'm a dirty old man, too."

"I'll bet Mark likes it," Betty says seductively.

"You think one hell of a lot of a guy that pinned your daughter and cheated on her the next weekend. Twice."

"Minor details. I've found my son-in-law."

The day and a half that Mark and Barry are in the house and the five days at the convention that follow are very difficult for Martha. A longing look at Martha from Barry as Lacey wraps her arm around him and puts her head on his shoulder triggers jealousy, guilt and affection, all in a swirling mass of emotions. Mark's overcourteous gestures, coupled with his conversation to other people that get back to Martha ("She's a wonderful girl; it's just that we never had enough time together during the school year to blossom. Marriage? No, never talked about that. I have to work, go to school. But she'd be the kind of girl I'd want")

183

have confused and depressed her. For Martha, the convention is incidental, a blur. More than one night, Pat hears Martha cry herself to sleep.

MARTHA: When I showed my mother that halter dress, all she could say was, "I bet you want Barry's hands all over you." If Mark would have raped me, it would have been fine. She must see me as this great temptress, having an affair with a married man. Wow, what could be further from the truth!

The convention was just about over and Barry took me to the bus station and he told me he had stayed away from me all week because of Mark. He basically likes Mark. As for me, it's all over with Mark; I've been hurt so bad I don't want that again. But with Barry, I just don't know. When he comes around me, I'm weak. I know he's married but he doesn't care that much about his wife. And I really don't want to get involved. But he's good, he's gentle, he's not a phony. Just to see Mark sucking up to my parents made me want to puke.

This isn't the first time my mother has shoved a guy down my throat. I went to the senior prom with Smittie, and all of a sudden he was the golden boy. My mother has no concept of a developing relationship. She always says to let the man win, but she doesn't practice what she preaches. Look how she treats my father. For her, it's like luring a man into a cage and then doing what you want. She wants to make sure I get married off. I'm afraid of marriage. I can recall years and years when things between my parents were really bad. They were going to the minister for counseling quite a bit.

A lot of it is because my mother has never been satisfied with how things have gone in her life. She constantly puts my father down. When I was in the third or fourth grade I remember her calling him yellow for not standing up to people, for not making decisions. My mother has no confidence in my father; she has destroyed him, in a way. And he has come a long way, for not even graduating from high school. She should be proud of him, but she always complains she doesn't have more.

Sometimes I sit down and cry because I see people

who have good marriages and a nice home and everything. How come I'm so afraid of marriage? Maybe I'm afraid of falling in love because I associate it with marriage, and marriage hasn't been so peachy around here. I wonder if I have the potential to spend my whole life making a marriage work? Maybe that's why I can empathize with Barry. I can see how a relationship can fall apart, and that doesn't make him this great adulterer; it just makes him a lonely man.

I think my mother is proud of what I'm doing in school but I think she hates me in a way too, for doing all the things she wanted to do. She takes that out by telling me something's wrong with me; I don't have the natural instinct to be a mother. I don't know much about my own sexuality. Sometimes I even wonder, Is Martha Neumeyer a lesbian?

Sex! Why such problems? Here my parents went crazy when I was seeing Len Morris and he never touched me. The Mark they love so much was really the horny one. Talk about aggressive! The first date with him I went further than I went with any other boy. He got his hand inside my pants, and that was the first time I'd been touched down there. But we never had intercourse. Close? Yes. I almost went on the pill once. It isn't that I have this big idea about preserving my virginity for the honeymoon night, but I just couldn't do it.

There must be some kind of book that guys read, some routine they follow when they're trying to make you. Like Mark. First a tender kiss, followed by the Frenchie, the passionate kiss. Then a kiss on the neck, which is my yuckie spot. My stomach just turns when that happens. The hands start moving, always top to bottom, and then the disrobing begins. And Mark was forceful about it and he got aroused in a minute.

Barry was the exception to the book. He was so gentle. It was on one of those convention nights during the school year and people started pairing off and there I was in the hotel room with Barry. When he kissed me I felt so warm inside, more wonderful than ever before. He wanted to go further but I said no and he didn't push me. I wish he would have pushed hard and I had to fight him off. Then I'd have known for sure there

185

was only one thing on his mind. We just sat up and talked the rest of the night. I felt like the spoiled woman the next morning—everybody knew we were together and thought we were screwing—but something great happened.

How do you tell your mother something so great happened with a married man?

The end of June, and the end of the first half of 1972, comes to Mariposa in a stream of sunny, warm, pleasant days. The golf course near the Neumeyers' house is crowded from early in the morning until the sun is low in the sky. Playgrounds are filled with children, now free from school. And at the green-shingled house at 97 Birchwood, all appears to be back to normal. Martha's company is gone; the living room and recreation room are neat once more; the five Neumeyers are once again about living their separate and, to varying degrees of intensity, family lives.

11

Blocked In

THE AIR IS STILL on this Saturday afternoon in July and, with both temperature and humidity in the high eighties, Mariposa seems covered by a steaming towel. A week of unseasonably hot weather has already caused Art Neumeyer's newly planted lawn to have yellow spots, and his pepper and tomato plants lean limply against their stakes at the back of the house. The only sound around 97 Birchwood is a soft metallic rustle as Art twists a plumber's snake into the line that leads into the septic tank. Periodically he retrieves the snake, shakes off the black, syrupy residue, then feeds it back into the pipe, which is just inside the garage door.

The stillness is broken by another metallic sound: the quick opening and then the slamming of the aluminum screen door. Art brushes the perspiration from his eyes to see Richard jogging toward the 1963 Chevrolet panel truck that he bought recently. Before Richard reaches the truck, which is mottled with orange metal primer, chalky body putty and flat black paint, the house's front door is thrown open again.

"Richard, I told you we needed some milk!" Betty calls to her son's back.

He grabs for the door handle and swings into the truck.

"Richard, if you don't get that milk, you can come back and get your sleeping bag and clear out of here. *Richard!*"

The engine of the truck turns over and a bluish-gray cloud of

187

smoke belches out of the exhaust pipe. Then the truck streaks down the street.

After a moment, Betty stomps down the cement stairs, two empty half-gallon milk bottles rattling in her hand. "That goddamn kid. Let's go get him, Artie."

"Betty, hold on a minute, what's going—?"

"That little son of a bitch. If he wants to live here, if he wants to be a member of this family, he's going to do his share. 'Got to get up to the station,' " she says in a singsong voice. "Everything for him, and the hell with everybody else."

Art wipes off his hands, and he and Betty drive to Main Line Gulf. They pull into the station just as Richard is climbing out of the truck. Art drives the car right into his son's path. Richard looks at these two faces staring at him through the windshield and begins to walk around the car toward the office. "Tell him, Artie, tell him he has to get the milk," Betty says, pushing the bottles across the seat toward her husband.

"Betty, this was your idea."

"Are you going to let him thumb his nose at us like that?"

Art snatches up the bottles and is out of the car before Richard can go around it. "Your mother said we needed some milk," he says.

"Just when I want to go someplace, all of a sudden she needs something," Richard says in a boyish tone. "I told her I'd get it later on."

"She needs it now, Richard. Get the milk," Art says, looking peeved. "Or else clean your stuff out today."

"Jeeesus Keerist! Give me the bottles." He grabs them out of his father's hand and starts back toward the truck.

Betty and Art ride home in silence. Art goes back to his work on the pipe and soon Richard brings the milk, leaving the truck engine running as he goes into the house. Back in the truck, he jams it into first gear with still another metallic sound, coarse and deep. The tires squeal and he is gone.

Art continues to twist the snake and retrieve the residue. Every fifteen minutes or so he flushes the toilet to see if the drain is cleared. Each time the murky water rises in the opening, so he goes back to work.

Art looks down at his right hand. The soft skin that was transplanted to cover the space where two fingers were amputated is reddish. Two thin lines of blood mark where the handle of the snake has worn through the rag Art has been using to protect that tender spot. He grimaces slightly as he runs his left hand over the flushed skin. He leans against Joan's sled, lights a cigarette and squints out onto the sun-drenched cement driveway.

Art Neumeyer was the only man Diamond Diecutting had who could operate the huge new European-made press. He had learned to run the press at Rabinowitz, and it was because of this special skill that Diamond lured him away from his first employer. So when the rush job came into the Diamond shop in the late summer of 1959, they pleaded with Art to come off his vacation and get it out. Art was annoyed. He had just moved from the city that April into his home on Tulip Lane, and he still had work he wanted to finish in the house and the back yard. Only his sense of pride that no one else could do the job brought him into the shop that week in September. Also, he needed the overtime money.

On September 3, the machine was balking and the job was falling behind schedule. Sheets were sticking in the gripper bars, constantly causing Art to shut down the machine and remove the jammed mass of paper. When still another sheet jammed, Art routinely pressed the red stop button as the gripper bars entered the hesitation phase, just before they would come down, in a scissors motion, to grasp the next sheet.

Art thought nothing about putting his hand where the gripper bars came down. He had done it thousands of times with the machine off. This time, for some reason, the machine continued the cycle. The hesitation was just that, almost a baiting, and then the bars came down. The gripper bars held his right hand for only an instant and then released and moved on through the cycle. Art pulled back a mangled hand. The machine that he took so much pride in operating was splattered with his own blood.

189

The shock and the intense pain blocked out any thinking for a moment. When his mind cleared, Art's first thoughts went to his family: How would he support them as a one-handed cripple? Someone in the office called an ambulance, but as the minutes went by none came. People tried to fan Art; others unthinkingly blew cold air on the hand, exacerbating the pain. Eventually, a cab was hailed and Art rushed to the hospital. His hand wrapped in towels already soaked through with blood, Art was forced to wait still another hour before he was given any medication to kill the pain, because there was no doctor free to see him.

As Art and the salesman who had come with him sat in the emergency room, Art told him about a friend who had had a similar accident and was left with only two stubs on his hand. Hearing this, the salesman insisted Art be seen by a hand specialist, not only the intern on duty. The hand was pieced together, and a huge bandage the size of a boxer's glove applied.

Betty at first was supportive, not letting on how concerned she was about the family's future. Each day for the next two weeks, after taking Richard, who was just starting first grade, and Martha, a third-grader, to school, she would travel into the city to be with her husband. Each time she walked into his room, Betty could picture him lying there without a hand. She visualized their losing the house and facing a life of poverty.

Two weeks after the accident, Art was released from the hospital. Inside the huge bandage, his index and middle fingers had already turned dark, and by the middle of the week he spent at home they were black with gangrene. The surgeon told Art there was no longer a choice. Betty accompanied her husband back to the hospital and came home that afternoon just as her two children were returning from school. She sat them down in the living room and said, without any introduction, "Your father is going to lose his fingers."

Martha screamed.

Betty reprimanded her, saying, "There isn't any time for that now; we've all got to pull together." Richard sat silent. Betty expected more of a reaction from the boy, who screamed and cried, becoming almost breathless in his tantrum, each morning that Betty left him behind to go to be with her husband.

The next day the fingers were amputated and a skin flap was cut in Art's stomach. The hand was sewn into the opening, thus providing the blood supply the graft needed. Art was groggy for a few days after the operation, but once he was clearheaded, he was stoic about the loss. He said he was lucky; he could have lost the entire hand.

Betty did not feel so fortunate. "Why couldn't it of happened to Billy or Mike? None of them worked like you," she said. "Why to you, Artie, why do it to us?" she asked plaintively.

"I wouldn't wish it on anybody else, Betty," he replied.

Betty seemed to have weathered the initial shock, but during the five weeks Art recuperated in the hospital she began to show the strain. Art's family had given her no support and showed little interest. She had heard stories of amputees becoming alcoholics and dope addicts. She looked at her husband and saw a man with a tough outer crust but with low self-esteem and wondered what kind of life they faced. Betty's temper flared often; beatings and punishments for the children became more frequent. Juggling two children and a husband who, once he was released, required frequent trips to the city for checkups, she felt alone, abandoned in her struggle.

Betty was enraged that Art could have done this to her. After all, when he married her, he had vowed to work hard, to give her the security she had never known in the hand-to-mouth Santangelo family. She felt sorry for him, but she also blamed him for reneging on his promise.

BETTY: I know I was irrational. I really couldn't blame Artie for the accident but I was so frightened. He was everything to me, my rock, and now he was crippled. I'm insecure anyhow, and it brought out all the insecurity I ever had. Sure, it all worked out, but who's to know that? Richie's screaming still haunts me; that kid felt abandoned. If anybody would have listened, I would have screamed too. Even my own family didn't really jump in to help.

191

I'll never forget my mother saying, "What are *you* going to do now?" as if it was my problem and I would have to solve it alone. So who did I scream at? Poor Artie! He was the only one around, so he was the target.

Art could see and feel Betty's rage and, looking down at his bandaged hand, knowing it was no longer whole, he wondered if Betty could ever love him again or even accept him. Would his children respect or just pity him? Would his wife think of him as a man, an intact man?

The bandages became smaller, and then there was the day near the end of the year when the last bandage came off. In what looked like an uncommonly wide space between his thumb and ring finger was a mass of reddish skin, bristling with the hairs that once had been on his stomach. As soon as the swelling went down, Art began to put the hand in his pocket, out of view. For the next two years few people saw it, except for his wife and children.

Art was afraid to touch Betty or the children with the hand. When he made love to Betty he kept it at his side or behind a pillow. When he went back to work four months after the accident, back to the same machine that had maimed him, he kept the hand plunged deep in his pocket as much as possible.

Months later, his damage suit for $100,000 came to trial in a city two hundred miles away where the machine's distributor, Bushwick Consolidated Press, was located. In the suit Art claimed that he had pressed the stop button but that because of faulty wiring the machine had continued its cycle. His lawyer had an electrician ready to testify, but as the trial opened the judge immediately disqualified him, saying that the machine was licensed in the distributor's state, not Art's. An electrical engineer who showed what could have happened to cause the machine to malfunction was, in Art's eyes, ridiculed by the judge. To Art, the judge was plainly on the side of Bushwick, a large local company with thousands of employees.

Art had been advised by his lawyer to have Betty and his two small children in court to keep in front of the judge and defending corporation the real victims of the accident. As she sat there, with a child leaning against each arm, Betty saw the trial unfold; to her it was a "whitewash." It seemed as though Art's witnesses were constantly demeaned and the company's representatives and experts treated with respect. Betty pounded her fist into her lap more than once during the four-day trial. Martha sat in the courtroom with tears streaming down her face, hearing the defense lawyer say, "Don't let emotions rule; this man has lost two fingers but he still has full use of that hand. Don't be swayed by a man who drags his children into court to play on sympathies. We have proved beyond reasonable doubt that the machine was functioning up to the highest standards. We cannot say the same for the operator." Richard sat by in silence, playing with his fingers, his face devoid of any emotion. Then, during a recess near the end of the trial, the seven-year-old boy broke.

The family was in a restaurant near the courthouse when Richard refused to eat and made loud noises which eventually developed into a full-scale temper tantrum. His own nerves frayed, Art finally shook his son by the shoulders and then made him sit in the car alone. When the family finished their meal they found Richard curled up on the floor in back, rigid. When his parents tried to talk with him, he would alternately say nothing and then scream at them. He tore up a box of tissues and scattered them throughout the car. After some coaxing he allowed his parents to pick him up, and they hurried back to the courtroom. Both Art and Betty agreed that Betty's frequent separation from the boy at the time of the accident had taken their toll, but they thought he was "in a phase and would grow out of it."

The trial ended on a Friday. As Art and Betty drove back to Tulip Lane, they had little hope of winning a settlement. In Art's opinion, the judge had been bought by Bushwick. On Monday, the verdict was phoned to them: Bushwick was not at fault. Art had violated safety rules and caused his own injury.

Diamond Diecutting had at first been sympathetic to Art, but when he persisted in bringing suit against a company whose machinery and spare parts were vital to the business, they turned cold: Drop the suit or lose your job. Even before the trial was held, Art was fired. With the $5,000 he received as a disability compensation from the state, he fulfilled a lifelong dream by starting his own diecutting business along with two partners. But even with the launching of Bestway Diecutting, the friction at home that had been evident since the accident didn't ease. It intensified.

When Art lost the court case and didn't press for an appeal, he had reconfirmed to Betty that he was yellow, that he didn't stand up for what was his. They fought. Betty called him, among other things, "a fucking coward." Art said she was "a greedy bitch." Sometimes the fight was held off until the children went to bed; sometimes emotions ran so high that the fight started when Art got home and lasted until midnight. On more than one occasion Betty stalked out of the house and didn't come back until the next morning.

Art desperately wanted to restate his manhood in some dramatic way and regain the respect of his wife. He—like Betty— wanted to save this marriage which had gone sour. There was only one thing they could think of that would serve as a symbol that he was still a man and that their marriage would last. Although they had planned to have only two children, they agreed they must have a third. In the fall of 1960, Betty became pregnant, and in June of 1961 Joan was born. She was to be "something to look forward to," a child "who will take our minds off other things."

Joan was a lovely baby and they enjoyed her, but her birth did not resolve the Neumeyers' problems. Art's two partners were not as diligent as he and Art was putting in ten- and twelve-hour work days plus most Saturdays with no thought of a vacation. Betty admitted she was possessive; she demanded that Art be home more. Art explained that if the business was going to succeed he had to give it maximum effort.

In 1966, after nearly five years of struggle to keep both a business and a family together, Art Neumeyer took a hard look at Bestway Diecutting. Although the business was grossing $300,000 and employed up to fifty people, he could see that it would be a long time—if, in fact, ever—before it would turn a profit to match the amount of work he was doing. One partner had already left, and the remaining partner seemed to have lost interest in the company, leaving Art to run the office and the small factory and to solicit business. Art knew that if he made the company successful, he would have to share the rewards with a man who was putting nothing into it, often not even coming into the office for days at a time. As Art looked at the pressure at work and the continuing bickering at home, he took what he calls "the easy way out." He closed the shop and filed for bankruptcy. The next week, with his newly obtained managerial skill, coupled with his back-shop experience, he went to the company he had started with while still a teenager and asked for a job. Rabinowitz Diecutting hired him at once. He was again an eight-to-five employee with a steady income.

Still, the tension did not ease. Betty was indignant about Art's remortgaging the house to pay off the $3,000 in business debts he had personally signed for when Bestway's credit had been overextended. When the Neumeyers were on edge, often their anger was directed toward the children. Betty would beat Martha and Richard with a thick leather strap or slap them across the face, leaving welts. The children learned to take punishment. When faced with losing a night's television or getting a beating, Martha would opt for physical punishment, cry, and then watch television, soon forgetting the sting. Richard was oblivious to his whippings and often would not cry at all.

One day after Martha had been especially sassy to her mother, Betty called Art, and when he came home he was commanded by his wife to mete out a severe punishment. Martha tried to run away when her father came toward her, and he chased her into the bathroom. He lunged for her, lost his balance and pushed her through the glass sliding doors of a shower stall. Martha's back was badly cut, and Art realized how out of control he had been for a moment. As the parents swept the shards of glass from their bathroom floor they decided they needed outside help. They would see their pastor and try to work out some of their problems.

Pastor Winfield pointed out to Betty that her husband was trying to be an honorable man by paying off his debts and that bankruptcy for him would be a further assault to his integrity and manhood. The pastor showed Betty and Art what they basically believed—they had a good relationship, but it would take continual working on; they had three healthy children with the normal amount of growing problems. With Art's new job and steady salary, loans were soon paid off and the acute marital problems gradually subsided. Art continued to get comfortable raises and, in 1968, instead of putting an addition on their Tulip Lane house, the Neumeyers decided to buy a bigger house, eventually settling in The Knolls, the prestige section of Mariposa.

Art looks down at the opening in the pipe. The water level has gone down some. He calls in to Betty to flush the toilet, and when she does the rush of water sweeps away the rest of the debris that has been blocking the line.

After cleaning up, Art goes around to water the back yard. Martha is sitting in the sun, writing a letter to her roommate, Pat. She squints into the sun and gives a faint smile to her father and continues:

> . . . heavy, heavy thoughts about Barry. God, how could something like this happen to me? Married, two kids. But he has that way about him. I've just stopped talking about him to my mother because if I even mention him, she makes me feel like I really am something awful. Glad I have you to tell about these things. Nobody else understands! Anyhow, didn't go to the WACs as is obvious by the postmark. That would have killed the summer, and this might be the last one at home. So they'll have to march without me. Just decided it wasn't for me—would be doing it for the lousy money. Summer, yeah, summer? Kind of a drag. One guy at work is kinda cute and we went out a couple times but nothing serious. Renting a cabin for a week in August when my father is on vacation, whoopee! We've been there before, it's up near

"Say, Daddy, where is the cabin anyhow? I want to tell Pat about our vacation."

"Up near the border, around Wyattsville."

The afternoon drags along. Art listlessly goes about measuring the steps inside the front door for some indoor-outdoor carpeting. Martha reads for a while, then cuts out material she will make into identical dresses for Joan and herself. Betty leafs through the Saturday paper and finds that *The Godfather* is playing at a neighborhood theater. She and Art plan to go to the seven-thirty show. Art's mother calls from upstate, saying she's in a depressed state, and asks if she can come down to spend a week. Art tells her yes. Betty says she will never come, pointing out that she has never been to the house on Birchwood in the four years they've lived there.

Near dinnertime Art fans charcoal in the hibachi he has placed on the driveway. Martha strips the husks from the ears of corn and Joan sets the table while Betty quietly prepares the salad and the huge piece of steak she has defrosted. Going into the refrigerator for salad dressing, she comes across a Tupperware container of spaghetti that has been lost amid the leftovers.

"Mark really liked my cooking, didn't he?" Betty says to Martha's back.

"They all did," she replies.

"But he made such a fuss over it."

"And don't tell me you weren't making a fuss over him."

"Martha, you're almost twenty-two and you're still afraid of boys," she says sarcastically. "I just have to push you a bit."

"I just turned twenty-one a few months ago, Mother, and I don't need any help."

"Did you hear the way that Barry talked to his wife when he called her? Even when Artie and I were having our roughest times, it was never like that."

"I don't make a practice, Mother, of listening in on other people's conversations."

"Coals are ready; everything else in shape," Art says as he comes through the front door.

"And leave some of it bloody, OK, Daddy?" Martha says.

Two male voices, with each short interchange, grow louder. They are coming from across the street, and the entire Neumeyer

197

family goes to the front window. "I don't want that piece of junk in front of my house!" Mr. Giordano shouts from his front lawn to Richard, who is standing by his truck.

"Happens to be a public street," Richard says, tossing his arm into the air.

"Then park it on your own side."

"Trees hit the top."

"I've got another car coming in here tonight, Richard, so don't give me that kind of crap."

"He won't park it in front of his own house because he's ashamed of it," comes a high-pitched voice from inside the Giordano house.

The Neumeyers watch silently as Richard walks jauntily away from his truck and toward his house.

"Damn kid," Art says. Once Richard is inside the house, his father says in rapid order, "If you can possibly walk away from trouble, why don't you? I don't want you parking over there anymore. This property is our security. We've had BB pellets through our windows already."

"You'll go out there and your tires will be slashed," Betty says, her eyes bulging. "Mrs. Giordano will egg her husband on; did you hear that thing?"

"I'll call the cops," Richard says. "They don't own the street."

"How can you prove it? Oh, God, Richie, why do you have to make us all uptight?"

"Relax, Ma, they aren't going to do anything but bitch about it."

"Rich, what did I tell you about the language?" Art says.

"Supper ready?" he responds.

"You damn kids don't care about anything but yourselves," Betty says angrily. "I have to live on this street day in and day out. Yes, supper is ready. Go wash!"

As Richard washes in the small downstairs bathroom, Martha meanders past, her knuckle at her lips. She leans against the wall. "Geez, you sure know how to get them going."

"I learned from a pro."

Martha smiles.

"Giordanos don't know what a famous truck that is. When Ron and I were at Sandy Point last week the pigs were swarming all over it, trying to catch us with some stuff. I fooled their asses."

"OK, big talk, what?"

"Had half an ounce of the most beautiful pot tucked up in the frame."

"So, big deal. What else did you and Ron do besides fool the cops? Sandy Point is supposed to have all the action these days."

Richard looks down at the water running out of the sink. "Oh, we just made it from beach to beach. Who told you it was happening out there? Nothing."

"If you'd sit still for a minute, you might find out," Martha says, giving her brother a light kick in the rear.

With supper on the table and the family already seated, Richard comes up from the basement. He hesitates at the front door. "Unbelievable."

The tone of his voice is enough to bring Betty and Joan to the window. Mr. Giordano is standing on his front lawn, and his wife is visible behind the front door screen. His daughter has just parked her car, bumper to bumper, in back of Richard's. One of the Giordanos' friends, who had his car in the driveway, is backing his car in front of Richard's. The bumpers touch and he turns off the engine.

"Will everyone please sit down and eat," Art shouts from the table.

"Artie, they boxed Richie in," Betty says, her breath whistling out her nose as she exhales in exasperation.

"I do not want to hear another word about it," Art says, his voice even louder.

Betty is the last to fill her plate, and as the family begins to eat she returns to the window. "Giordano's doing something under the hood."

"My truck?" Richard rises out of his chair.

"Sit down," Art says firmly. "*Betty*. I want to eat this meal, and I do not want to hear about the parking situation."

Betty gives her husband a dirty look as she returns to her seat.

"Can't we talk about something enjoyable once in a while?" Art says. "Wasn't always like this. Conflict, conflict, conflict all the time. Steak OK for the cannibal?" He smiles at his daughter.

"Could be a little more bloody, Daddy, but because I love you so much I'll say it's perfect," Martha says.

"Bridget called this morning when you were out, Artie," Betty says evenly as she salts her ear of corn. "Seems like she's not going to divorce my brother. This week, anyhow."

"He's no prince, Betty, so don't go defending him—"

"Conflict, conflict," Martha singsongs. Both her parents stare at her momentarily, then become more diligent about eating their meal.

While Betty is dishing up the dessert of canned pears, Art, without saying a word, walks out the front door. Family members one by one tiptoe to the window to see him going across the street and then ringing the Giordanos' bell.

Mr. Giordano appears at the door. The two men begin talking, although no one in the house can hear what they are saying. Art appears to be talking calmly through the screen, his hands at his sides. He drags on a cigarette and listens to Mr. Giordano's response. Art's right hand suddenly shoots out, pointing toward the truck and making a sweeping motion up and down the street. Then both Art's hands reach toward the screen door, almost in a plaintive gesture, and slap to his sides in exasperation.

Art crosses the street, and the members of the family scramble back to their seats at the table. "Where you been, Artie?" Betty asks innocently.

"That truck can rot out there," Art stammers. "They're working on the car in front, and the carburetor on the one in back is shot. What do they think we are, idiots?"

"Get the camera, Artie; take a picture so we'll have it for evidence."

"Joanie, get the camera, the good one, the Japanese one." Turning to Martha, he says, "On Monday you go down and take out a summons so they'll pay for your shots from the dog bite."

"I'd have to miss work and everything for a couple of lousy dollars," Martha says.

"You are going down and they are going to be in court or pay that bill."

"Don't forget, Martha, you had to miss a week of work after the bite." And Betty smiles. "But they don't know you were at the convention."

"Talk about honesty," Martha says.

"Never you mind," Betty retorts sharply. "Are they being honest boxing in Richie's truck and not caring about your leg?"

The phone rings and Martha answers it. She walks to the corner of the kitchen, away from the family. She is through in a few minutes, just as her father is sitting down for a cigarette after taking the pictures. "Who was that?" he asks.

"Some guy at work. Went out with him a couple times and I told him we'd go out again when he got a job. Still doesn't have a job, but he wanted to go out tonight."

"And?" Betty asks.

"And I told him I was busy."

Betty rolls her eyes. "Joan would never drop a guy after three dates! You never give them a chance."

"He was kind of a jerk, Mother, do you mind?"

"Michael gave me a note and says he wants to go steady," Joan says, her face in her hands as she giggles.

"Give your sister some lessons, honey. We're going to the show. And Richard, you call the police and tell them you want to use the truck and you're boxed in."

Fifteen minutes later Betty and Art are ready. Richard has been on the phone most of the time to the Mohawk County Police Department.

"Those pigs really help. This guy tells me to get in the truck and bash both of the cars out of the way, and when they sue, tell the judge they boxed me in."

"Don't you do any bashing, Richie," his father says.

"Just watch out there. They have to use their cars; then get yours out," Betty adds.

201

"I'm going with Ron tonight; we'll use his truck."

"Artie, the hell with them," Betty says. "Let's go."

Evening brings northern breezes to Mariposa, and the house at 97 Birchwood becomes comfortably cool. Richard has already left, and Martha and Joan play a game of Money. Much to her delight, Joan is winning. Martha pulls out some old Ferrante and Teicher records and the dual pianos resound off the walls, much louder than her parents would put up with if they were at home.

With Joan in bed, Martha sprawls on the couch, restlessly trying to find a comfortable position. She looks at the magazines on the coffee table. *Response*, a Methodist women's magazine and the only one the Neumeyers subscribe to, gets no more than a glance and is pushed aside. *Family Circle*, which Betty bought at the supermarket, then *McCall's* and *National Geographic*, both of which are passed down monthly from a friend, are flipped through and discarded. Almost unconsciously, Martha begins to read "The Knolls News," the monthly newsletter of the civic association. Her eye jumps from an unsigned letter—"It is deplorable to attend meetings only when something threatens the value of your home!"—to a column of short news items—"P.S. The Association has acquired a Polaroid camera for use during sewer construction. Residents may take as many pictures as you feel necessary." She flips the page and the underlined *"We are the largest, noisiest and best civic association around"* catches her eye. "Mr. Bradford's group is opposed to the downzoning of this land and to any low-income housing in this area. His community is integrated now and he does not want this balance threatened." Moving on, Martha finds an article on using fresh fruit and vegetables for centerpieces, an offer for a Las Vegas weekend for association members, and then the want ads, which she scans. "WANTED: A day care center, state and community funded, desperately needs toys for children. . . . NEEDED: Used clothing and toys for Navajo, South Dakota and Mohawk Indian tribes."

Martha is dozing when her parents come home near midnight. From the look on her mother's face, Martha knows something

202

has happened. She says nothing but looks at her mother expectantly, sure the silence will not be long.

"I have never seen such a depressing movie in my life," Betty says, plopping onto the couch. "Artie, how about a whiskey sour. I need it."

"I thought it was great," Martha says. "A little blood and guts, but great."

"Italians were never like that, Martha," she says. "That baptism scene and all those people being slaughtered."

"Your father had his own bookie, Betty; there was organized crime in the North End," Art says. "And what about the store owners that didn't go along?"

"There were windows broken, but it was never like murder. That picture is so far removed from the way Italian people lived."

"Uncle George handles hot goods. Where do you think they fall from, the sky?" Martha says.

"All right; go ahead, both of you, and pick on me."

"Honey," Art says, "we're not picking on you; that's just the way the world is. How do you think we got Richard's tickets taken care of?"

"Your godfather is different, Art; he just does nice things."

"I just gave him my notification for jury duty, and I'll never have to serve. That's the grease that makes the world go around."

It is quiet in the house. A sudden wind whistles through the locust trees, and a few large raindrops hint that a full-fledged squall is due. Martha is the next to speak as her parents look into their whiskey sours. "Honesty, your magic spell is nowhere."

"Whaaa?" Betty says blankly.

When Richard looks out at his truck Sunday morning, it is still stalemated by the two cars. He calls the police department, and this time a squad car comes out and one of the officers goes to the Giordano's front door. Soon Mr. Giordano comes out of the house in a bathrobe and slippers. He snorts in anger as he pulls his daughter's car into his driveway.

That afternoon, Betty and Art visit three real estate offices. They tell the agents they want a smaller house, closer to shopping, and are willing to trade their equity in the house on Birchwood for another that may not be in as prestigious an area. Betty repeats a line to Art that he has heard many times before. "Just call me from the city that we're going to move, and by the time you get home I'll be packed."

12

High Noon

ART REACHES OVER and stops the dull buzzing of the alarm clock. He immediately stands up and walks to the bathroom. One of the paper suppliers Rabinowitz buys from gave him a heated lather dispenser a few Christmases ago, and Art applies a puffy white mound before shaving with a double-edged blade. Betty opens her eyes a slit and eases herself to a sitting position on the bed, where Art finds her when he comes back to the bedroom to dress.

They say nothing to one another on this morning in late July. Art has never been one for early morning conversations, and Betty is plainly too sleepy. By the time Art is halfway through his bowl of Sugar Frosted Flakes, Betty is in the kitchen making lunches for Richard and Martha. She calls down the stairs to Richard, who must be up before seven if he is to get to work by eight. This morning Betty will break her routine of going back to bed after the lunches are packed and Art is off to work. She is going in with Art to pick up Joan, who has spent a few days with Jon, one of the Rabinowitz salesmen, his wife, Becky, and Wendy, their daughter, who have a country home about fifty miles outside the city.

"Betty, you going to eat anything?" Art says. "It's a long trip in."

"Teeth hurt too much this morning" she replies. "Took some aspirin."

Richard comes into the kitchen yawning and looks down at

his father's breakfast. "You're eating junk. Nothing in that but worthless crap."

"Then I must be full of worthless crap," Art says dryly. "Let's get moving Betty or we'll miss the train."

A little over an hour later, as Art and Betty are arriving in the city, Richard and Ron, who quit his job at the mental hospital, pull into a parking lot behind a single-story, medium-sized brick building. The lot is only half full and, inside, half the machines will lie idle today. The defense contract boom that swept Mohawk County swelled a small shop, Perfection Metal Fabricating, into this larger facility. But now, with the boom past, only twenty-five workers are needed where sixty once were employed.

Richard punches in, and for the first time in five days the numbers are in blue. (The line of red numbers show he has been from three to seventeen minutes late.) He changes into a flannel shirt and a pair of greasy jeans and goes to his bench. A cardboard barrel half filled with rectangular pieces made of a dull-finish alloy awaits him. For the last two days, he has been drilling five large and two small holes into these pieces and then filing down the burrs. Richard had no idea what he was working on until yesterday, when someone told him it was part of a wing assembly for a 747 airplane.

"Look at this fucking thing." A voice with an Italian accent comes from behind Richard.

"What is it, Tony?" Richard asks, looking at the blueprint the man is holding.

"Fucking killer, that's what it is," he says, looking over his shoulder to see if anyone is watching. "See this? The bracket for a pod for under the wing of a fighter. The pilot squeezes the stick and *ffffttttt!* twenty thousand bullets go out."

"So tell them you won't work on it, Tony; tell them to stick the pod and all right up their asses."

"Killer stuff."

"Tell them."

"It's only a job," Tony says weakly, looking again over his

206

shoulder to see the plant foreman walking their way, talking with another man.

Richard watches them as they disappear behind a wall of shelving that holds some of the thousands of pieces of metal that Perfection has fabricated. On the shelves are the mundane, like a partially assembled popcorn-making cabinet—the type that would be used in movie theaters—which was never finished because the Japanese entered the market with a lower-priced product. There are hundreds of small, nondescript pieces of various kinds of metals that have gone into tools, machines, aircraft. Then there are the pieces that Perfection made with pride and for profit during its heyday in the 1960s: a bronze plate, looking like a Roman warrior's shield, that fended off the heat rays on a Saturn rocket; a tiny potty chair used by Apollo spacemen that had to be remade because it did not come within the .005 tolerance demanded by the government. This piece is the brunt of a standardized Perfection joke, one that Richard heard his first day of work: "They must have measured their assholes to get the specifications on that one."

Richard eyes the pieces assigned to him, picks one out of the box, clamps a molded pattern on it and presses the button to start a drill press. The low, monotonous hum blends into the chorus composed of the high whine of turret lathes and the padded thumping of the stamping machines. He drills five small holes in one side, repositions the piece, changes the drill bit and drills two larger holes in the opposite side. Brushing his hair out of his eyes and taking the first look at the wall clock, which is barely visible through its greasy glass—it is 8:07—he unclamps the piece, tosses it onto his bench and reaches into the box for another.

Richard's movements quickly become programmed, his face passive. Only as ten o'clock nears does he slow down, looking at the clock every few minutes. At ten a throaty buzzer sounds, the machines wind down to a stop and the workers head for a small table that holds a huge coffee urn and boxes of doughnuts that the company provides for this midmorning break. Richard and Ron each take a doughnut and fill Styrofoam cups with milk and lean against a pile of empty skids. They say little to their

207

fellow workers, all of whom are older and whose concerns are different. The workers were not much interested in Richard's trip to California; he is not interested in their talk about organizing a shop union.

During Richard's two short periods at Perfection he has gained the reputation of being a good worker, and the foreman has told him he could work himself up in the company. This holds little appeal for Richard. The men who have worked there for twenty or thirty years often do the same tedious work Richard does. The highest-paid men, earning $4.25 an hour, operate hydroform machines that shape parts out of sheet metal, but their work is repetitive also. New technology has provided new machines for industries like Perfection, but instead of helping to ease the boredom they have increased it, as the worker more and more becomes an extension of the machine. One new drill press the company recently bought is programmed by computer tape. Its operator does little except watch for the "change tool" light to flash on so he can put a different drill bit in place before the machine goes into its next phase.

By lunchtime Richard has a load of finished pieces on his workbench. When the buzzer sounds he walks quickly toward the men's room to wash, and then he and Ron head for the truck.

Sitting in the front seat, Richard quickly gobbles the sandwich, pear and cookies his mother packed him. Then he reaches beneath the seat, pulls out a small Baggie and shakes some of the brownish dried mixture onto a cigarette paper. Deftly, he rolls the cigarette in his fingers to eliminate air pockets and licks the paper to seal the cylinder. He twirls the paper on both ends and lights the cigarette, inhaling deeply and noisily through his nose and mouth. He leans back in the seat and closes his eyes.

"Goddam fine stuff," he says, passing the cigarette to Ron.

"You know, I think this job might put me back in the mental hospital."

"It sucks but who gives a shit. Like I said, we're going up to Canada and we'll just truck until we find a good place, then we stop."

"Just like last weekend."

Richard inhales deeply, and his thin chest pulls away from beneath his shirt. "What was wrong with that, man? We did a hell of a lot of trucking."

"And not much finding."

Richard looks at him through half-closed lids. "Blow it off, man, you got to get out there and look for it. It ain't coming into your house. When I had this gig on the Coast with the Santa Claus . . ."

"One-night stand; so what?"

"Chicks were crawling all over us. 'Hey, Santa, I want a Mercedes for Christmas.' "

"So what?"

"It was cool, that's what. Don't be a drag, huh?"

"I'm just trying to be realistic."

"Bullshit!"

"We're always the preview of coming attractions, and the feature never comes."

Richard's eyes are closed, and he says nothing for fifteen seconds. Then his eyes flicker open and he looks sideways at Ron. "What was that, man?"

"Nothing, Richie. Let's get back in; it's time."

"Don't expect nothing to come to you, Ron. I had to get out on the road to get my head together. You listening, Ron?"

RICHARD: Indoor bullshit. Four walls all day long. The job is definitely freaking me out, and I get pissed off at everything when my mind goes bad on something. I got to see daylight. Deliveries or a gas station.

I don't know. When I came back from California, I'd seen a lot of stuff and I tried to bridge the gap; I fixed up my room like I had it in California, with dark lights and stuff. But the shit is piling up on me again. I'm trying to study up on farming and leatherwork so I can get out of the city. I waste so much time just getting back and forth to work, an hour and a half every day that I could be reading up on stuff or practicing my guitar. But when I'm locked up all day long, I got to get out at night. You can't sit indoors and read a fucking book.

Man, I know I say a lot of different things, and to some people it might seem like I'm jumping around. Like I want to go back to school this fall. I want to get an apartment. I got to get rid of the truck; the insurance is killing me. I'm going back to California. It isn't that I'm confused. I just got a lot of stuff to do, and now I can just move and get things done. I'm just into a lot of things, and when they don't work out I just drop them like a hot coal.

My parents think I'm jumping around and it really gets to them, especially my father. He hates me. If I would be a regular citizen right now, they wouldn't hassle me, but they know I'm different from Martha and they let me know about it, about what a bummer I am and how fantastic she is. If I get into ideas they like—like college—then they treat me good. But since I split from college, I'm nothing in their eyes.

What would bring it all together right now would be if I had a chick. I just want one good chick to rap to and run with. I had a good one last year—Merta—but then she said they had this Huntington's chorea in their family and she had a good chance of having it and she couldn't stand for anybody to get close to her because she might die from it. Then right before California I was digging Phyllis, and her boyfriend came back. She was a bitch anyhow.

California was definitely a necessary thing to do. I figured out how to live the way I want to live. Like I want new stereo equipment and I'm going to get it with Master Charge. Then I'll work my ass off for a while to pay it off. I needed to get miles away to think about stuff like that. I always allowed myself to be sheltered at home, to take the easiest, safest way. I can cope with trouble now. I proved that by going all the way across the country and back.

Another thing that brought me back was I didn't know how much my friends depended on me. When I talked to Randy long distance he said he'd send me the money right then if I'd fly back. He'd just lost his girl friend and he didn't have anybody to hang around with. And Ron. He didn't have anybody either. His parents are getting a divorce and he's with a shrink now.

It wasn't anything like being homesick, but I did feel more guilty than homesick. I really felt guilty about my father, because I heard he was looking at pictures down in my room and he fell asleep on the bed. I didn't think he had it in him.

I think we might make it at home this time, but I don't know. One word—"haircut"—and I'm leaving. The day my hair gets down to my shoulders is the day I'm going to be happier. It's growing too slow for me. Why cut your hair? Some people say deodorants are bad because they stop you from perspiring and you're supposed to perspire. Hair wasn't meant to be cut. It's great to have it blowing all over the place when you're driving a car.

But California did a lot of stuff for me. I'm just not going to let my mother and father hassle me any more. I can give them as much shit as they give me. And the rest I can let slide. We can argue about welfare and I can leave them boiling and I can just walk away and forget it. I recommend getting away to everybody so you can see who you are and what you really want to do.

Richard and Ron head for the back door of the factory. Richard squints into the midday sun and pulls out his sunglasses. Once inside the plant, he puts them on.

Just after eight o'clock this morning, Betty and Art step out of the air-conditioned train and into the muggy terminal in the middle of the city. Where they had been in the company of all-white and neatly dressed commuters, they are suddenly plunged into a smorgasbord of people. Betty looks vaguely confused as a group of men gesturing with their hands and speaking Greek push their way past as she and Art head for the subway. Blacks, Puerto Ricans, Chinese, white-collar workers and blue-collar workers swirl past the slow-walking Neumeyers. Betty rolls her eyes as the subway doors close and she is squeezed into Art by the crush of humanity. At Art's stop, the pungent smells of the printing industry and the sour odors from restaurant garbage cans cause Betty to screw up her nose. Art looks at her, smiles—his first smile of the day—

and says dryly, "Now you see why I don't come home in a good mood every night."

As they walk toward the building with RABINOWITZ DIE-CUTTING fading into the brick, Betty tells Art to walk still slower. "Don't know why they send Wendy to camp anyhow," she says, breathing heavily. "They live in the country. Summers are a good time to get to know your children. And they give a lot of camperships to inner-city kids. Joan doesn't need to hear that kind of talk. She doesn't have that bad a home to stay in."

"Neither does Wendy; that's not the idea, Betty. Just a chance to get away, be with other kids."

"Get away." Betty huffs. "No more after her, Artie, don't forget that."

"She's my baby too."

Mort Stern and Tony Napoli are already at their desks when the Neumeyers come into the office, and both men come over to say hello and make brief comments on the hot weather. The receptionist makes Betty a cup of coffee, and she sits quietly by Art's desk as the telephone begins ringing and the tempo of activity picks up.

A half hour later Joan bursts into the office, followed by Jon, the salesman. "Mommy, Mommy, I had the best time! We fed the chipmunks and everything!" she says excitedly. Betty smothers her daughter in her arms, closing her eyes as she did when she greeted Martha after a three-month separation. Joan struggles to get free and gives her father a hug and a kiss. The office staff says nothing but smiles at this happy family.

"There's a ten o'clock showing of *Butterflies Are Free*," Art says, looking up from the newspaper.

"What's the rating on that?" Betty asks in a loud voice.

"Rating? PG."

"We'll take a pass on that, won't we, Joan?" Betty says with the same volume.

"I guess so," she answers softly.

"They put a PG rating on any kind of trash nowadays."

Joan and Betty are soon outside, heading for the subway. The temperature is near 90, the humidity high, and Joan keeps rubbing her arms as if she is trying to clean them. Betty runs her arm along Joan's back and says, "If you want the museum, you got to take the dirt, the smell, the noise."

The Natural History Museum is just opening when Betty and Joan arrive, and soon they are transported from the hot city into the coolness of the African room and confronted by a herd of stuffed elephants. Moving on to a display, Betty asks Joan to look carefully at it and tell what makes the difference between the fertile Nile valley and a sandy plain.

"Different animals," Joan says, pressing her nose to the glass.

"Look, honey," Betty says, "what does the Nile have that the desert doesn't?"

"Different vegetation."

"Look," Betty says impatiently.

"I don't know, Mommy; I told you what I thought it was."

"Water!"

Joan looks sheepishly at the plastic animals drinking in the plastic Nile. She turns quickly because of some young voices behind her. A lady about Betty's age in a fashionable pants suit is rounding up a group of elementary-age youngsters wearing Fredonia Fun Club T-shirts. Some of the children are blondish, suntanned; others are black.

Joan looks at her mother questioningly and Betty promptly responds, "It's good for these underprivileged children to come in groups." She whispers to Joan, "But certain children don't need day care." She smiles broadly. "They get so much more out of a trip with their mother."

Betty continues her quiz as they walk through the museum.

"What does extinct mean? Read the sign."

Joan is silent.

"It means animals are no longer around."

At a slice from a giant sequoia tree, Betty points to a marker at a circle and reads, "A.D. five fifty."

"I don't know what A.D. means but B.C. means before Christ," Joan says proudly.

Joan has not been quick to answer the specific questions her mother has put to her—much like a teacher in school—but she has

213

been fascinated by the stuffed animals and by the complex displays and dioramas that other children pass quickly. The pollenization of apples, farm crop rotation, cutaways of a chipmunk's nest, earthworm holes and a mole community—all have her asking Betty questions. "How does all that dirt get through the worm's body?" "What would happen if the bees got tired one year; wouldn't there be any apples?" Betty has Joan read the information plates and encourages her to look up facts neither of them know in the encyclopedia the next time she's at the Mariposa Public Library.

Betty reads the plate at a display containing the ruddy duck and waves to Joan, who is looking at loons. "This is interesting, honey, the way the ruddy duck mates," Betty says. "You might have to use this some day." She gives her daughter a hug. "The male dives beneath the water and chases the female. When she screeches, that's his sign to swim out in front of her. If she likes his tail feathers, they swim away together and mate."

Joan looks at her mother quizzically.

"You'll understand someday, honey," Betty says.

As they wait for the subway to take them back to the train station after their two and a half hours in the museum, Betty nods in the direction of a women's room. It is off to the side, its entrance between two candy machines. "That used to be my favorite place to vomit when I was pregnant with Martha," she says proudly. "And sometimes I'd be off at almost every stop, I was so sick."

"It's so dirty down here, Mommy," Joan says, rubbing her arms and looking at the wet newspapers, cans and candy wrappers lying between the tracks.

"Honey, that's the city. If you want a museum, you have to take the dirt. It wasn't always like this. We have to come in more often for these half-day trips. It's good for you."

"I don't mind the dirt; I'll come every day," Joan says excitedly.

On the train home, Betty's eyelids are drooping and she asks Joan to come and sit in her lap, telling her daughter, "I just want to feel a little closer to you. Let's take a little nap."

Joan kisses her mother on the cheek and says, "I want to see out the window, OK, Mommy? You sleep."

BETTY: I love the city, but Artie really catches me when I romanticize about the old neighborhood. I really wouldn't want the kids to be growing up there. I'm glad we're going to the suburbs and not to a North End apartment. The last time we drove through the North End I wanted to cry. The milk company was boarded up; my father's fruit stand is now an office for garbagemen; an old ice cream shop I used to go into is one of those check-cashing places for people on welfare.

Our old apartment building at Eight sixteen Bushing looked so sad. On summer nights people used to bring out canvas chairs and talk, and our babies would be sleeping in their buggies. Now there's dog dirt and broken wine bottles and garbage cans overflowing and stinking. It's disgusting. We used to have a beautiful wooden door, and now it's that banged-in metal kind. And just a hole; no doorknob.

Joanie will never know how good the old neighborhood was. It doesn't even make any sense to show her, because how could I explain? Like the apartment on Rush Street where I grew up. There was a vacant lot across the street, filled with jagged rocks. After we saw Ziegfeld Follies and those tiers and the dancers, we acted it out right there in the lot. It was our playground; we used to weigh rocks and dirt to sell in our play store. But even the dirt was clean then. The last time I went by there it was filled with rusty cans, mangled baby carriages, all kinds of trash. And this ferocious German shepherd was barking at the top of the hill like he wanted to eat somebody.

It is about six forty-five that evening, and the family has just sat down for dinner. Art has brought home the bad news that the cabin they were hoping to rent is already taken. "We had to wait around for you two to decide if you were going to be here," Betty says, looking first at Martha and then at Richard. "It's your fault and don't you forget it." Neither child answers Betty so she turns to Joan, and her voice is suddenly calm. "Tell your father about our nice trip today."

"I love the city and the people are interesting and the subway is too noisy and you can buy all kinds of things," Joan says, standing up at her chair.

"What about the country, up at Jon's place?" her father asks.

"That was good too, but sometimes you get bored because all you do is walk around and go kite flying and feed the birds."

"Tough life." He smiles. "Stay out of the city. I can't wait to get home and breathe some decent air."

"Paradise is Mariposa, a regular nirvana," Martha says, crossing her eyes. "What about you Mommy?" she asks in her little-girl voice. "What did you like best about the city? Most of my friends think you need a passport to get in; I don't think they've ever been there."

Betty looks down at her plate. "Sometimes it seems like we're living just for us," she says slowly. "Maybe we're too self-centered. There were these kids from a day care group—"

"Betty, you couldn't wait to get out of the city," Art cuts in.

"I know, I know," she says. "I was just thinking on the train coming home how nice it would be if Martha was a missionary. There are so many kids in the city, they don't know who their parents are, don't—"

"Missionary to some undeveloped place, fine." Art cuts her off again. "But the parents—or whoever keeps those kids—are getting welfare and food stamps, and the food stamps go for booze and cigarettes and the kids go hungry."

"Which reminds me," Richard says. "Any more beer?"

"You are really turning into the boozer." His father stares at him. "It smells all over you. How many did you have after work?"

"Just two." Richard smiles.

"Maybe it's like the Bible; the poor you will always have with you," Betty says.

"Our generation worked very hard to work our way out of the city," Art says. "Now it's their job to work hard and escape. If your friend McGovern would get elected, he'd just hand them everything without any work."

"I assume that statement was directed at me," Martha says.

"Even with all my compassion, there's one thing I can't stand and that's a free handout," Betty says. "You notice, Martha, he

216

never poses for a picture unless there's a black person in the picture."

"OK, he's turned into more of a politician than a humanitarian, but God, he wants to do something for people and not just build bombers."

"That man would kill middle-class families, Martha," Art says, his voice growing louder. "I already pay fifty or sixty dollars a week in taxes. The welfare family does great; the big guy has his tax shelter. Loopholes don't mean anything to us because we don't have any extra money to work with if we found them."

"So what do you do, starve people and put the illegitimate kids in institutions? You don't know what it's like; you weren't raised in a ghetto. In our minorities literature class I—"

"It just so happens I *was* raised in the ghetto, Martha, and you were raised out here with grass and trees because I worked for it. I hitched on the back of trolley cars. I played hooky from school. But I made it."

Martha mumbles something.

"Speak up; what is it?" her father says.

"I just don't see," she says, "how we go to church, quote the Bible. . . . It just seems that to be an American you've got to be your brother's keeper."

Art's and Betty's eyes narrow. "Start paying taxes and paying your own way, then come back and preach to me," Art says.

"We're the hypocrites, Martha," her mother says sarcastically. "Maybe your magnificent generation is going to find the answers."

The doorbell rings. Richard calls down to Randy and Ron to come in.

"Finish your meal like the rest of us," his father says.

"Finished."

"There's still some peas and meat left; we aren't millionaires you know."

"Lost my appetite," Richard says, snatching the can of beer from the table. He and his friends are soon out the front door.

"Betty, if he wants to stay here, he's going to have respect."

Betty does not look at her husband. "Eat up, Joanie, or else I'll be sure you caught something in the country."

217

The boys climb into Richard's truck, which in the last week has been redecorated. There is carpeting and a mattress with a clean sheet on the floor, two Indian-style tablecloths on the sides and a poster of a grotesquely muscular Tarzan.

"I'm in the mood for some action," Richard says as he slows for the red light at Main Line Drive, then lurches into the intersection with the green. He quickly gulps down the rest of the can of beer and tosses it over his shoulder into the back of the truck. He belches loudly and asks Ron to open him another.

"C'mon, Rich, I don't want to be a baby-sitter again."

"Yeah, California cool," Randy cuts in. "Heard that you had three beers last weekend and you were out of it. Ron had to lead you around by the hand."

"Bullshit, man. Open the beer, huh? I'm just getting a buzz on, and I ain't letting it go till I drop tonight. Whoopee!" He shouts out the window to two girls riding in a convertible with the top down.

"Slow down, Rich," Randy says. "Let's get acquainted."

"Dogs. We'll find better stuff tonight. Got to be like this Barry dude from Martha's school, balling every chick in the state, including my sister. Let's go over to Moonshine East. I heard there's all kinds of ass over there."

"Yeah," says Ron. Randy lays his head back on his hands and says nothing.

After a 75-mile-an-hour ride the truck pulls up in front of Moonshine East. There are no cars in the parking lot and only a few on the street in front. A sign on the door reads: CLOSED FOR REPAIRS.

Richard streaks to the Barnacle, five miles away. Although there are a few unattached girls at the bar, Richard says they are all dogs and wants to play shuffleboard. While he does, he talks about making telephone calls from California and charging them to nonexistent numbers. "Called Phoebe and talked for a half hour on her birthday. Learned it from *Steal This Book*. All kinds of ways to rip off."

Fifteen minutes later, Richard finishes a game.

"C'mon, this shithole is getting to me," he says. "Nothing happening. Let's go to Buzzy's."

In the parking lot of Buzzy's Hideaway, Randy takes out one of the three marijuana cigarettes he has rolled for tonight. The boys pass it around, smoking it down to the roach.

Richard shakes the remaining marijuana onto the top of an empty beer can and attempts to light it, then sniff the smoke. Spilled beer along the rim frustrates his effort.

At the door of Buzzy's Hideaway is a 6-foot-4-inch man with a baby face but muscles that strain at the sleeves of his bright red shirt. He collects $1 each for admission from Ron, Randy and Richard and then asks Richard for proof of his age.

The band is just starting their first number as the boys go to a table on a raised balcony away from the bar and dance floor. As they play "Ain't Got Nobody to Depend On," colored lights flash on the stage. Along the bar and at tables near the dance floor are at least twenty girls, mostly in groups of threes and fours, who do not have dates. The unattached boys, tonight in the minority, walk over and ask various girls to dance. Ron, Richard and Randy look on, saying nothing.

"Look at that piece of ass," Randy says, pointing to a tall, attractive girl with streaked hair and a short miniskirt.

"Well, go on, ask her to dance," Richard says.

"What about you guys?"

"Don't see nothing I'm interested in," Richard says. "Let's go outside for a joint."

The effects of the marijuana wear off more quickly, and twenty minutes later the three boys are sitting in silence, full glasses of beer in front of them, watching the dancers moving in front of the bandstand. "Should have seen the place I went to in Michigan," Richard says. "Must have been five hundred broads there."

His friends say nothing.

"Who's buying the beers?" Richard asks, breaking the silence.

"We got full ones," Randy says. "All right, you can buy, Rich, and when you come back I'll show you how to hold a whole puddle of beer back with a single hair."

Richard returns with the glasses and Randy asks him to lean toward him. "Ouch!" Randy pulls a long hair from the back of Richard's head.

Randy forms the hair in a circle and pours half a glass of beer into it. "Get down closer to it, Rich," Randy says, "and you'll see what's holding it back."

Richard looks closer.

"Get down there or else you can't see it," Randy says.

Richard puts his face a few inches from the beer. "So what? The hair—"

Randy slams his palm down in the puddle, drenching Richard's face and shirt.

The beer dripping from his nose and off the uneven growth on his chin, Richard stares at Randy. "Let's get the fuck out of here. This place brings me down."

13

On Vacation

THE FIRST SUNDAY in August dawns clear, and by 10 A.M. Mariposa is alive with people on the road in pursuit of recreation or those already playing under the brilliant blue skies. On the golf course near the Neumeyers' house, the fourth hole is the scene of a jam-up as the soft northerly wind has been easing balls into the lake. And, on a street a few miles from his home, Art Neumeyer takes a roundabout way to the delicatessen to avoid having to go by Parkside United Methodist Church, where but a handful of people are present for worship. This morning, in lieu of a Sunday suit and tie, Art is wearing his white swim trunks, a terrycloth beach jacket and a blue hat with a green dolphin on it.

When Art returns home with ham, cheese and fresh rolls, he finds Betty at the counter, packing soda, grapes and plums into the cooler. Martha is sitting at the kitchen table in a lavender nightie, nibbling on an English muffin.

"Let's get going before we have to park a mile from the beach," Art says, putting the package on the counter.

"A few minutes, honey, and I'll have these sandwiches ready," Betty says. "Martha, if you want to go, better get something on."

"Crap," Martha says with little emotion in her voice. "I don't know if Carol and Theresa are going or not. At school, we pick up and do something in ten minutes. Here it takes a week to plan one afternoon."

"Beach express leaves in five minutes," Art says cheerily as he wraps his arm around his daughter and then slaps her on the rump. "Richie still home?" he asks, suddenly flickering with sternness.

"If you got home in the middle of the night you'd be in bed too," Betty says. "Anyhow, I don't need his beery breath this morning."

"Did I hear it right? He quit Perfection?"

"Exactly. He and Ron gave up their two-sixty-five-an-hour jobs so they can make one eighty-five in a bicycle factory. Artie, get me one more piece of aluminum foil for this sandwich. Martha?"

"I'll wait for them. Go ahead."

Art is midway through his two weeks of vacation. After the Neumeyers' plans fell through for the cabin, they decided to spend the time around Mariposa, taking day trips to historic sites or to the beach. Art, Betty and Joan have visited a President's home, a craggy overlook that has a lighthouse and the zoo near their old neighborhood in the North End. Next week they plan to go to Washington, D.C., to see the Capitol and the Smithsonian Institution and to visit a retired Marine officer they knew when they lived in Florida. One of the reasons Art and Betty have not gone away for any length of time is that they do not want to leave Richard at home unsupervised. The levels on the gin and vodka bottles in their liquor cabinet have mysteriously dropped, and Betty mopped up some sticky rings from the top of Richard's desk when she cleaned last week, pronouncing them the result of sloppy screwdriver drinkers.

By the time Art, Betty and Joan load the car and reach the expressway, it is living up to the name regular commuters have given it—"The Creepway." Cars are bumper to bumper and some cars dart into even the smallest space in the next lane, futilely attempting to make better time. Art stays in the middle lane, turns the air conditioner on medium and stares ahead. When the Neumeyers reach exit 13 they turn off, leaving the traffic jam behind. Most of the cars on the expressway are headed for public beaches in the state park some six miles away. Because the Neumeyers live in Myrtle Township of Mohawk County, they are allowed to use

222

the township's private section of beach. Art slows at the guard-house of Breezy Beach as a young suntanned boy with a life-guard's uniform looks at the blue sticker on the bumper before waving him through.

"There's a spot over—" Betty stops. Art turns the car in the opposite direction. Betty and Art have been making efforts not to be "on each other," as Betty puts it, during the vacation. Last night in bed they agreed it had been a very tense year for them, the summer had been a disaster and they wanted to make the most of the already fragmented vacation.

On the walk to the water's edge, Art rents a beach umbrella for $1, leaving the required $5 deposit. He, Betty and Joan slog through the sand and find a spot to lay down their old bedspread, the beach towels, a chair for Betty, and the cooler.

"Artie, we should do this every day," Betty says, hugging him around the knees as he stands above her.

"Fine with me," he says, giving her a wry smile. "Just tell Rabinowitz they can reach me right here."

Joan, clad in a flowered bikini, the top of which is having trouble staying up, comes running over to them. "Daddy, Daddy, there's a million shells over there! Come on, let's get some for my collection."

"Go ahead," Betty says. "I want to read this anyhow. One of our progressive ladies at church said it saved their marriage." She takes *Open Marriage* out of the bag and turns to chapter one, "Why Save Marriage at All?"

Breezy Beach is moderately crowded this weekend midmorn-ing, with three quarters of the space near the water and half the sand farther away staked out with chairs, towels, umbrellas, plas-tic sand pails and coolers. Art and Joan walk hand in hand toward a part of the beach near a breakwater where the waves lap lazily at the shore, bringing curds of foam to evaporate on the clean sand. They look for air holes that bubble up as the waves recede, laugh-ing to one another as they dig frantically in pursuit of a clam that is burrowing deeper. The wet sand goes flying from Joan's beach shovel and splatters against Art's thin legs. He playfully boots her in the behind and she sprawls onto the sand, as if the kick had been powerful. Art picks her up over his head and, caveman style, trudges across the beach. Joan's face is red from laughter. He winds his way through people on the beach: a quiet family from the Middle East, serving an exotic dish with yogurt out of a Tupperware container; a mother with peroxide hair reading a movie magazine and, without looking up, occasionally yelling at her daughter not to go too far; an older couple, very suntanned —he with a captain's hat and she with a net over her bright red hair styled high on her head—reading the Sunday paper. And finally Art is back to Betty, a pale figure under an umbrella in a one-piece bathing suit that looks one size too small. Her ample breasts are partially exposed, and rolls of fat ease past where the bathing suit ends on her legs.

Betty, who is a fast reader, has finished most of chapter one of *Open Marriage*, learning about concepts like "The Four-Burner Wife," "The Fidelity Trap" and "The One-to-One Relationship." As she looks up to see Art and Joan approaching, she closes the book with a loud noise. "This isn't for us, Artie. It might help some people who can't get along, but we don't need this stuff."

"It wasn't on my reading list anyhow," Art says. "How about some food?"

Betty hands out sandwiches and drinks, then opens the bags of potato chips and fruit.

As the family begins to eat, a trim woman with an even tan stops in front of the umbrella. "Well, the high rollers from The Knolls are spending some time with the little people." It is Maureen Kelly, a neighbor from Tulip Lane.

"Yeah, high rollers," Betty says with a smile. "That's why we're on a free beach instead of a cruise ship to the islands. Hanging on by our fingernails in the old neighborhood and no different now."

"Only we bite the nails more," Art adds.

"How are things back there? Haven't seen you for months, and Pam Brown only has some of the gossip." Betty goes no further as she knows that Maureen and Pam, although both Catholics and members of St. Anselm's Church, do not get along.

224

"Rash of marriage problems, but otherwise everything's the same."

"Seems there's something in the air; lot of it in our neighborhood, too," Betty says.

"Can't get away from it," Maureen says.

"I wish we wouldn't have."

"Wouldn't have what?" Art asks.

"Moved from Tulip," Betty says in a low voice. "Maureen, remember Martha's confirmation party? The whole block was there." A warm smile covers Betty's face, almost as if she could see the party in progress. "It was like one big happy family, everybody in the same boat, everybody with young kids, big mortgage. It was wonderful."

"Betty, you wanted more room, you wanted a dining room."

"So what, Artie? I wish I could be back there right now."

A house in the suburbs, on a peaceful street like Tulip or Birchwood, was beyond the farthest reaches of their imagination when Betty Santangelo and Arthur Neumeyer married in 1950. Betty, a delicate 98 pounds, came down her apartment steps on August 27 with the neighborhood children lining her route to the waiting car. It was, in her words, "the first significant day of my life." Her school days had been a time of holding back because of her illness; her short career as a secretary had been a limbo until she could marry and bear children. On that sunny day in August she rode in a rented Cadillac limousine to Appleton Hill Methodist Church, walked up the aisle on her father's arm and was given in marriage to a thin young man her parents warmly approved of. At that time Art Neumeyer was making more money a week than Betty's father.

Art was a severe figure with his pencil-thin mustache and slicked-back hair, his face not entirely yielding to the happiness he deeply felt on his wedding day. But there was no question about Betty. Dressed in a floor-length satin gown that had been borrowed from a friend, she was beaming. She carried a small bouquet of white roses and wore a crown headpiece of artificial

225

flowers with a fingertip veil—she had visited every bridal shop in the North End before choosing it.

Art was not a churchgoing person, so the ceremony was for Betty's sake. Her brother had been baptized at Appleton Hill, she had been confirmed there, and inside of a year it would witness Martha's baptism. After the fifteen-minute service, the couple had their formal wedding pictures taken at a studio and then went to the Paradise Inn where a reception for some hundred guests was held. Anthony Santangelo, cigar in hand, was in an expansive mood that evening, telling stories of the first time little Betty walked, the first time she rode a carousel. It did not faze him that the entire wedding was being staged on $500 of borrowed money. His string of bad luck with the horses had lasted throughout the summer of 1950.

Art and Betty went to a fine city hotel, the Georgetown Manor, to spend their honeymoon night, and when they opened their suitcases they found them stuffed with confetti. They laughed as they made wonderful, legitimate love, occasionally spitting out a piece of confetti.

The next morning, Betty's brother, George, brought her a jacket she had forgotten. When George went back to the North End late that morning, he ran from drugstore to fruit market, hollering up to women who sat in the windows, telling the men at the newspaper stand. He had found his sister and her new husband having breakfast in bed! Elegance North Enders had only heard of or seen in movies was being lived out by one of their very own girls.

Betty and Art had made a week's reservation at a mountain lodge, but they returned to the air-conditioned hotel after one night in the hot, humid, insect-filled natural wonderland. They went to baseball games and movies; they walked slowly, hand in hand, along the busy avenues as working people surged by; they ate restaurant steaks and hot dogs from street vendors.

Apartments were scarce in the North End, so Art and Betty had to settle in a mixed residential and commercial area in the middle of the city. Betty called their first home a dungeon because it was on the ground floor, sunlight was nonexistent and the windows that

226

faced the street were covered with an iron grate. For $22 a week, the Neumeyers had a furnished room-and-a-half, the room being the bed-living room and the half being a bathroom. A closet had been converted into a kitchen that was barely large enough to cook in, so the young couple either set up their table next to the tub and ate in the bathroom or, when Betty cooked special meals, they would light candles and eat in the living room. Dishes were washed in the bathroom sink and drained over the tub.

Betty was in her second month of pregnancy when they married, and with no ventilation in the tiny kitchen she would often have to interrupt the preparation of a meal to go into the bathroom and throw up. But even comically small quarters and morning sickness didn't alter their enthusiasm and joy for living. Evenings they would sing together or talk about buying a gas station where they could live upstairs. Art talked about having a daughter just like Betty. Betty admitted she wanted a baby girl also. Betty was conscious of a new life beginning for them as married people, and she tried to convince Art they should say grace before meals. She wanted them to have "good and graceful habits." Neither had said grace in their own homes, but Betty wanted this to be a tradition they would hand down to their children.

Of course, there were the squabbles that mark most new marriages, such as the night Art complained that Betty's corned beef and cabbage didn't taste as good as his mother's and Betty threw the pot at him, or the time Art was being unusually slow in getting up to come to breakfast and Betty picked up his bowl of cereal and sent cornflakes, milk and bowl sailing across the tiny apartment. Often after these fights Art would "fix her wagon," as Betty now jokes to him. He would take her rage and turn it into passion, and they would make love.

Four months after they married, the Neumeyers found a three-and-a-half-room apartment in a building on Sterling Avenue, which had almost all elderly Jewish residents and was a fifteen-minute ride from the Santangelos. Art and Betty moved into the $50-a-month apartment with only two tables that Art had made and a kitchen set Aldrich's Department Store had lent them, which was to serve until the one they had purchased with part of their $900 in wedding gifts was delivered. Art painted and wallpapered the large kitchen and made a breakfast nook in one corner. In the bedroom there was a double bed and soon a bassinette, as the time for Betty to give birth drew near.

When the labor pains became intense on a cold, rainy night in March, Art and Betty decided they would go to St. Joseph's Hospital. Betty had had her overnight bag ready for weeks, she and Art were excited, but it seemed that the little things she had hoped for hadn't occurred. Her maid of honor, whose reputation for being late was legendary, had postponed a baby shower until it didn't happen; Betty's mother had strangely been of little support. Betty went to the hospital knowing little of what to expect.

When the young couple arrived at the iron gates of St. Joseph's, they were sternly reprimanded for coming after the first shift had left, when the staff was small. The nun pointed Betty toward the admitting desk and slammed the gate shut in Art's face. It flashed into Betty's mind that giving birth was a criminal act, that she was about to be punished. Betty arrived in her room, her brown teddy-bear coat still on, and went to the window to see if she could spot Art. She couldn't, and as she looked into the night she felt so depressed that for an instant the thought of jumping out the window, committing suicide, flashed into her mind.

The next day she was wheeled into the delivery room. The last thing she remembers was the itchy powder they sprinkled on her face before they clapped on the gas mask; she was strapped to the table and couldn't rub her nose. Eight hours later, a flushed-face baby girl was set down beside Betty Neumeyer. It had been a difficult breech birth but her dream had come true. She had had a baby and had lived to see it.

Betty and Art were loving, concerned parents, both of whom read the child care books and fussed over water temperatures for little Martha's bath and over her clothing, making sure it was not too itchy. When the pediatrician said Martha needed four ounces of a ready-mixed formula at each feeding, Art went from store to store frantically looking for four-ounce containers. Hours later he came home, looking as if his daughter faced imminent starvation. There were twelve-ounce and twenty-four-ounce cans, but none with the amount Martha needed. Finally Art called the doctor who, after he finished laughing, taught Art some simple arithmetic.

The Neumeyers lived on Sterling for four more years, during which time Richard was born without complications. It was a happy apartment, the scene of their first birthdays and holidays as a family. Their bedroom was crowded—a double bed, a child's bed for Martha and a crib for Richard—and Betty loved it that way, since it allowed her to reach out to either child during the night.

In 1956, some friends returned from Florida and told Art and Betty about good weather, palm trees and jobs that were going begging for skilled people. Betty had been suffering from mild rheumatism, and Art convinced her that warm weather would make her feel better. Also, Florida was a Promised Land in the mid-1950s, where young couples bought houses and picked oranges from their own trees. Betty was reluctant at first, not wanting to leave her parents, but Art's persistence won out. In March they withdrew their $1,000 in savings, put their furniture aboard a moving van and told the driver to meet them at a friend's house in Opa-Locka.

By the time the van reached Opa-Locka, the Neumeyers had not only found a house to rent but Art had gotten a job. It paid $85 a week, $5 more than he was making at Rabinowitz. The Neumeyers were dizzy with their good fortune. This, their first daring act, had been a roaring success.

Art had to work the second shift, four until midnight, and once the house was settled Betty found herself alone and lonesome in the evenings. When they went to the beach for two hours in the morning of a workday, had their lunch and watched the children play in the sand, Betty was happy. But when Art had to leave for work she would beg him not to go, crying to him that she was miserable. Often he would come home and find her still in tears. Betty was, at that difficult time, receiving plaintive letters from her mother, who was missing the daughter she had never given much attention to before. Her mother's barrage of letters and phone calls confirmed to Betty that she was indeed lonely and that she and Art had made a big mistake by leaving the North End.

Art liked Florida and wanted to stay. After weeks of tears and hurt feelings on Betty's part, he agreed to let her go back for a visit, thinking she would then be ready to think about Florida as their new home. When Betty came back she was content for only a few days; then her tears began again. This time Betty became almost hysterical and threatened to leave Art if he wanted to stay. Art yielded, as he would do again years later, when he closed his business. One day he came home from work, told Betty he had sold their car, bought a truck and cashed in Betty's insurance policy to pay for her and the children's air fare home. "The Florida disaster," as Betty would later call it, was over. Like Richard, they had left home with a bankroll and returned broke.

BETTY: In Florida we had a real house to live in, we had a friendly block, so why wasn't I happy? You don't take a city girl, a neighborhood girl, and transplant her just like that. I missed my family, the aunts and uncles, the birthdays, the Sundays together. I know I nagged Art, I know I cried a lot, but I just couldn't overcome that horrible feeling of loneliness. I'm human; I missed the familiar things.

For Art, he was probably happy to go to Florida, to make a break with the old neighborhood, to start fresh. Maybe he even wanted some distance from the family, so he could prove that he could take care of Betty all by himself. Why is it that too old we get smart? If Artie would want to go to Florida tomorrow, I'd be ready this afternoon. Too old I want adventure. I'm probably a little ashamed of the way I got him to bring me back— no, I'm not! I knew what I wanted and I resolved to myself I was going to lie on that bed and cry until I got it. I met a girl at church whose husband got transferred and they had to move. It's not even a hundred miles from her family. She wants to go back and I advised her: "Lie on that bed and cry. He'll take you back."

Betty and Art lived for three years in the North End after re-

turning from Florida, but by 1959 they could see the neighborhood was changing. Houses coming up for sale were no longer
being bought by the sons and daughters of the Jews, Poles, Slavs,
Irish and Italians who lived in the North End. Young couples were
moving to newly developed suburban areas while black families
were taking their place as the next generation in the neighborhood.
Art began to talk about not wanting his children to go to school
with children "who came from families where they see their
father drinking all night and using all kinds of curse words." One
night a newly arrived black family had a fight in an apartment
house down the street from the Neumeyers and a husband pushed
his wife through the glass door in the lobby. Art and Betty date
their decision to take flight from the city from that night.

Houses in Mohawk County's newest developments were then
selling in the $20,000 range, but as Art and Betty began house
hunting they knew they could not afford that much. They were
eventually shown the house on Tulip Lane, which was nine years
old and priced at $14,500. They liked the house, but even the small
down payment of $600 was a problem, so Art worked two jobs
for several months to amass the money. Monthly payments were
around $100 a month, more than they were paying for rent, but
within a carefully worked-out budget they could be met. A garage, three bedrooms, screened-in porch—it was to them a
dream home. The elementary school was two blocks away, a
shopping area a few minutes' walk and the street teemed with
young playmates for the Neumeyer children.

Tulip Lane, suburban living, was a whole new world for the
Neumeyers. Richard and Martha prowled around a vacant lot,
among weeds and squirrels and mosquitoes. Art looked out at his
back yard and planned where the swings would go and where he
would charcoal-broil hamburgers. Betty sat in the spacious kitchen,
complete with modern wooden cabinets, appliances and a large
window over the sink, and cried with joy.

Martha adjusted, adapted, made new friends. Her brother, who
had at first followed her around like a puppy dog, was made to
feel unwelcome in the company of Martha's new friends and
turned even more sullen and withdrawn. By the time Martha had

231

reached high school, brother and sister were in open warfare. Richard looked down on her friends, calling them "creeps," and criticized the music she liked, the clothes she wore to school.

Mariposa High School was proud of its tracking system, which allowed A-track students like Martha to have accelerated studies and smaller classes. B-track students like Richard and those in C-track received more vocational subjects. Students in the various tracks were virtually separated into castes, with the A-track students dominating all phases of social and academic life. While Martha strove for good grades and acceptance into a good college, Richard toiled over the well-worn cars in shop, dreaming of the day he would have his own car. Martha aspired to be a teacher, Richard to work in a pit crew of a racing team.

Although Martha turned into an outspoken teenager, challenging her parents' beliefs in politics, race and religion—as she continued to disdain household work—Betty and Art were willing to accept her nonconformity. After all, she was going to college; she would eventually make them proud parents. Richard, branded an "underachiever" early in grade school, was living up to that title. Richard's surliness, his poor grades, could have no payoff; his rebelliousness was not acceptable to his parents.

Richard was truant from classes, on one occasion vandalizing a house under construction; Richard was a boy who knocked girls over to get a seat for the short ride to school. When his mother could get him to sit down and talk about himself he would say he was a loser, that "everything I try never turns out." Betty and Art prodded Richard to do better in school, sometimes in their anger comparing his poor grades to Martha's. They kept trying to drum a desire for a higher education into a boy who was barely passing.

Richard's senior year in high school saw him cutting more classes and entire days, going to friends' houses to drink wine or smoke marijuana when it could be afforded. More than once, Richard came home drunk on a day when he should have been at school.

When they first moved to Tulip Lane, the Neumeyer children were small, problems were relatively minor and money was in

232

short supply. Once Art closed his business and went back to work at Rabinowitz, there was more money for things the family had never had before—such as vacations. Art began to take his family for a week to the mountains, to the seaside, to Canada. Vacations for the Neumeyers were modest, but Art was adamant about not economizing. If the choice was between a clean motel without a swimming pool at $12 a night and one with a pool at $20, Art always chose the higher-priced lodging. "For one week a year, I'm not going to be pinching my pennies," he would say. But as money became more available, the Neumeyer children were older, their own lives were complex and vacation time for the last five years—although pleasurable—also had the undertone of being a juggling act, keeping Richard and Martha happy and not fighting.

Betty resigned herself to the fact that teenagers are more difficult to live with than younger children, but, when times were especially strained, she would often throw up to Art that geography had everything to do with the unhappiness in their lives. On Tulip Lane it was better; her father was alive; the family was intact, happy with simple pleasures, she would say. Why had they ever moved?

After spending fifteen minutes talking with the Neumeyers, Maureen Kelly is gone, leaving Joan to play in the sand near the umbrella, Art to listen to the baseball game, and Betty to watch the people on the beach and tell Art she'd like him to have a job where he could work at home. The Neumeyers spend another hour at the beach and then, hoping to beat the late-afternoon rush of traffic, they leave. On the way home Art buys a bucket of Kentucky Fried Chicken for his family and a dozen steamer clams, one of the delicacies he treats himself to more often on vacation.

There is time before supper so Joan has a shower, puts on a black leotard, takes the golf balls she has found alongside the fence at the course and goes down to where players must cross Pawnee Road going from a green to a tee. She sells good balls at twenty-five cents and scales prices down to a nickel for the worst in her collection.

Martha is lying on her bed with the radio playing. She fingers three white envelopes and slowly taps them against her forehead. She has not answered Barry's letters but has written instead to Pat, repeating that she does not know what to do, that she is attracted to him, but that it is foolish to try to foster anything. And she has told Pat that two currently popular songs have been plaguing her. This afternoon as she lies on her bed, by some cruel fate they are played, first one, then the other. "Daddy, Don't You Walk So Fast" is a child's plea to a father who is leaving; "If Loving You Is Wrong, Then I Don't Want to Be Right" is a song about a man with two children who is in love with another woman. Martha stares blankly at the frills around her mirror.

It is after six as the family gathers around the table. Martha and Richard, who has just awakened and whose eyes are noticeably bloodshot, are both quiet. Joan excitedly shows them $1.35 from her golf ball sales.

"At least somebody in this house has some sense for money," Betty says. "This kid is the new generation, not afraid to get out there and do something."

Joan looked puzzled. She does not understand all the praise.

"Don't look at me, baby, I'm on vacation," Art says to Joan.

"That was stupid, Richie," Betty blurts out.

Richard has been lazily gnawing on a chicken leg. "Yeah, the chicken's good. Little cold."

"Would you wake up, Richard!" Betty says, her eyes bulging.

"For Chrissakes, what do you want now?" he says, tossing the bone onto the plate.

"What did I tell you about language—" Art begins.

"Stupid. Leaving a perfectly good job"—Betty cuts him off— "and to work for a dollar less an hour."

"Eighty cents."

"Don't be smart to your mother," Art says.

"I was going crazy at Perfection; now I get off work at two and I can go to the beach every day."

"You *hate* the beach," Betty says, rising slightly out of her chair.

Richard reaches into the bucket of chicken.

"How about thinking of somebody else, Richie?" his father says. "Don't hog it all."

Richard's shoulders sag. "Everybody had some. OK, OK."

"Martha, eat," her father says.

"You know I'm trying to diet."

"C'mon, a little chicky won't hurt you. No-Cal chicky."

The telephone rings. It is Mrs. Donahue, who wants Betty to work a dinner party for her. Betty tells her that Art is on vacation and lies that they'll be out of town. "Couldn't stand it last time," Betty says, coming back to the table. "Her son had long hair and they told him he could not set foot in the house while they had their fancy guests in. Then one of these fancy guests went on and on about her son in college, how well he was doing, what kind of summer job he had. She knew. She was just rubbing it in."

Without saying a word, Richard gets up from the table and goes to his room. Soon after, Joan and Martha clear off the table, and the six pieces of chicken that are left are wrapped in aluminum foil and placed in the refrigerator. Their chores finished, the two Neumeyer girls go downstairs, leaving Betty and Art alone in the quiet living room.

"Artie, we just have to wait it out," Betty says, standing with her arms folded, to her husband, who has opened the Sunday newspaper.

"I don't know how much patience I have," he says, without looking up.

"He'll just see that he can't make it with one crummy-paying job after another. He'll get some direction."

"For the people and the peace of this house, I hope so."

"Where did we go wrong, Artie? Pam Brown never gave her kids anything, never went on vacations, never encouraged them to go to college. We did it all, Artie. Why is Richard so restless? They never even took Gerard to Little League."

"They took their vacations in their back yard."

"We had a back-yard pool before anybody on the block. The Browns' kids, Maureen's kids, they were over to our place all the time. Our kids never had hand-me-down clothes like Pam got. Like we had. I wanted them to have it, Artie, but maybe we gave them too much."

"Don't say 'them.' Look at Martha; she turned out just right."

"Look at Pam's Sylvia. There's an apple that won't fall from the tree. They talked her out of college. She's going to get luggage for her honeymoon and she'll never use it again. She uses the same kind of pots Pam does. She's not going to advance on her family like Martha will."

"So, we did what we thought was right. You read Dr. Spock till it was dog-eared," he says, finally looking up and taking hold of her hand.

"We just weren't strict enough with Richie. If he would just get married, that would settle him down."

"Betty, he's the product of an entirely different time. Two years apart, those kids, but it's another whole generation."

"He knows right from wrong, Artie, he'll never lose that, and he's really gentle. But he's never going to be what we hoped for, and the sooner we realize that, the better off we'll be."

"It's the freedom, Betty. What they had in college it's now in the high schools, and Richie just doesn't know what to do with it yet. I don't know. I think it all runs in cycles. They'll be wearing short hair in five years. And don't forget"—he pauses to gain her full attention—"this generation didn't invent sex. They even had prostitutes in Jesus' time."

"What does sex have to do with this?" Betty asks with annoyance in her voice.

"Don't know. Just thought I'd throw it in."

"It's his friends, Artie. Ron Bronowski is going to a psychiatrist and Randy Short is a regular boozer."

"Maybe Richard should see somebody like that, maybe he has to talk things out."

"A psychiatrist!" Betty exclaims. "He's not crazy! The boy is just growing up."

"Betty, this Eagleton guy isn't crazy either, and he needed help. He's a Senator."

"Would you want him as your Vice-President?"

"Don't want McGovern either, but it's no sin to go to a psychiatrist. It's just for a sickness, like having the measles."

"The measles!"

ART: They estimate that fifty percent of the population is mentally sick and not being treated. I don't think Richie has always been mentally stable; he had some psychosis or some inner fear and it should have been brought out in the open and cured. When Richie cracked up during my trial, we needed help. Parents can't help a child like that; we're too close. You need an unbiased stranger that you have confidence in. I've mentioned it more than once, and Betty always pooh-poohs the idea. I think at one time or another we all could use therapy. As for me, though, I really can handle any situation by myself. I don't need other people to survive.

BETTY: I could never really trust a person to be stable after they were treated for mental illness. Of course, it's better to be treated than not to be treated, but I'd never look at them the same. What Richie did during the trial was brought on by the circumstances. We were so edgy; Artie was taking tranquilizers before he went on the stand. Once Richie returned to the normality of his home he was fine, and there are no vestiges of that in him now. I just don't believe in professional counseling. I think a loving parent can talk things out with a child. Or another married couple can do a lot more for a couple that is having troubles than these so-called professional marriage counselors. Counselors just listen; they don't really solve your problems. What could I tell a counselor about myself? That I really want security, I want Artie to be home all the time, that I'm possessive? They'd find something in that and say I was sick or something. I'm just a normal woman, a wife.

From the back yard, the sound of laughter reaches Betty and Art. They give each other a puzzled look and silently go downstairs to the sliding glass door. Martha and Richard are playing badminton and Joan is retrieving the birdie when it floats into the evergreens along the back fence.

Martha taps a shot over the net and Richard, shirtless and shoeless, sprawls headlong onto the grass in a vain attempt to return it. "OK, sissy, I've been playing easy. We start the game now, and watch it because you are not going to score one solitary point." His first serve goes into the net and the second hits the shed, out of bounds.

Martha lofts a serve and Richard returns it, sending the birdie even higher. Martha tries to smash it, but the birdie catches in the strings of her racket. "Shit," she says softly. Joan jumps up and down, laughing and clapping her hands in glee.

Art slides open the door and walks onto the cement slab that is their patio. He watches Richard run up a three-point lead and then says, "How about letting the second string play?"

Richard forms a small smile. "If you think you can handle it."

"Me and Joanie against you and Martha; let's go."

Betty pulls a folding chair onto the patio and watches not so much the birdie going back and forth as the people, their faces and their gestures: Art, a cigarette hanging out of the side of his mouth, serving behind his back; Joan pounding her racket on the ground after she misses an easy shot; Martha sprawling in the bushes in pursuit of an out-of-bounds return; Richard grinning broadly as he slams the birdie across the net to his father's feet.

The score seesaws until the final five points, which Richard and Martha take. The game ends with Richard jumping high into the air to tap a shot that hangs on the net and then falls on the other side. "Get that man a beer," Art calls over to Betty.

"Coming up," she says as she turns quickly and goes into the house. Betty Neumeyer is crying.

14

Security

SEPTEMBER USUALLY MEANS the beginning of a new year for Betty as the church, the center of her social life, comes alive after summer's dormancy. But this September she finds herself less excited about predictable events, like a craft fair or Couples Club functions, and more aggravated by the summer, which she says has "dribbled away." She had talked about being at a paying job by August, and her deadline has passed. With Martha now back at school and Joan soon to start, Betty has renewed her pledge and has been scanning the *Mariposa Post* for jobs. Art has repeatedly told her they do not need the money, but Betty knows that to pay for Martha's operation Art had to sell the only investment they had: $600 in stocks. With graduation less than a year away, Betty has told Art she must earn some money. His casual response, "Don't sweat it; we'll get it somehow," might have comforted some wives. It is too cavalier for Betty. For the first time since they were married they are, as of a September 15 payment to a department store, out of debt except for the mortgage on the house. Betty does not want to finance the graduation trip with a loan.

Richard sold his truck and bought a bicycle in late August and is already grousing about how hard it is to get around on two wheels. He has toyed with ideas ranging from opening a pizza stand with some friends in California to taking night classes in welding to enrolling full time at a two-year college upstate. The forestry and conservation courses were filled, so Richard applied for a food processing and handling course that starts in January, saying that with the training he could travel around the country, supervising in canneries handling seasonal crops. Betty has generally been doubtful of Richard's various schemes, but she has offered mild encouragement. Art has been a study in silent skepticism.

The difficulties that the Neumeyers face this fall are, as for most families, known only to them and are discussed primarily within the four walls at 97 Birchwood. On the surface their life has once again taken on its normal pace—as the fully booked wall calendar shows on this, the third week of September.

On Monday Art bowled (after throwing the first ball, the dentist member of the team said soberly, "We don't have the team we did last year") and then attended an official board meeting at the church. Tuesday Betty had a Women's Society for Christian Service covered dish dinner and meeting. Thursday, Art has to substitute in the church bowling league; Friday they are going out to eat with several other couples and Saturday the Dupreys have asked them over for snacks, drinks and conversation. That leaves tonight, Wednesday, for shopping.

Otherwise these days, for Betty, have been filled with other people's problems, the course of other people's lives. Art's mother has been calling weekly, saying despondently how badly she wants to visit. A few days ago she decided she would not come after all. It is no surprise to Betty, but it angered her that she has been strung along. Art pointed out to Betty that she really didn't want his mother to come, so why should she be angry? Betty's answer was a tirade against "inconsiderate people who think I have nothing to do but wait around for them to decide to do something."

Martha's first call from college last Sunday brought the news that she is considering doing her practice teaching in a poverty area in Kansas City through a program that would guarantee her a job next year. Betty and Art were at first shocked, then incensed, citing the dangers that Martha would face. They told her,

"Wouldn't it be better to start teaching in a civilized setting with normal kids?"

Betty and Joan are clearing the evening dishes while Art looks through the first few pages of the newspaper. "What's happening in the world?" Betty calls over to him.

"This paper," he says, shaking his head. "You'd think the North Vietnamese were saints and we were horrible. We accidentally bomb some village and we're killers. They come in and slaughter in the South, that's fine; that gets two lines and no picture. Look at this!" He holds up a picture of a village leveled except for two poles and a few crumbled walls. A woman is picking through the rubble in the foreground and a child is following her, crying. "That's war."

"It's the same way with McGovern," Betty says.

Art displays another picture. "Look at this one."

Betty squints and comes closer. "People around him, shaking hands," she says, and then, softly, "almost kissing his ass." Then, back to her normal voice, "Falling all over him. When they show the President, he's got this stern look on his face and bodyguards all around him, pushing people back."

"Wonder who they're backing this year."

"Really will be a surprise, no?"

Wednesday night at the Neumeyers is the most routinized of the week. It calls for Art to drop Joan at Mrs. Shulman's for her weekly piano lesson, take Betty to the supermarket and help her get started, return to hear the last few minutes of Joan's lesson and then get Betty and the groceries and come home.

"Going to call tomorrow, Artie," Betty says as they drive up Pawnee Road to begin this Wednesday night's chores. "A dentist's wife wants somebody a couple days a week, like she said, to talk to her two-year-old. They have a maid already but she can't talk?" Betty's index finger pushes her nose into the air. "She's already pushing for me to work some nights, but the heck with her. We got so much stuff going on at nights I don't want to leave Joanie alone any more."

Joan, who has been going through her music sheets to see if she has brought "Fiddler on the Roof," says nothing.

"At official board, Perry Dawson brought up a resolution to switch six thousand dollars in benevolences over to the operating budget," Art says. "Going to vote on it next time."

"Artie, don't you dare vote for that. That money goes for the missionaries. It's the only thing that church does except keep the doors open."

"We got enough money in the benevolence fund, but we're running behind in apportionments. We haven't paid the conference for the past five months. If the church doesn't pay, the pastor's retirement fund doesn't get paid either."

"Forget about his retirement, Artie. We cut back, and the missionaries starve after they expect us to send them—"

"Betty, we can still pay them." Art cuts her off. "Nobody's starving."

"Cash in the savings bonds, that's what we ought to do."

"I wouldn't touch them with a ten-foot pole. Don Wheeler!" Don Wheeler has amassed twenty-one $25 savings bonds for the church through a chain letter he received a few months before and passed on to ten of his friends. It caused considerable scandal in the church and Pastor MacIntosh has said it was "downright immoral," yet he has not known what to do with this tainted treasure in a financially tight year.

Betty and Art wait until Joan is inside the door at Mrs. Shulman's, then drive to the supermarket. Art slowly pushes the cart as Betty checks her list and wanders among the colorful displays and products that beckon to the shopper. The aisles are clean, wide and covered with glistening tile. Muzak wafts "April in Portugal" throughout the store. Soon Art leaves to get Joan, and Betty cautiously picks her way along the produce section. Lettuce is selling at 49 cents a head, so Betty, continuing a habit she started a year ago, buys escarole for 19 cents. She buys a turnip sealed in plastic and then turns up the next aisle.

Bread crumbs are on her list, but the price here at Safeway is 43 cents and she knows they are less at Browns, where she often goes for Saturday shopping. Apple juice is three for 79 cents. Betty recalls that Browns charged 35 cents a can, so three cans go into the cart. Facial tissues are five for 89 cents and

Betty buys five, knowing it is far more than she'll need in the weeks ahead, but that she'll save the penny by not buying them individually at 18 cents apiece.

Betty's buying habits combine sharp bargain hunting, comparison shopping and what she calls splurging. She will watch for a penny's difference in canned goods, but she will pay much more for a loaf of Pepperidge Farm or Arnold's bread rather than buy Tip Top. She is convinced that Tip Top and Wonder Bread are stripped of their nutritional value. Each week she splurges on one or two items she considers real luxuries, like A-1 Sauce or peppercorns or Mallomar cookies. Having meat on the table each main meal is a necessity for the Neumeyers, and while Betty buys a good share of ground beef, she prefers to get the more expensive ground round, which is selling at $1.29 a pound. Also, Betty will buy some expensive convenience meats like turkey roll, claiming that it is actually economical, saving her time and providing as much meat per dollar as a whole turkey. Tuna-fish dishes are out for the Neumeyers. Art and Betty feel they ate their lives' quota of tuna casseroles during their leaner days in Florida.

On this Wednesday night, as Betty scans the shelves, a loaf of Pepperidge Farm white bread and one of whole wheat go into the basket, followed by shredded wheat, Sani-Flush, floor wax and a quart of milk (she buys most milk and eggs at the Cow Barn, claiming they are fresher and less expensive), then 100 bags of Tetley Tea, frozen broccoli, Baggies plastic bags, two cans of Campbell's chunky soups, clam chowder, French dressing, applesauce, tomato sauce, canned yams, Yodels chocolate cakes, Reese's Peanut Butter Cups, two cans of Cadillac dog food, frozen grape juice, pretzels and some paper towels.

She studies the price on Nescafé Instant Coffee and puts the jar back on the shelf, seeing that it is six cents more than at Browns. Betty has almost a full jar of Nescafé at home, but she likes to have a backup of often-used items and buys them when the price is right and not just when they are needed. When the items are rung up on the cash register, the total is $11.41, one of the smaller Wednesday-night bills. For each $5 in purchases, customers are allowed to buy a piece of stoneware that the store has been featuring. Betty already has three complete sets of dishes, but she has told Pam that Art likes the brown color and that the price—33 cents for a plate, for example—is too good a bargain to pass by.

Art has joked to friends that his wife has become fonder and fonder of the can opener as the years go along. Betty denies it but privately admits it is true. She always used to make her own Italian sauce but now buys Ronzoni for many uses. She used to cook more fresh vegetables but now relies heavily on frozen varieties, often buying the more expensive types where butter is already added and all the cook has to do is plunge a plastic bag into boiling water to prepare a table-ready vegetable. Just a generation ago, when her grandfather heard radio commercials on the Lanny Ross Show for Franco-American Spaghetti in a can, he would angrily switch to another station.

Each Friday night, after Art cashes his $250 check on the way home from the train station, Betty receives $50 for food. Last Saturday she spent about $20 at Browns on food and drugs, $10 for meat at Freddie's and $3 for milk and eggs at the Cow Barn. With the $12 spent tonight, Betty has used up $45 of her food budget. She has purchased less meat than usual because the freezer is reasonably well stocked with chicken, ground beef and some chops.

As Betty's food budget is usually exhausted by the end of the week, so is the rest of the money that Art has available to keep his family housed and clothed and to provide for other necessities and comforts. In addition to the $50 for food, Art gives Betty $20 for clothes, and the rest of the money is taken in cash or put into a checking account to meet other obligations. On a weekly basis, Art budgets: commuting, $18; car $10; mortgage, $60; church, $12; personal, household and car insurance, $20; bowling, $8; piano lesson, $5; phone, $5; electricity, $5; fuel for heating, $6. This leaves $31 for Art's, Betty's and Joan's spending money and entertainment, for dental and medical bills, for incidental expenses for Martha, for household improvements and repairs and for a long list of incidentals, including newspaper delivery, garbage collection and a never-ending demand to buy cookies and candy from Girl Scouts, Little League, Midget Football and church groups. When Richard is contributing for room and board, Betty puts his money aside to pay for his clothes and miscellaneous expenses, like the college application fee. Art's annual bonus—about $1,000—goes for Martha's expenses. Betty's catering jobs pay for Martha's clothing and for her air fare to and from school.

Although Art Neumeyer is making more money than he ever expected to, the family is living under the constant threat of having an unforeseen expense shatter their budget. Finances have caused no end of discussions and arguments for as long as Betty and Art have been married. Tonight, after the groceries are put away and Joan is in bed, Betty looks at the $4 and some change that she has left in the food envelope. She fixes her gaze on Art, who is looking at a baseball game on television. Sensing he is being watched, Art glances up to meet her blank look.

"What's up, babe?"

"Artie, what are we going to do when we get old?" she asks, almost mournfully. Then she answers her own question. "We're just going to be poor and not have anything."

"Not now, Betty," he says quietly.

"It's obviously something you don't want to talk about."

"I'll talk about it any time you want to sit down and discuss it calmly and rationally."

"And who says I'm not rational and calm right now!" she shouts at him.

"See?"

Betty walks slowly toward Art, her eyes narrowed. As she is ready to begin talking, the front door opens and Richard comes in. Betty's and Richard's eyes meet. Hers continue to glare. His eyes are glassy. He gives her a silly grin and starts down the stairs, missing the first one and almost falling. Art and Betty look at each other.

"That kid's hair is a mess—" Art begins.

"Forget his hair." She cuts him off. "It's *us*, Artie. It's us who don't have a penny in the bank. What are we doing in this house anyhow?"

"Betty, damn it, you came out here with your tongue hanging out."

"That was when we were living in a four-room apartment, four flights up."

"Betty, if they would give you the moon, you wouldn't be happy. Why not the sun?"

"Richie hasn't fallen far from the tree. He's got a place to sleep, food to eat and a third of a bathroom to use. He's got what he needs."

"What exactly do you want, Betty?"

"Right now?"

"Now, today."

"I'd like to have the diamond I never had. I'd like to have a mink so I could dress up elegantly."

"When Martha is through with school and Rich settled, we'll afford those things. I'll get them for you if that makes you happy."

"Like hell. We'd better start saving for our future. Don't think your kids are going to support us when—"

"Nobody will have to support us," Art fires back. "Can we talk about something besides money once in a while? I am paid very well for what I do."

"Paid very well," Betty says as if he has just told her the earth was flat. "So you get a raise every year and it all goes to taxes. Benefits, Artie. We need benefits. Medical benefits, retirement benefits. The men in the factory have better benefits than you do."

Art reaches over to turn off the baseball game, now drowned out. "You don't want to look on the other side of it, do you Betty? If I was working in the factory I'd be making maybe ten thousand with overtime. I make five thousand more than that, and you're worried about a couple of dollars in benefits."

"You really are thick, aren't you, Artie? Don't you realize that you had the brains to get out of the factory and that's what they pay you for? What do those other jerks make who work in the office?"

"With profit sharing and everything, they make about forty thousand, Betty, and they also happen to own the business."

"Something you're never going to do, that's obvious. When Mort's kid Sidney came into the office, that should have been your sign to move on."

"Well, I didn't, and I'm not indispensable. Other guys can do the same job I can."

"Do one daring thing in your life, Artie. If you would just have guts and assert yourself, you'd tell them you don't want the two hundred or whatever raise they give you each year and tell them you want dental coverage so I can get my rotten teeth fixed. Artie, my mouth is falling apart!" Betty Neumeyer is screaming at her husband.

"Nobody has full dental coverage."

"Bull—shit," Betty says, distinctly pronouncing each word. "Street cleaners right up to the President get benefits. Ninety percent of the people I know make as much or more than you, plus they have benefits and a pension."

"What do I do, Betty, go up to the boss and say I want this, this and this?"

"Exactly. In exchange for this, this and this."

"In exchange for me still working for him. That's not much of a bargaining position. You push them hard enough and they'll say, Let him go."

"And we'll be worse off?"

"You're damn right we will!"

"Artie, you don't realize you have somebody who will go along with you no matter which way it turns out, good or bad."

"Betty, the first week there wouldn't be a paycheck you'd be a nervous wreck. Now, let's get serious. OK, what did I get for a raise last year? How much? Tell me! Well, it was twelve hundred and fifty dollars, an increase of almost ten percent, eight and three-quarter percent, to be exact. Now what do you have to say?"

"What I have to say," she says, looking at him defiantly, "is, Where is it?"

"The cost of living went up, and I just gave Martha a four-hundred-dollar car."

"Up to last October we were paying off a car loan. Where's that sixty a month?"

"I'm eating it, Betty," he says sarcastically. "We are giving the kids a lot of things. Joan has a piano; she has Mickey Mouse sheets. I put a rug in Richard's room. The Roto-Rooter man. It all goes, that's where it goes."

"And what do we get, Artie?"

"Listen, the diecutting business isn't all that good. Our office is way overstaffed. If they wanted to, they could do without me, and if I push them that's what they'll do."

Betty puts her hands on her hips and lets out an audible huff. "You're just rationalizing your way out of an unpleasant situation because you don't have enough confidence in yourself. You made a whole wall of excuses, Artie. The youth of today has it over us, you know that? They're not so worried about everything. They're willing to take chances. I would take chances, Art, and you haven't got the confidence."

"You're talking like a crazy woman, Betty," Art says, getting off the chair and heading for the back of the house. "In one breath it's security, retirement you want, and the next thing it's like let's strike out. You can't have it both ways."

"I married a jerk," Betty says icily.

Art turns toward her, his face barely visible in the darkened hallway outside Joan's bedroom. "Thanks. Thanks for the compliment."

Art and Betty use the bathroom separately this night. In the bedroom, their eyes do not meet. Betty slips beneath the covers on her side of the bed; Art turns off the light and gets in on his side. Back to back, in silence, they search for sleep.

BETTY: I don't know what gets into me when we talk about money. I'm like Jekyll and Hyde. I've always been the one to live modestly, but if we have to scrimp on everything—like the Browns do—then it isn't worth it. I used

248

to be very tight about money, so bad I wouldn't even buy underwear, only winter coats and shoes for the kids.

Now I love the affluence of being able to rip off a big sheet of aluminum foil and not have to worry about washing it and using it again. Now I buy a liner for the wastebasket instead of using paper bags; it's an unnecessary expense, but it's so much more neat. We can't possibly save that much raising three children, and I want to live. Why not have wine with our meals? Why not spend a few dollars getting my hair done? When we were first married I didn't even make brownies because you had to use two eggs and nuts and I figured why put two eggs in a cake when you could fry them.

I'm much better to live with when we can afford a pot roast or ham or chops when we want it. Not that we don't eat a lot of ground meat; we've had years of training. But one illness would wipe us out anyhow, so why not have the memory of wine, a pot roast and foil? I really get angry at myself for arguing with Artie about how we're doing. We're really affluent compared to the Artie and Betty of twenty-two years ago. But he just doesn't push himself enough. He's the backbone of that company, and they should pay him plenty. I don't know, maybe I'm greedy, maybe I'll always be wanting something that we don't have. That's what Art tells me anyhow.

The Neumeyers have never been people to take on enormous debts, but neither are they able to save when earnings are higher. Art's saying, "Whatever I make, you spend, Betty," is not far from the truth. The Neumeyers are not conspicuous, but continuing, consumers. Up until five years ago the Neumeyers didn't have a savings account of more than $100; today, it is about $300. Their biggest debt—besides the house, of which only $2,000 of the $20,000 mortgage has been paid—was in 1968 when they bought the Chevrolet, paying $2,500. Although the Neumeyers are not spendthrifts, they do continue to buy things for themselves and to list the items that will be purchased when the money is available.

For instance, Art is continually improving his house, adding paneling or rugs; Betty is continually buying accent pieces to beautify her home. The family owns eight still and movie cameras, none of them expensive, but all of them saved because each is good for a certain kind of use, is lightweight or otherwise has some redeeming characteristic. On the list of things to buy are: a higher-powered pair of binoculars for Art; a queen-sized bed to replace the double bed they've used for fifteen years; a sofa to replace the old one, which is becoming worn at the seams. But as the Neumeyers buy and plan for more, they also conserve. Many of Martha's and Richard's toys were used by Joan; Art takes exceptionally good care of his car; Betty's good coat with a fur-trimmed collar is years old. The Neumeyers have no difficulty meeting their basic needs and go a reasonable way toward meeting optional needs. But, as Betty often says and Art secretly knows, they live very much on what he makes. If he were out of work for even a short period of time, the Neumeyer family would be hard-pressed immediately.

It is now five days later, Monday, and Betty is about to try to help the Neumeyers' financial condition. She walks out the front door to the car of the dentist's wife, to start her new job. She was supposed to begin last Thursday, but the woman kept changing her plans, which has already caused Betty to have misgivings. As she told Pam Brown over the weekend, "You don't even do that to a teenage baby-sitter. I'm a mature woman and I have to do things on a scheduled basis, not just when she feels like going out."

On Tuesday, the dentist's wife calls fifteen minutes after she is supposed to pick up Betty to say she would like her to work that afternoon and evening because of a change in her art class and because she and her husband want to go out for dinner. Betty is irritated but says she will work the afternoon. She tells the woman again she does not want the job to interfere with her being home at three thirty for Joan. Thursday the woman comes on time. Friday she calls and says she isn't feeling well and won't need Betty that day.

Betty calls her later in the day and says she doesn't need the job.

Over the weekend Art and Betty halfheartedly visit several more houses for sale they found through newspaper ads. One, although it is no older than their house, is in such rundown condition that Art feels it would take months of work and thousands of dollars to get it into shape. Other houses are rejected because they are too far from shopping or public transportation or because Betty does not like their layout.

By Monday, Betty is back at home, spending a lot of time on the phone telling friends like Lillian, Francine and Pam that she has the "blahs." "Or, like the kids say, I'm in a funk. Don't know whether it's battle fatigue, depression or old age." By midafternoon she has spent over three hours on the phone but has managed to dust and vacuum the house. She is taking down the curtains—a week before their scheduled bimonthly washing—when the telephone rings.

Betty has been recommended by her friend who owns the gift shop for a job with a security agency whose personnel manager is calling. He cannot say where she'd be working, but there have been numerous thefts in the jewelry department at a large department store and the agency has been called in to find the thief.

"Does something like this sound interesting to you?" The voice comes over the line.

Betty looks around as if to get a consensus from the dusted tables and chairs. "Well—well—" she stammers, "this is quite a surprise. Yes—yes, it sounds very exciting."

"I have a few questions then. Would you mind answering them?"

"No, no, I'll answer anything," Betty says with a nervous laugh.

"If you got personally close to an employee—liked an employee—would you have any trouble reporting that person if he or she was suspected?"

"Of course not." Betty almost shouts into the phone. "As a consumer, I don't believe in stealing; it adds to the price of everything I buy."

The questions go on: about Betty's background, her previous work experience, her husband's job. "Are you, or have you ever been, a member of the Communist Party?"

"Heavens, no!"

"The store is open in the evenings, and that's when we think the

251

trouble is happening—or on Saturdays. Could you work evenings and weekends?"

The smile fades from Betty's face. "I'd—I'd have to see about that."

"I'm sorry that I can't give you our number; it's company policy to withhold our name until you've been formally accepted. I'll call in a couple of days. Will that be enough time for you to decide?"

"Fine, fine."

"By the way, the pay is about a hundred and forty dollars a week, some of which is normal salary and the rest our supplement."

As soon as the man hangs up, Betty calls Pam Brown. "You'll never guess, Pam, they want me to be an undercover agent," she bubbles. "A hundred and forty a week too! It would have been such a great job."

"You're not taking it?" she says incredulously.

"Next week I'm going to take out a learner's permit, and I'm going to get a driver's license. Opportunity might knock a second time, and I want to be ready for it."

"With that kind of money, you could take a cab."

"But it's nights, and what about dinner? It just wouldn't work out. But you know what, Pam? It did a lot for my ego. I may not get elected but at least I was nominated."

That night at dinner, Betty excitedly tells Art about the job and Joan jokes about her mother wearing a mustache so nobody could tell who she was. Richard is not there and no one knows where he is or why he's missing the meal, but the happiness of the moment transcends any possible friction over him.

After dinner, Betty leaves the dishes in the sink and sits beside Art as he has his cigarette. Joan and Cynthia, the girl from down the block, have made up after one of their periodic tiffs and are setting up cardboard stores and houses in the hallway to play dolls.

"Read that letter from Martha," Betty says. "The kid hasn't been on campus one weekend. Says she's tired of living out of a suitcase. She's overcommitted and I think she loves it."

"Probably gets to be a drag after a while," Art says.

"That kind of a drag I could live with," Betty says. Her eyes search the top of the coffee table. She moistens her finger and touches the small marble slab to remove a tiny piece of newsprint.

"You've got it made. Work isn't any fun. Just . . . just work. Stay home and enjoy yourself."

"Stay home and rot," Betty says tonelessly.

There is silence for a few moments, and then the front door opens. Art and Betty look down to see Richard and Ron standing there. Silence again.

"We missed the pleasure of your company at dinner," Art says with a wry smile.

"Got laid off," he blurts out.

"You what?" Betty says, rising up off the couch.

"Anyway, me and Ron are going to Pennsylvania where the floods were. Going to work on the river."

"The river!" Betty says, her voice higher. "Just like that you're going. You made application to go to college. What about that?"

"Catch it next year," he says. A small smile shows first in his eyes and then spreads to the rest of his face. "Got to get my stuff . . . my . . ."—he hesitates—"my shit together." Richard noisily clumps down the stairs with Ron close behind him.

"Why, Artie, tell me why," Betty pleads.

"Why what?" Art says, looking down at the newspaper.

"Don't be stupid about it, Artie. Artie! Look at me!"

Art finishes the paragraph he had started to read before he looks up. "You said you were bored. Well, now you won't be bored any more. We're back to open warfare."

15

"And Stay Warm"

IN THE GARAGE at 97 Birchwood, Art lifts a cardboard box full of odds and ends—dishes, salt and pepper shakers, a flamingo-shaped Souvenir of Florida vase—onto the card table so the customers at the Camp Fire rummage sale will be able to see them better.

In one of the bedrooms upstairs Betty finishes stitching the letter B onto Joan's cable-knit cheerleading sweater. Joan pulls it over her head and smiles delightedly at her new uniformed self in the mirror.

In the bedroom downstairs, Richard has just gotten out of bed and is looking through his dresser to see if he has enough warm socks to take on his trip.

The Neumeyers of Mariposa have many things to do on this Saturday in October. An activity like the rummage sale marks a commitment family members must follow through with, although they are doing it with little zest. But for Joan and Richard this Saturday brings the promise of new adventures: being a cheerleader for the Broncos' football team and preparing to go to Pennsylvania to clear up the flood-ravaged Susquehanna Valley.

In front of the house is a sun-faded blue 1965 Mustang that Richard bought yesterday for $150. Because it does not have insurance and therefore no license plates, it has been in the garage overnight. Today Art pulled it into the street to make room for the rummage sale, thus taking the chance that the Mohawk

County Police will not notice it or the Giordanos report it. The rummage sale is supposed to begin at eleven o'clock, but it is fifteen minutes past the hour as Art looks out to the rain that has been falling lightly on and off for the past two hours. A woman Betty does not know by name but whom she has given the nickname "Bubblehead," because of her incessant talking and pouffed hair style, is supposed to be on duty now, and Art is impatient to get on with his other work. For the Methodist church's craft fair he is making recipe holders in the shape of a whale and small easels that hold a photograph. By eleven thirty Bubblehead arrives, gushing that she just couldn't resist the temptation: a friend lent her a 1972 Cadillac and she has been driving around Mariposa for the last hour hoping some of her friends would see her.

"I have this sixty-six Nash, and it would really blow their minds," she says to Art. He smiles weakly at her barrage of laughter. He leaves her to her wares: stacks of games that children have outgrown or grown tired of, a set of glasses that Bubblehead received for her first wedding fourteen years ago that she wants to get rid of, old sweaters, a couple of phonographs that need a tube or a needle, a metal saucer for skimming over snow, rusty garden tools, books, a stack of *Saturday Evening Posts*.

By noon a few people have come to browse in the Neumeyers' garage, and the $3.25 that has been made rests in a cigar box. Inside the house, Richard is buttering an English muffin as his mother comes into the kitchen.

"Going to go over to Roeders' to see about some insurance for the Mustang," he says, yawning.

His mother stares stonily at him. "You don't do any asking any more, don't want anybody's advice."

"Listen, I got the chance for a job that pays twice as much."

"Everything is always so perfect until you do it, Richie. But when you do it, it never turns out. When are you going to grow up and stop running from one thing to another, huh?" Betty snatches the dish he's used and sends it clattering into the sink.

"Don't hassle me today, I got a lot of shit to get together."

"You always do, Richie. Has it ever entered your mind that

255

where you're going in Pennsylvania is Appalachia and the unemployment is unbelievable there?"

"They got unemployment; we got us a job," he says breezily.

"Don't think this house is just a stopping-off point for your travels, Richie. Either you settle down or . . ." She looks down and doesn't complete the sentence.

The doorbell rings. Ron Bronowski, rain dripping from his blond hair, stands there with an unsure grin on his face.

Soon the two boys are in Ron's truck. "We got to get hip boots and all kinds of stuff before we go," Richard says excitedly as he shifts nervously in his seat. "This is really going to be tough shit, and we have to be ready for it."

"Can't we get the stuff there? They got stores, don't they?"

"We got to be ready to go to work the first morning. Right off."

"Is this a sure thing?"

"When I was coming back from the Coast I met this dude who's like a foreman. All we do is meet him in front of this diner on any morning—I still got the name and everything. And we go to work for four bucks an hour."

"Last night it was three fifty."

"OK, smart-ass, it's three fifty more than you're making now."

"What if this whole thing doesn't work out and we're stuck out there?"

"This guy was begging for workers. We're in."

Clancy Roeder is what Betty calls "a real John Bircher," although he is not a member of that organization. It was Betty's feeling, if Richard walked in with long hair and baggy jeans, that even though Roeder handled the family's life, automobile and property insurance, he would not make much of an effort to help him. Clancy Roeder is proud that he has voted against every bond issue in Mariposa and for George Wallace in the 1968 election, and he proudly displays a bumper sticker: REGISTER COMMUNISTS, NOT GUNS. Betty has joked, "We're McGovern liberals compared to him."

Before Richard rings the doorbell at the Roeder house, Betty has called Clancy, asking him to "see what you can do for Richard." Clancy meets Richard and Ron at the door and, with a face that shows no emotion, leads them into a small, cluttered office. The close quarters immediately amplify the body odor coming from Clancy, who has been working on a leaky pipe in his basement. He is a large man with pale, fleshy cheeks and hair so closely cropped that his scalp shines through.

Clancy looks at Richard's license, which shows he was penalized five points almost three years ago for driving without a license. "This put you into assigned risk then, and you're probably still there, but we'll see what we can do," he says making some notations at the bottom of a legal pad that is filled with names, telephone numbers and dollar amounts. "Clean record since then?"

"Nothing that shows up on the record," Richard says, smiling at Ron.

"If you keep it off here," he says, holding up Richard's tattered driver's license, "it don't mean shit."

If Richard's driving history were a matter of record, he would not have a license. He has had at least three accidents, all due to reckless driving: he hit a parked car and drove away after the crash; he ran one Volkswagen into a fire hydrant and rolled over another. And he has had two tickets for moving violations—one for speeding and another for failing to stop at a stop sign—both of which were fixed by Art's "godfather."

"If this company won't pick you up, you're in assigned risk and that's going to be about seven hundred and fifty dollars. If they pick you up, maybe about five eighty-five," he says after totaling up a row of figures. "You could save a hell of a lot just by going on your father's policy, Raymond."

"Richard. My old man's not too hot for that idea. OK, I'd appreciate the best you could do, Mr. Roeder. I got the money for the down payment, so let's get some coverage because I got a job in Pennsylvania I got to get to."

Back in the car, Richard asks to drive and stomps down on the accelerator, fishtailing away from a stop sign at the end of Clancy Roeder's street. "This chick I met told me this place in Pennsylvania is pure Freaksville," he says. "Freaks from all over coming there to work. Man, it's going to be beautiful. Work your ass off during the day, and come back to some fine chick and some joints and a cold beer."

"I just want to see this guy and his diner," Ron says.

The garage sale, like the rainy day in Mariposa, drags on. Although it is to benefit the Camp Fire Girls, only a few of them make an appearance. The various mothers who have agreed to give time come, saying that activities like tap dancing rehearsal or music lessons prevent their daughters from being there. Even Joan has little time to spend in the garage, as she has to be at the football game for most of the afternoon.

It is after one o'clock, and Betty is in the kitchen baking some cranberry bread for Richard to take along on his trip. She has assembled a pile of plastic forks, napkins, and other items for him. Art kisses his wife lightly on the cheek and calls for Joan. Soon she comes running into the living room and they are off for Mariposa Public Park and the game.

Competitive sports are a big part of the lives of many Mariposa boys, and playing Midget League football is no small honor. But since the time Richard was old enough to play there has been a change in thinking on the part of some parents as to the value of competitive sports, with the hardest questioning put to contact sports such as football.

Benjamin Caruso, Joan's principal, was a football player from age eight through college, but he has found himself discouraging his own students from playing that sport. He cites medical studies that have shown that the bones of preadolescent boys are still growing, and shocks from a block or a tackle could stunt the growth or otherwise cripple them. There has been a movement in Mariposa to organize more soccer leagues and for certificates to be handed out in lieu of trophies. Every player gets a certificate under the new system, and outstanding soccer players or members of the championship team simply have that noted on their certificate.

But, as this rainy Saturday afternoon at the park shows, football is still popular in Mariposa. The coach of the Broncos, a red-faced Irish policeman, stalks the sidelines in the best Vince Lombardi fashion, wearing a rain slicker and football cleats. Farther down the sidelines are ten cheerleaders, Joan among them, who huddle together for warmth and then periodically break out to cheer, "Give me a B. Give me an R. . . ." They cheer to empty stands. The fathers who have come out in the inclement weather congregate near the bench to watch the Broncos do battle with the Raiders.

After the Bronco fullback slips and then tumbles head over heels even before he reaches the line of scrimmage, the coach screams, "Open up that hole! Come on, you guys, you're like a bunch of pansies out there. Hit 'em!" He stalks some more and, when the halfback stumbles through the line for a one-yard gain, he forms a T with his fingers and the captain tugs on the referee's shirt to ask for a time out.

The ten cheerleaders break into "One, two, three, four, who are we for . . ." as the five boys from the bench join with the nine coming off the field, their coach and two assistant coaches. The players wear pants and jerseys of top-grade Dacron. Their helmets are made of a shock-resistant plastic. From a distance, with their equipment, which costs $138 per player, they look no different from a professional team. It is only when the faces behind the awesome face masks come into view that illusion is shattered. These nine- and ten-year-old faces are covered with peach fuzz and a look combining dejection and fear as their coach lectures them.

"You're like a bunch of girls out there," the coach says, so angry he cannot even look at his players. "You've got to hit 'em, knock them down. What are we out here for in this weather? We are out for one thing. To win! Let me spell that: W–I–N. And wipe your nose, Billy, for cripe's sake."

Billy quickly raises his arm to his face but bumps into his mask. His father, who has been standing next to him, jerks at the helmet, pulling it back. The boy's sleeve finally reaches its target.

The whistle blows and the Broncos take the field again and continue to slog through the afternoon to a 0–0 tie.

When Art picks Joan up for the ride home, he asks her how the game went and what the final score was. She leans against the window and says to her father, "Oh, I don't know. Not too high. Not too many touchdowns I don't think. I hope that garage sale is over. I'm tired."

"That coach is a bum anyhow. Ought to try some razzle-dazzle stuff, running around end and passing. Just keeps on sending them up the middle."

"Huh?"

Joan looks out the window, and as the hot air from the heater warms the car, her eyelids flicker but never really close.

JOAN: Cheerleading is fun because we all get out there and yell and scream and cheer the team on. The only thing is that I don't know any of the boys who are playing. They all go to another school. I don't like the practicing much, but then at the end of the year we have cheerleading competition and maybe we can win that. But it's fun to have the team letter on your sweater and to feel that without the cheerleaders the team really wouldn't have the spirit to go on and really play a good game. We are very important to the team, just like the sponsor mother, Mrs. Craig, said.

I think I look very cute in the skirt and sweater, but the most important thing isn't that. Looks don't matter. It's your enthusiasm. That's the stuff that wins the games. If it wouldn't then the team with the prettiest cheerleaders just couldn't get beaten by anybody.

Later that evening the Neumeyer house is quiet. Art has stacked the remnants of the garage sale on one side; the stuffed teddy bear with the missing eye stares forlornly from the heap of undesired items. Joan is in bed. Richard's knapsack is partially packed; an unopened bottle of vitamins his mother bought for him has been placed on top of a stack of flannel shirts and thick socks. Art and Betty sit in the living room, Art vacantly watching a one-sided football game and Betty leafing through *Family Circle*.

260

"Isn't there quicksand or mud or something along rivers?" she says.

"Betty. Sure there's mud, but there'll be a lot of people around doing the same thing. Who said he's going to get the job anyhow?"

"With our luck he'll get it and like it."

"He hates the outdoors. Give him a week and a cold and his allergies and he'll be back."

"Dead on our doorstep," she says, with fatalism in her voice.

"Ready to expect the worst, aren't you?" he says with irritation.

"Damn it, Artie," she says, "he could die out there, and what do you care about it?"

"I care."

It is three days later, Tuesday night. Richard has announced he will leave tomorrow and, although Betty did not prepare a special dinner—Art warned her against doing that—she cooked one of Richard's favorite meats, flank steak. But now, at eight thirty, a large portion of the steak is in the refrigerator, brown and cold. Richard did not come home for his last meal. Art and Betty sit in the living room, each reading, each having trouble concentrating.

With the sound of a car stopping in front of the house, Betty goes to the window, then quickly sits down. "He didn't see me," she whispers.

"Just like we planned it, Betty, no big deal, OK?" Art says, patting her on her folded hands.

"No big deal," she says sorrowfully. "I'll try, Artie."

Richard comes through the front door, mumbles "Hi" and goes to his room. In a few moments John McLaughlin's guitar resonates along the basement paneling and then abruptly, in mid-song, is silent. Betty and Art know the pattern well. They have complained about the loud music more than once. Richard has just locked himself into a small stereophonic world with a pair of headphones.

Fifteen minutes later, Betty stands up. It is late in her day, and by this time each evening her eyes are often fine slits. They are wide open tonight, dark brown dots on a fleshy cheek which is pale and looks almost sallow in the soft living room light. She says nothing to Art as she goes downstairs.

Richard sees her coming toward his door, but he does nothing. He stares at her for a minute, then looks away. When he looks back at her, his mother's lips are moving. He removes the earphones. "What was that?"

"I just said remember that we used to pray before we went on trips together."

"I remember."

"I'm not going to make a big deal out of it this time, Richie. It hurts too . . ." She hesitates. "So just take care of yourself. Call us every week. Collect. And stay warm." She moves toward the bed.

Richard's face is passive. His fingers dance nervously on the headphones that lie on his stomach.

Betty leans over and kisses her son lightly on the cheek. "I love you," she says, almost mournfully.

"I love you too," Richard says, and quickly places the headphones over his ears.

Betty walks up the stairs. It is not until she is standing in front of her husband that she begins to smile. "I just got something that even topped Martha making *Who's Who.*"

"What?"

"Never you mind. I'm getting ready for bed."

Minutes later, Art goes to his son's room and finds him just as Betty did, his ears covered and his eyes fixed on the door. This time Richard slips off the earphones and fidgets with them as if he were somehow adjusting them.

"Be careful, Richie," his father says. "Don't let anything happen to you because—because—well, remember we love you."

"Yeah, sure," Richard says and replaces the headphones. Art stands in the doorway for a moment. His son's eyes move about the room, finding nothing safe to rest on. Then Art waves to his son, just a few feet away, and turns to go upstairs.

As Art is shaving the next morning and Betty is lying awake in their bed, they hear the front door open and close. By the time Art finishes the last few strokes of the blade and Betty has put on a

262

robe, they hear the sound of an engine starting. As they look out the front window, the faded blue Mustang speeds down the street. Art finishes his preparations for work, saying little to Betty. Once he is gone, and Joan has gone to school, Betty goes back to bed and sleeps until noon.

" 'The only Christian running for President,' " Betty reads, holding up Parkside's bulletin, as if it could be viewed through the phone receiver. It is two weeks since Richard has left.

"What are you talking about?" Lillian says.

"Haven't you got your mail yet?"

"Sure, phone bill and the *Reader's Digest* sweepstakes."

"It's in the 'Grape Vine' this month. The pastor tells us that McGovern is the only Christian running for President. Would you call that an endorsement or not?"

"The nerve! Well, he's been hinting at it all along."

"Joanie's class is having mock elections, and she made up a whole bunch of Nixon stickers. I'll have them all over me Sunday." There is a hesitation. "Sunday," she repeats.

"For God's sake, Betty, you sound like the voice of death, or at least doom."

Betty lays the bulletin on the kitchen table and sits down. "I don't know, Lil. It's the middle of the morning and I'm still in my nightgown. It's just so . . . Did you see in the papers where they had to operate on the girl who had glass slivers in her throat? Nice man gave her a candy bar. It's so sick any more. The whole world is sick. It was so simple when we were growing up."

"Nothing that happens any more shocks me."

"Guess so."

"How about the girls going to lunch next week?"

"Sure. Fine. Any day. I'm available."

Since Richard has left, Betty has spent hours sleeping on days that she does not have any commitments that take her outside the house. In the afternoons she has fallen into the habit of having a glass of wine, a rarity for her, saying, "It perks me up." She has told Art she does not feel well, although she cannot pinpoint an illness. Otherwise, she has performed the necessary tasks of vacuuming and washing and cooking. Her evening meals have not seen fresh vegetables—except for salads—since Richard left, and she has concentrated on easy-to-prepare cuts of meat and casseroles, using many bottles of prepared spaghetti sauce.

The mood around the house at 97 Birchwood has been subdued, melancholy. Art and Betty have not argued for two weeks. Conversation, when it hasn't revolved around day-to-day experiences like a late commuter train or the need for some new garbage cans, has been on a now-familiar theme: "Where have we gone wrong?"

Art and Betty Neumeyer, who have idealized family life and made sacrifices for their children, are now seeing that the mold they carefully formed for their two older children is not fitting. It doesn't seem to matter to these two children that Art and Betty are giving them everything their parents never had when they were younger—attention, objects, opportunity, encouragement. Especially Richard; he has plainly let them down. He is acting out and saying that he wants to experience other things in the world; meanwhile, his parents are branding his life not only a waste of time but an embarrassment to them, a slap in the face for all they have done for him. Although he is not harming them directly, he is not conforming to their sense of order, their goal orientation.

In the past nine months it has become more and more apparent to Martha and Richard that their parents' lives are not the kinds of lives they want to have. Martha does not aspire to be a mother and homemaker; Richard does not want his life revolving around something as ephemeral as a job, steeped with responsibility, cemented in sureness. Martha and Richard know of their parents great sacrifices, but they wonder to what avail they have made them. As the lives of Martha and Richard take on the violent shifts and changes endemic to a budding adult, they are trying to avoid following in their parents' path.

There have been better times in the Neumeyer family, but it has never been devoid of tensions, of friction. Betty has said she is a demanding wife. Richard has had acknowledged problems from youth—problems in getting along, in concentrating, in feeling worthwhile. But these months have seen friction become almost the keynote of life in the Neumeyer house. Betty has been most openly affected. Her skin looks paler than usual; she is not sleeping well; she is having trouble keeping herself busy—a quality in which she has always taken pride. Since turning down the undercover work after the job was formally offered, she has not even considered other employment.

For Art the most alarming thing is that Betty is drinking during the day. He has not said anything to his wife, but it has been disquieting to him to come home to an evening kiss from a woman with wine on her breath. Betty is not drinking heavily; Art knows that. But he knows she is drinking small amounts regularly.

On a Friday afternoon late in October, Betty is dozing on the couch, an empty wine glass on the table. She has spent a good part of the morning on the phone, but after lunch she felt drowsy, so she lay down. An hour and a half later, she woke up, but still feeling drowsy she took a glass of wine as a tonic. Soon after finishing it she fell back asleep. The phone rings and her eyes flicker open. The afghan wrapped around her shoulders, she goes to the phone.

"I have a collect call for—"

"I'll accept," Betty says, her eyes opening wide. She runs her hand through her hair, which is matted in the back from her nap.

"Well, how's it going?" she says eagerly. "Your allergies acting up? Been raining a lot here."

"Here too," Richard says in a subdued voice.

"We've been waiting and waiting for a call, Richie. You could be dead and we wouldn't know it."

"Just been busy, that's all."

"Working?"

"One day."

"Job isn't exactly what you thought?" Betty says, a smile coming over her face.

"I can handle the work. Like it's kind of irregular."

"So come home and get a regular job."

"It'll get better; I'm going to stick it out here," he says, trying to sound more confident.

"Another dream that didn't come true?"

There is silence on the other end. "Something'll come through," he says, in a voice that takes Betty back five years to an unsure boy in junior high school.

"Do what you think is best," she says, the smile now off her face. "Either way, it's OK."

"Yeah, well, I'll be going."

Betty rarely calls Art at the office because of the long-distance charge, but as soon as Richard hangs up she dials her husband. Art says little as Betty tells him of the conversation. "I just couldn't be hard on him, Artie. He sounded so depressed. I just couldn't rub it in. Anyway, this is the first year he can vote. He says he's coming home for election day."

"Now let's not do anything special just because—"

"Election day, Artie. Rich'll be home! Did you hear me?"

16

"Be Not Content"

On the Monday before election day, Joan takes special care in dressing for school. She pulls red knee socks onto her thin legs and then slips a red, white and blue smock over her already brushed hair. Next, a matching pair of hot pants goes on. She brushes her hair again and brings a red ribbon to her mother, who ties it into a large bow at the back of Joan's head. Joan has been, almost since she started grade school, a clothes-conscious girl. She was encouraged by her mother to dress smartly, and she herself liked shopping for clothes and putting together different outfits such as today's patriotic ensemble. But her interest in getting ready for school has not always carried over into interest for school itself as Joan has gone from grade to grade, teacher to teacher.

In years past—last year in particular—Joan would seize upon any excuse to stay home: a scratchy throat, a trip her mother was making, bad weather. This year, the bored fifth grader who rarely finished her work has turned into an attentive sixth grader who has a perfect attendance record. Working in small groups of mixed-ability children, called clans, in the open classroom of Mr. Bruce and Mrs. Ferris, Joan has blossomed in the more relaxed setting. She has learned from better students about word meanings, a little more about geography—she still has trouble conceptualizing what a continent is—and math. In a free period called "inquiry" Joan has read about astronomy, rocks and the seaside and, because she has been encouraged to do craft projects and not only written reports, she has earned praise from the teachers for her work. Basically, she has been able to utilize her strengths and downplay her weaknesses.

Socially, her acceptance has not been that much better than last year, but Joan has never been one to pout over a lack of school friends. She is not an unfriendly child at school; she is attractive, not obnoxious, yet for some reason she is not popular. Mrs. Durgin, her fifth-grade teacher, felt that children dislike manipulation, and Joan is a manipulator. This year Mr. Bruce, her homeroom teacher, says, "It's chemistry; some kids take to each other, some don't. In Joan's case I can't figure it."

In her classroom today, Joan spends the morning completing a comparison chart for the two Presidential candidates and the afternoon involved in a mock election. With placards and speeches the sixth graders emulate their elders, playing up their candidate and playing down the rival. Joan gives a speech in support of President Nixon. Although every other speech receives some applause, the class is silent when she finishes. The quality of the speech wasn't the issue; there were better and worse. As Mr. Bruce repeats late in the day to Mrs. Ferris, "Just chemistry, a strange chemistry."

The lack of response doesn't dampen Joan's spirits. She leaps into the air, cheering loudly when the vote is tallied: 42 for Nixon, 18 for McGovern.

Joan bursts through the front door at three thirty exclaiming, "Mommy, Mommy, we won! Nixon won the election!" Betty greets her daughter with a weak smile, says she's happy and then asks Joan if she would like some milk and cranberry bread. She has made several loaves for Richard when he comes home to vote. Joan's enthusiasm is still undampened, this time by her mother's lukewarm response. She goes on to tell all the details: the beautifully drawn elephant and donkey, the coordinated red, white and blue outfits of the McGovern cheerleaders, the fact that she did not stumble over a single word in delivering her speech.

Joan's enthusiasm for the election is reflected by her sister in

Kansas, who is planning to hand out McGovern literature on election day and then spend election night at McGovern headquarters, watching the results come in. But except for the fact that Richard might come home, tomorrow is not a very special day for the older Neumeyers.

On this Monday night, after Art comes home from bowling, he and Betty sit for a few moments in the living room. Almost with irritation in his movements, Art leafs through the pages of pre-election-day coverage to get to the other news inside the paper.

ART: I haven't paid much attention to the election this year; in fact, I very seldom pay attention to what the candidates say. I'm a Republican but I also base my vote on past performance, and I think Nixon is trying to get us out of Vietnam with an honorable peace and he's doing the best he can with the economy—who ever controlled it? There is no way to control the economy if we keep on putting more people on government payrolls and unions get bigger increases. Prices have to go up.

In a democracy, a man can run a campaign any way he wants to, and I think Nixon is doing his just right. Why should he get in an open debate with McGovern? The last time he did it, he lost to Kennedy, so why risk it? Debates only prove who is the slickest talker anyhow, the guy who can call names louder. If McGovern had the same lead Nixon does, he wouldn't want an open debate.

Nixon is not a great President, but McGovern is awful. Three years ago he started running for the presidency and he thought all the kids would get him in and look at him now. They aren't marching to his tune. And he switches all the time. First he comes out with a thousand-dollar income credit for every family. Then he finds out it would bankrupt the country and he turns around.

I didn't vote for Goldwater because I thought he was impulsive. I voted for Kennedy and Kennedy did one good thing, and that was make the Russians back down in Cuba. But then there are the so-called great Democrats like Roosevelt. He was awful. It's Roosevelt's fault we went to war with Japan. He knew that Pearl Harbor was coming and he didn't do a thing.

BETTY: Politics is a very disgusting thing because it's just a matter of money. I see the campaign like one big commercial. It's really not like a democracy was intended to be, and I feel that we are fairly intelligent people and we can see through it. What about the unintelligent people, people who have the right to vote but do not have anything to help them decide?

I usually vote Republican, but I voted against Goldwater and I thought Kennedy would do a good job, so I was for him. I think face-to-face debate is really good because, if anything, we can at least sense who might be telling the truth. McGovern is talking out of both sides of his mouth, so I could never trust him, and anyhow if all those programs he wants for the poor were brought out, what would we get out of it? The good old family in the middle class—the Neumeyers—would be stuck again.

I'm voting for Nixon, and as terrible as this is to admit, he's the lesser of the two evils. We just don't have great Presidents any more, men like Lincoln. I'm just worried that with the polls and everything people are going to be overconfident and figure Nixon doesn't need their vote and then McGovern could win. McGovern will really bring out the kids' votes and . . . this might be selfish . . . I'm happy. Rich will come home and I'll be more than glad to have his vote cancel out mine.

Betty has been having more than her usual amount of trouble sleeping nights, and on election morning she wakes at 5 A.M., sure she hears someone at the door. Art assures her Richard has a key and goes back to sleep. Betty cannot. She listens for more sounds until the alarm clock startles her at 5:45.

The day drags on, and Betty finds it difficult to get involved with her housework. She keeps going to the window to see if the Mustang is outside. She runs to the telephone when it rings, as it does a half-dozen times during the day. But each time it is a friend. Perhaps her most stimulating conversation of the day—the one that takes her mind off Richard—is with Pam Brown, and it revolves around religion. Pam attends the Catholic church and last Sunday, during the time when worshipers are supposed to extend a sign of peace to one another, she saw two women in the row in front of her turn to each other and from ten feet give each other first a shocked look and then one of unbridled hate.

Betty has worked for one of the women, Melissa, at the Mari-Knolls Beach Club. The other woman, Peggy, was one of a group of Mariposans who adamantly fought the beach club's existence, claiming that the new proprietors, Melissa and her husband, were allowing boat owners other than Mariposa residents to tie up and come in for a drink or food. Peggy claimed undesirables and blacks from Union Heights would be next.

Pam tells Betty that Peggy switched her church membership the next day and is removing her children from the parish school. "I come to church to pray and then I'm forced to give a handshake to her!" she told Pam.

"I remember the time the pastor wanted to try something different with Holy Communion and he had this one big loaf and everybody was supposed to share, to break off a piece," Betty says. "Most people passed it by. He heard about it the next day. Who wants all those germs? They did it in the time of Christ, sure, but they died at eighteen and nineteen too. We do it the old way now. Much more sanitary."

Betty and Art vote as soon as he gets home. A few minutes after they return to the house, the phone rings again. Betty walks slower this time toward the kitchen to answer it. "I have a collect—"

"Yes, I'll accept." Betty cuts the operator short, but there is little anticipation or excitement in her voice.

There are a few seconds when neither party speaks. Then Betty simply asks, "Where were you today?"

"Working."

"On the river?"

"Naw, that's a bummer," Richard says, sounding more confident. "I'm working with this electrician, wiring buildings and stuff."

271

"Electrician? You never did anything like that."

"It's simple. Only thing is, the building is cold."

"Do you have . . . ?"

"Yeah, I got plenty of clothes. Well, I just wanted you to know I wasn't going to be home to vote today."

"Well, you could have let us know before now," Betty says, her tone turning angry. She looks at the two loaves of cranberry bread on the tile counter and her fist clenches at her side.

"Yeah, well, didn't have time."

"Richard, you think about positively nobody besides your own selfish self," Betty says, her voice now louder. Art walks toward the back room extension, but Betty waves him away.

"I gotta go."

"Just go then. Don't care about anybody!"

"So I got to call long distance and get hassled. Every damn time."

"It's just because you're not going anyplace. You're bumming around."

"OK, see you."

"*Good-bye!*" Betty slams down the phone.

In a telephone booth in Wilkes-Barre, Pennsylvania, Richard Neumeyer smiles into the receiver. "It is going to be some cold day in hell before she sees my ass again," he says to his friend Cary, whom he met the one day he worked on the river before he was fired for not being strong enough to do the work.

"What happened?"

"Same old shit. Will your old lady really let me stay at your place?"

"Yeah, she doesn't care. Come on, let's see what's going on."

The Mustang pulls away from the curb and starts down the road along the Susquehanna River. Huge chunks of curbstone are missing and side streets stand forlornly dark, their street lamps uprooted by the floods. Jumbled asphalt looks like tilled soil and appears to have sprouted an unseemly crop of rusty wagons and carriages, broken branches, hunks of porch railings, all of it mired in a bed of dried silt.

"How did you do with Vicki last night?" Cary says.

"You know, no big thing," Richard replies.

"Ball her?"

"Yeah," Richard says, inhaling deeply on his cigarette.

"That broad carries a mattress around on her back."

"She wasn't exactly hard to convince, man. But what a dog! Doris found out already and she's plenty pissed. Now there's a chick I can see some future in, trucking around the country or something."

Back in the living room on Birchwood, Betty moves toward the sofa, a tissue in her hand. She blows her nose loudly. Art is pensive as he stands in the hallway. He looks up at the clock. "Want to watch the returns?"

"No, Artie, who the hell cares?"

"Let's go to bed then."

"A whiskey sour first. If I go to bed like this I'll be up all night."

The drinks in their hands, Art and Betty Neumeyer sit silently in their living room. "Blue Boy," a paint-by-number picture, looks down from the wall, his childishly arrogant pose and face indifferent to the problems of his creator, Art.

"It's different this time," Betty says. "I feel more immune, like I had an anesthetic or something. He can just hurt you so many times; then it doesn't hurt so much any more."

"Tell me how much it doesn't hurt as you sit there bawling."

"I'm not bawling," she says. "Must be an allergy or something."

"What for, Betty, why the heartache? He's here, he saves a few dollars and he's off again. New adventure. Meet me here, kid, and I'll give you a job. I tell you, Betty, the first week away might be fun but then it's no clean laundry, no set place to go, no meals." Art stands up and starts pacing in front of the coffee table. "I'm just as sick at heart, Betty. But I'm annoyed. This time it's clear: we are being used."

"He's too young. I don't think he'd intentionally—"

"Damn it!" Art slams his maimed right hand into his left. "Intentional or not, we're being used. I'm a very bad father to say

273

that, I know. But he'd be just as well off someplace else far away, causing us less heartache instead of being around with those bummy clothes and us on the edge of our seats wondering when we'll say something and off he'll go."

"All I want to know is what he's going to do about college. I bought sheets and towels on sale for him; I got a whole bunch of things ready. He could get an acceptance any day, and then what is he going to do? I don't even know where to reach him."

"Betty, be realistic; that kid ain't going to college."

"Joanie said he told her if he isn't accepted he's going off to California to live."

"Let him go; let him send us postcards; let him go for a year, two years. He's not coming home again just to rest up until the next adventure. This time I'm doing it my way. When he gets home, he gets the rules. And when he gets the rules, he's going right back out the door because he isn't going to like them."

"Like what, Artie? Why are you going to make sure he walks out?"

"He's got to prove he's grown up. He gets his hair cut, not a crew cut but neatly trimmed. He shaves. He puts in his application with all the companies you can get a decent job with, like the telephone company, the gas company, civil service. No baloney like 'I'll do it tomorrow.' And he gets decent clothes."

Betty goes to the kitchen and gets two tissues from the box. She rinses out their glasses and puts them in the dishwasher. "Were you any better, Artie? I can remember more than one paycheck you lost at cards. I just sat there and watched you throw it away."

"I had no father, Betty, to try to knock some sense into me. And don't forget, from the time I was sixteen I had a steady job. This kid is being a bum. He's not man enough to admit that in life you have to work so many weeks and earn the money, then you take your vacation. You have a good time on your vacation; then you go back to work for another year. For him, his life has been one big ball."

"It's too much, Artie, too much turmoil. I don't want to suffer like this. I want to live, to walk into a store with you and just look

274

at jewelry for an hour. Just be together. Good times like we used to have."

"So we consider him gone and then we get rid of this monster; all we need is a two-bedroom house. I could cut the expenses by one fourth. All we got left is Joanie, and if Martha or Richie come to visit we can have a pullout couch."

"We don't have to have a room downstairs with his things in it, really. It's just a heartache."

"So you cry and I don't, but it hurts just as bad, Betty. When does a parent's obligation end? I mean, who says that a child is the only one who can have fun and experience things?"

"I still don't look forward to them all leaving, Artie. I want to be a grandmother. That's not too much of an ambition. Instead they go off and they don't get married like they're supposed to."

"You also have the right to have peace of mind, knowing that your son is here or someplace. Not go to bed wondering where he's sleeping."

"This last time he left so quick I could hardly get his clothes washed."

"Well, that's over. He could be twenty-five and still be stopping here to rest up before he takes off. We're never going to be used by him again."

"Never?" Betty says softly.

"Never."

"Remember when we said we would never say never? Remember when we said we wouldn't have anything to do with Martha if she kept seeing Len Morris, and in the final analysis we were ready to change our minds because she wasn't going to come home?" Betty's voice, which has been low throughout the talk, is steadily rising. "Remember we got panicky but we won anyhow and we didn't know we were going to win?"

"We're going to win this time, Betty, and on my terms. We've run it your way almost every time and look! You can nag me for what happens, but you won't have to blame yourself, OK?"

"I'm just afraid I'll have to bury him," Betty says, the short-lived passion gone from her voice. "I'd rather lose him than bury him.

He's not going anyplace but down. He doesn't know much. Really."

"He's going to grow up. If he comes home and I want to go to Christmas Eve dinner I can't even take him, the way he looks. I wouldn't go into a restaurant with him."

"You're missing it entirely, Artie. What if he was a retarded child; would you be ashamed?"

"What does a retarded child have to do with one that won't grow up?"

"It was our weakness all along; we never were firm with him."

"Well, let's end our weakness right now. I see kids in the city every day, on drugs, filthy—"

"Artie, don't! Don't tell me about that, I have enough problems."

"I think Richie is past the stage where you have to worry about him getting into drugs, sleeping on cold floors or ten people in one room. I'm not saying him."

"I don't know, Artie, I'm so confused. I told Richie I'd never compare him to Gerard Brown, but look at Gerard. He minds the other kids when Pam goes out. Does work around the house. Pays all his medical bills. Takes his father to the train. Had food on the table when Pam was in the hospital. Hair two inches below the ear. Calls his father at eleven to see if he can stay out."

"We've been lenient. We always wanted them to be independent."

"I suppose then it's my fault, Artie," she says, turning hostile.

"Both of us. Now it's going to be the other way. And if he can't take the rules, then he can find somebody else to support him. Things were relaxed around here after he came back from California only because we made all the concessions. If I'm not home and he comes home, you just tell him not to unpack until I talk to him. Just put it to him that way."

"That is, if he ever comes home again."

"He'll be back."

"If he's not, then we should make it official. Sell his stereo so we can rent the room or something."

276

"Don't bring things into it that complicate it. Don't sell anything."

"I can't look at the room, Artie; can't you see that?" The tissue mops at Betty's cheek.

"I think he read too many of those damn books written by capitalists who talk about how to be a bum. And they get rich in the process. What was the name of that one he was reading?"

"*Be Not Content.*"

17

The Children They Were Never Allowed to Be

"Alison, now pick out the one you want," the suntanned woman in the white tailored slacks says to her daughter.

"I don't care which one, Mommy. Just any one," says the girl. She is about Joan's age and wears a pleated plaid skirt and matching vest.

"You're bored, that's your problem!"

"I don't want another coat. I told you before we got here."

"You pick one out right now. The saleslady doesn't have all day."

Betty and Joan watch the lady shake a credit card at her daughter. The girl goes to a clothes rack, reaches in and grabs a tweed coat with a fur collar. Betty and Joan move behind another rack of clothes and Betty shrugs her shoulders. Her daughter repeats the gesture and they walk on. Joan is holding a bag containing a pair of purple pantyhose that will match the smock Martha made during the summer; as yet Betty carries nothing but her purse. She and Joan have been to three stores already and spent an hour and a half in pursuit of a long dress that Betty will wear to the big social event of the church year: the Couples Club dinner dance, which is less than two weeks away. Arriving in the women's department she looks through the offerings: a simple black dress with covered buttons for $49.95—too expensive, she tells Joan; an orange and green stripe for $24.95—"It would make me look like a circus tent." After a few minutes she comes to a multicolored print on a black background, close-fitting at the waist, falling away in a slight flare to the ground. It is $19.95, reduced from $35.00. Betty takes it from the rack and, with Joan, goes into the dressing room. Ten minutes later, she takes out two ten-dollar bills, a single and the change. "It looks really nice, Mommy," Joan says. "Daddy will love it. You look pretty in a long dress."

It is Thursday evening near nine thirty, and Art by now will be waiting at the corner of the building to meet them, so they hurry out of the store and into a cold, windy night. Soon they are huddled together on the front seat of the red Chevrolet as Art turns the heater to high. On the way back to the house, Art turns off Main Line Drive, and it is he who first sees the panel truck much like Richard's old one, and the familiar outline of Ron's head of blond hair.

Art and Betty look at each other and Betty says one word: "Hurry." He presses the accelerator almost to the floor and speeds along Pawnee Drive, only slowing down at the stop signs. As the red Chevrolet reaches the corner of Birchwood, Betty bumps her head on the ceiling as she tries to stand in the car to get a better look down the street. In the vicinity of their house the dim outlines of at least a half-dozen cars are evident.

"It's there, I see it in the street light!" Betty exclaims. "He's home, Artie, Joanie!"

Joan sits up straight and expectantly squeezes her mother around the neck as her father hurries down the street. The dim outlines of the cars grow clearer. When the Chevrolet is ten houses from 97 Birchwood, Betty slowly sinks back into her seat. She is silent. Art releases the accelerator.

Once inside, he says simply, "Let's call Ron's house and see what's up."

Ron is not home but returns the call the next morning. He tells Betty he left Wilkes-Barre at the end of the first week. The river job hadn't worked out—only "brutes," as Ron calls them, were being hired—and he didn't want to stay around. When he left, Richard was hoping to get steady work with a carpenter or electrician, but Ron doesn't know if it worked out. Why hadn't he called,

Betty asks, to tell them how Richard was doing? He just hadn't thought about it, he replies, in a bland, emotionless voice. Where could Richard be reached?

He doesn't know.

It is Saturday, early in the afternoon, as Art drops a quarter into the waiting mouth at the toll booth, the light changes to green and he is off. It is quiet except for the song on the radio which crackles and fades as the car moves out of the station's range. Betty, Art and Joan are on their way to the wedding of the eldest daughter of Art's sister, Florence. As Art and his sister grew apart soon after each was married and Betty has never felt accepted by his family, visits like this have never been pleasurable for the Neumeyers. Duty, rather than love or interest, is the key motivation today. When they were first married, Art and Betty visited Florence and her husband, Hal, and Art's mother, who lives with them, more often, but the visits were never reciprocated and Betty began to feel slighted—a feeling which has blossomed into deep resentment.

"You know, I'd give anything to be going to that Quaker retreat this weekend, Artie," Betty says suddenly as the car speeds along. "There's so much on my mind; it would be good just to clear it out for a while."

"You could have gone; Joan and I could have represented the family. It's only a niece."

"Not on your life. We never did things separately and we're not starting now. Do you think Florence and Hal would believe I was on a retreat?" Betty goes on, talking faster. "It's OK for her to have a filthy house and spend all her time listening to those fundamentalist tapes. But if anybody else has religion she turns up her nose at it."

"OK, OK, Betty, I just—"

"And the way that other guy—what's his name?—pats her fanny and stuff, don't tell me there isn't some switchy-switchy going on."

Art looks in the rearview mirror. "Is she sleeping?"

"Yes, she's sleeping," Betty whispers back angrily.

Art stares at the road ahead.

280

"Artie, I'm sorry, I don't want to be my usual ugly self," Betty says, putting her hand on Art's knee. "You've never been anything but swell with my family."

"And?"

"It's just that I hate them"—she pulls back her hand—"hate them, Artie! They think Joan is spoiled because we dress her pretty. Your mother does not know to this day that my father died. They are so holy they wouldn't let Martha play her Beatles record when we used to go up there years ago. Everything. Let's forget about them, Artie. Let's forget about everything. It'll only be a couple hours and then we have a nice motel room to ourselves. Artie, I've been looking forward to this like a second honeymoon. We can have breakfast out; somebody else can cook my eggs. Oh, honey!"

A trace of a smile breaks Art's stern look, and he gently slides his hand along the seat. Ever so slightly, Betty lifts up her left buttock and Art's hand slides beneath. He gives her a gentle squeeze and leaves the hand there as the car speeds north.

At the motel, Betty hangs up her "basic blue" dress that she has brought to wear at the candlelight wedding that night. It is a simple yet attractive dress cut just at the knees, its only decoration a narrow band of white trim down the front. Joan is staying overnight at her uncle and aunt's house, so she is already in the $6 pink dress that Betty bought for her at Easter. After brushing Joan's hair, Betty says, "Zero hour; let's go."

Florence, Art's sister, says a hurried hello to Betty and Art as they come into the house and then she disappears, leaving the Neumeyers standing inside the front door, their coats still on. People are swarming around the house, everyone seemingly with something urgent to do this afternoon. The Neumeyers make their way through the kitchen and toward the extension Hal has built for his wife's mother. Betty gives Art her "I told you so" look as they pass the sink, which is filled with dirty dishes.

In the extension, the first thing that catches Betty's eye is not her seventy-year-old mother-in-law, who is walking toward them, or the pale-faced girl who is to be married. It is the dress hanging from the top of a closet door.

"Oh, Mother, that's a pretty dress," she says cautiously.

"Yes, I'm going to wear it to the wedding."

"Is everybody going to wear long dresses?"

"Sure, Hal's mother wanted to wear a long dress she just got."

"Everybody?"

"Yes, everybody in the family."

"Am I in the family?"

"What do you mean?"

"I'm not wearing a long dress and neither is Joanie. We have them, if only—"

"Oh, there was no time to let everybody know. We only made up our minds last week."

"A telephone—"

"We better get back to the motel and get ready; it's kind of late," Art cuts in as he takes Betty by the arm.

"You just got here, Artie," his mother says.

"It takes me hours to get myself together." He smiles weakly.

The door on the red Chevrolet is not even closed when Betty virtually screams at Art. "Last week she wrote me to bring chopped liver. You mean to tell me she couldn't let me know?"

"Baby, let's just go over here to the shopping center and get a long dress and that'll do it," Art says calmly.

"God damn it," she says, starting to cry. "They don't care about anybody. If they can humiliate me, they would just love it."

"Let's get a dress. We don't have much time."

"My girdle is back at the motel; how can I try on a dress? And I am not an impulse buyer, Artie; I'm not just going to run out and get a dress because of them. Let them all laugh; let them turn up their noses at the people from Mariposa. They're jealous of everything we have."

At six thirty, Art and Betty arrive back at Florence and Hal's house as the family is ready to go to the church. Betty's eyes are puffy and red but she says nothing. At the church she remains silent as she watches the women in long dresses standing in the vestibule or being escorted up the aisle. Florence and her mother stand talking, borrowed mink stoles around their shoulders, as Betty runs her hand along the buttons on her cloth coat.

282

"Did she bring the chopped liver?" Florence asks her mother.

"Betty, you brought it, didn't you?"

Betty stares at Florence. "Mother, tell Florence *she did* bring it," Betty says, clutching Art's hand tightly.

Buster, Florence's son, a boy Betty has described as looking as if he hadn't washed his neck in the last year, is ready to escort the Neumeyers to their place in the candlelit church. "Let's go, Betty," he says. His liquor-laden breath makes Betty turn away. She puts her arm in his and they walk slowly up the aisle, his crooked smile and Betty's poker face a strange combination. "I'm gonna put you on the groom's side." Buster turns to her. "Not too many of his people showed up."

Betty's eyes are straight ahead and without the slightest trace of emotion on her face, she says, barely moving her lips, "If you do, I'll kick you right in the ass, Buster."

The afternoon that started out badly continues to follow that course. The Neumeyers are put in the wrong pew by Buster and have to stumble over other relatives until they are settled. Then at the reception Buster pushes one of the younger children, who falls and cuts his head, and Betty and Florence are on the verge of a confrontation over it. After Buster is sent to his room, Betty goes into it to get some Kleenex from her coat and the boy greets her with "What the hell do you want?" She says nothing and goes to the bathroom for toilet tissue to blow her nose.

By the time Art and Betty get back to their motel, the dream of a second honeymoon night has long been out of the question. The solitude they planned for is present, but the mood is gone. Sex for the Neumeyers would be an impossibility in a situation like this. Sex is for happy times, or times of making up. It is not for a time when Betty feels she has been consciously, publicly humiliated.

As they lie in bed, Betty collects her thoughts before delivering what Art knows will be forthcoming, some sort of declaration. "That's it," she says as her arms fall to the pressed sheets. "We are never coming up here again. Starting this year, we are not exchanging Christmas presents. We are going to stop living a lie. They pulled out pictures of every damn one of their kids; did they have the courtesy to ask how Martha was doing? The only grand-child your mother has that's doing anything. Did she care? I am not going to be a hypocrite. When your mother dies, I am not going up." She hesitates. "Unless you ask me."

Art is still, his eyes closed.

"Say something. Why do I always have to be the one lashing out? How can you stay so calm? Why didn't you just say we were leaving when you saw what they were wearing and how they were putting me down? I would have loved that, Artie. I would have walked out right behind you."

He rolls over to look at her. "I would not do anything to hurt you. I am sorry you didn't know about the dresses. We do not have to come ever again unless we mutually agree to. OK?"

"You've spent twenty-two years with me, Artie," she says, almost pleading. "And only half that with your mother and your sister. Less with your sister, because she got married. I've always been willing to start over again. They could have a wonderful relationship if they would just accept me. Artie, you have to realize that there just isn't a relationship."

"I never said there was," he says slowly, enunciating each word.

"Right from the start. You brought me home and—remember?—your mother sent you out for ice cream. 'You're not the first girl Butchie ever brought home,' she said to me, like I wasn't going to be the last one either."

"Betty," Art says, propping his head up on his hand, "I always said my life began with you. What more do you want?" He eases his head down and turns over before saying quietly, "I was nothing till I met you. OK?"

Arthur James Neumeyer was born in a small Pennsylvania town in 1928 to Freda and Karl Neumeyer. Karl, a salesman—of what, Art does not know—took sick the next year and as the Depression was just beginning, died of pneumonia. Freda Neumeyer felt she could not survive with her two children, Arthur and Florence, so she placed them in a state orphanage and went to the city and eventually found work as a dressmaker.

Art and Florence spent the next nine years at Bakersville orphanage, brother and sister by blood but just two more children in the eyes of the staff. Boys and girls slept in different dormitories and had different activities, and there was no effort made to cement family ties. What Art remembers of the orphanage is that "you worked for your keep and it was just work and school and that was all. No monkey business." Much of their food was grown on the grounds. In those Depression days potatoes were a staple. Gobs of potatoes were served at many meals, potatoes that were picked by Art and the other children during long, backbreaking hours in the fields. One of the first jobs Art was given was to go down row after row, picking potato bugs from the plants. In the orchards, apples were gathered, not to be eaten outside of mealtime. Any child caught eating apples while at work was given a dose of castor oil to purge the forbidden fruit. One of Art's earliest memories of his older sister is of the day she saw him eating an apple and told on him, thus subjecting him to still another spoonful of castor oil.

As best as Art can recall, his years in the orphanage were neither happy nor unhappy. They were not lonely; they were not warm. "When you start off your life in an orphanage you don't know there's any other kind of life. My childhood was really nothing," he says. He can remember going fishing on occasion, he can remember swimming in the creek and almost drowning, but otherwise his childhood memories are few.

There were neither housemothers nor houseparents in the dormitories at Bakersville, nor privacy, just long rows of beds on every floor, squeezed together to make room for children like Art whose parents either could not or would not take care of them during that period. At the foot of his bed was a wooden seat that lifted off, and within the box beneath was contained everything he owned: a few changes of clothes, a worn toy or two. If it didn't fit in the small box, a child could not keep it.

During the years at the orphanage, Art recalls that his mother visited, but not that often. So when at the age of eleven Art was told by his mother that she had remarried and that he and Florence could come to live in the North End, it was not just that Art was going to live with a stepfather (his first stepfather), Charles Newcombe. To him, it was as if he were also going to live with a stepmother and stepsister. He had been an orphanage child since he was twenty months old.

Once Art, his mother and sister were together, a certain closeness developed. Art got along well with his sister outside the confines of the orphanage, and he found his mother, although not an overwhelmingly warm person, at least ready to feed and clothe him and buy him a baseball cap or an iron car, unreachable luxuries at Bakersville. Art barely remembers his stepfather except for the fights Charles had with his mother during the three years of their marriage. He was not interested in his stepchildren, avoided playing with them and appeared to be a stern, unapproachable man who liked quiet and didn't like to be bothered.

As a twelve- and thirteen-year-old Art frequently played hooky, and the truant officer was a regular visitor at his home. Art and a gang of boys from the North End broke an occasional window and were involved in petty thefts from markets and candy stores. The grade school principal told Art's mother, "You have a budding juvenile delinquent on your hands there," but Freda couldn't take Art's minor problems seriously. Her own life and marriage had been in turmoil, taking up much of her attention and energy.

Once his mother was divorced, Art seemed to straighten out. He began working to help the family, delivering groceries, selling soda outside a factory, then tending rowboats and grooming horses in Pierrepont Park. Slowly, through these years, Art Neumeyer began to see that everyone had not been brought up the way he had. He began to see mothers and fathers and their children enjoying a picnic in Pierrepont Park. He saw grandparents proudly walking their grandchildren in strollers along the wide streets. He saw fathers tossing a ball to their sons. Slowly, he realized he had missed something in his growing-up years.

As soon as he was sixteen, Art quit high school—he was in the tenth grade—and got his first full-time job. Rabinowitz Diecutting hired him for 55 cents an hour to sweep the floors and fill in where he might be needed: gluing or folding or packaging. With his newfound money, Art became somewhat of a gambler, dice being his favorite game. He would play at lunch and at quitting time. As the night janitor also liked to play, a payday game could go into the late evening. Art grew a thin mustache, as was the style, and bought a wide-brimmed hat and overcoat with big lapels that underworld figures popularized. He liked to hang out at Peppy's Pool Hall and to lean over a table with a cigarette dangling out of his mouth, lining up the money shot. One night he and Billy Tompkins came out of Peppy's, their coat collars up and hat brims down, and were promptly grabbed and bent over a car fender to be searched. This pair fit the description of two gangsters the police were looking for. Art and Billy were heroes around Peppy's for weeks because of the incident.

Whenever he went out with a date Art never tried to economize. Buses were a nickel, but Art might just as well hail a cab. Hot dogs from street vendors were a dime, but Art would take his date to a good restaurant and if she wanted a steak she had it, even if it cost a quarter of his take-home pay. "I was more or less like my son," Art admits. "It was, Enjoy today and worry about tomorrow later."

If Art Neumeyer presented a tough appearance with his gangland getup, it was a masquerade. Beneath the stern exterior was a shy young man who treated dates with respect and courtesy and would avoid a fight rather than look for one. But that masquerade was an essential part of being accepted in the North End. So it was natural, with the war still on, that Art and his friends should offer to serve their country. It was apparent that the war would soon be over, but not to be in service before the end would have been a disgrace. With a maximum amount of buildup at the pool hall and at Rabinowitz's, they went down to the recruiting office. His two best friends were accepted quickly, but Art was told to stand aside for another physical examination. He seldom went into specifics when his friends asked why he was declared 4-F. Art Neumeyer was found to have a hernia and varicose veins in his testicles.

After the war was over and cars were in production again, Art bought a year-old Nash for $1,300 and found that his popularity

287

with the girls increased tremendously. It wasn't a rare weekend when he'd take one girl roller skating on Friday, another horseback riding on Saturday and still another to dinner and a movie on Sunday. It was at the age of nineteen, with this newfound acceptance and the freedom of his own car, that Art Neumeyer finally succeeded in doing what all the fellows at work and the pool hall bragged about. In the phraseology of the day, Art "got his first piece of ass" on a cold night in the back seat of the Nash, shielded from the world by windows steamed by the two participants within.

On New Year's Eve in 1949, Art wasn't planning to go to the party, but his sister Florence complained that she wanted to go and couldn't get there unless Art took her. He was only going to drop her off and stay for a few minutes, but then he saw a girl in a black dress, with skin "as white as a ghost." (Betty Santangelo was sick with the flu that night and almost hadn't come herself.)

Art managed an introduction and spent the rest of the evening getting to know the girl he would marry before the year was out. Betty was a thin girl with short brown hair and a shy, ready smile, and Art was immediately attracted to her. Once he met her mother and father and sensed a warm, whole family, he wanted to be a part of it. He had never experienced a father who would put his arm around his shoulders, a mother who loved to laugh at her husband's silly jokes. Betty often says, "Artie married me as much to get into my family as he did because he loved me."

Betty came to the marriage a product of an intact family that, while it was a revelation to Art, had not met some of her basic needs. Art came to the marriage from an emotionally bankrupt and fragmented family. Both vowed that their children would have a better start in life. What Art missed as a boy, he would give to his son; what Betty missed, she would give to her daughter. Together they wanted to create and raise the children they were never allowed to be.

It is Wednesday night. The wedding is four days past, but the wounds have not yet healed. On the telephone to her friends, Betty has retold the embarrassment of being the only family member in a short dress. When friends have come to the house, Betty has modeled the long dress she will wear to the Couples Club dinner dance Friday, telling them how easily she could have taken it and how wonderful the weekend would have been if Art's family had been considerate enough to tell her what everyone else was wearing. Art has heard the story many times and has said nothing.

Art, Betty and Joan are all lying on the bed together watching the movie *Giant* on television when they hear what sounds like the front door opening. They look puzzled and then a familiar voice calls out, "Is anybody home?"

"Richie, Richie!" Joan squeals and, tripping over her nightgown, goes running toward the front of the house.

Art and Betty follow her. When they reach the living room they find their daughter in the arms of a scraggly-haired boy who has two scraggly-haired companions standing behind him, one of whom has a scraggly-haired afghan-looking hound on a leash. Richard looks toward his parents and then directs himself to Joan. "What's this I hear about you being for Nixon at your school?"

"He won, didn't he?" Joan says.

"Yeah, he won, the creep."

"Not enough of our younger generation turned out to vote for his opponent," Art says icily.

"America got what it deserves. Got me a place to live, so I came back for some stuff." Richard makes eye contact with his parents. "OK?"

"Sure, Richard," Betty says.

"We'll go back in the morning. Been sleeping with this dog . . . always sleep with this dog . . . so he'll stay in my room."

Betty's look stops Richard from going any farther. "This is a one-dog family," she says. "If you and your friends want to stay, that's fine. The dog stays in the car. I don't want those long hairs all over the rug."

"I always sleep with this dog," Richard says defiantly. "If my dog can't stay here then I'm not staying either."

"Would your friends—I'm sorry I don't know your names—

289

mind taking the dog out to the car and we can talk this over," Art says, his eyes smoldering.

"Nothing to talk about. If the dog can't stay, I can't stay."

"The dog can't stay," his father says.

"Well, I better get my shit together and go. Come on down and see my room," he says to his friends.

"Take—the—dog—out," his mother says, pausing after each word.

The three boys take the dog to the car and then come back into the house and go down to Richard's room without saying a word. Twenty minutes later, with armloads of clothes and a shopping bag brimming with odds and ends, they come back up the stairs. Art and Betty look almost mesmerized. Joan runs up to her brother and gives him a kiss.

"Well, I'll see you around," he says.

"Do you have an address?" Betty asks softly.

"Yeah, you want to take it down?"

She goes to the kitchen for paper and jots down his address in Wilkes-Barre.

"Yeah, well, good-bye," Richard says.

"Good-bye," his parents say together.

James Dean fills the television screen in the bedroom with his famous boyish grin just as Art walks in and flicks the set off. Soon after, Joan is in bed and Betty is in the bathroom shaking two Bufferins into her hand.

"Why, why?" Art says, looking down at the yellow bathroom rug.

"He isn't dead or anything, Artie; he's just a closed issue," Betty says, looking down at her plump pink palm and the two white pills. Then she tosses her head back and swallows the pills.

It is nearly seven thirty on Friday night when Betty hears the car pulling into the driveway. Art has been getting home late because the railroad is on strike and he is forced to drive into the city. Betty had her hair done earlier in the day, and an hour ago she applied lipstick, powder and perfume. Since then she has been waiting in her bathrobe for her husband, sitting on the couch, staring into space. The last seven days in the lives of the Neumeyers have been "some of the worst of my life," Betty told Lillian Rose this afternoon. Tonight she has prepared herself with little enthusiasm, although she and Art have been looking forward to the dinner dance, which was such a success last year.

Art comes through the front door and Betty smiles weakly toward him. With a rakish smile on his face, he grabs her and kisses her on the neck and says seductively, "Is your husband still home?"

"Artie, that ride is driving you loony." She smiles. "Is that disc jockey still saying that?"

"Every morning." He sings out the words: " 'Is your husband still home?' I'm locked in the car with a madman. Boop-boop-be-do."

Betty hugs her husband. "You're the madman."

"And how would you like Frank Brown, first thing in the morning? Madman? Of course I'm a madman." Art juts out his bottom jaw in his best monster pose and stalks slowly around the living room, his eyes shifting from side to side.

"If Pam didn't have to take the car to school those few blocks, her husband could drive, too."

"Either way, I'd still be a madman," he says, continuing to stalk about the living room. "Scotch on the rocks, please."

"Artie, what's gotten into you? I'm not really up for this thing tonight."

"Betty, my dear, I have made a firm resolution to have a good time tonight. We used to have good times when we were broke. Now that we're the poor slobs among the rich snobs in The Knolls, why can't we still enjoy ourselves? Tonight all the troubles of the world are going to be put aside and we are going to have a time. A double Scotch on the rocks. I'll get it, baby. Get your dress on so I can take it off later."

In a half hour Betty and Art Neumeyer are at Parkside United Methodist Church, along with twenty-three other couples and one widow, standing at prayer before the dinner is served.

". . . Fellowship and gaiety are wonderful parts of our life, and

291

let us share them tonight," Pastor MacIntosh says, "but let us always be mindful of what Jesus Christ would want us to focus our lives on, what he would ask of us. Amen."

"Do I or do I not have the most beautiful wife tonight?" Art says to Dave Bismark, his bowling partner, as conversation begins after the prayer.

"Sure, Artie, anything you say," he says, putting a platter of sliced turkey roll on the table. "My kitchen crew worked over the punch pretty good before anybody got here, so I got to get back in there."

Platters of ham, bowls of beets and cranberry sauce, boats brimming with turkey gravy are served up in the noisy fellowship hall. Bill Freeman spills coffee on Lottie Lippman's dress and suggestively reaches below the table, leaving his hand in her lap as people at the table howl.

"Freeman," Art hollers, "you are fired for being drunk on duty."

"Drunk, sir?" he says with mock indignation. "Didn't I spill some coffee on one of you ladies?" He reaches under the table to Betty and she pushes him away, laughing.

After the ice cream topped with crème de menthe is served, the couples walk upstairs where the band is ready to play. In Mohawk County in the past few years there has been a resurgence of the "big band sound," and groups like the one performing for the Couples Club—fifteen men in all—have formed to play the songs of Glenn Miller and the Dorsey brothers. "Around a golf course, I'm under par . . . but I can't get started with you," coos a little-girl voice as the band runs through the first number. The singer is blond, red-lipped, ten pounds too plump, but with a warm and evocative voice, bringing back memories of stars like Helen O'Connell.

Betty and Art are on the dance floor, cheek to cheek, their hips close together. Other couples who rarely touch in public now have their chance, and the floor is soon filled with men and women dancing—some talking and laughing, others staring over their partners' shoulders. As the faster numbers are played, the crowd thins out and a few dancers gain all the attention. One is the pastor, who dances with his twenty-year-old daughter plus a variety of churchwomen, as his wife isn't here. Benjamin and Polly Morris, both of them attractive, trim, black people, move easily and rhythmically to the cha-cha, samba or jitterbug. And Sophie Cogley—branded the church's activist because of her antiwar stand and various campaigns—bobs around the dance floor shimmying and shaking to the upbeat songs of the Beatles and the Rolling Stones.

Betty and Art smile readily and go in and out of conversations with the ease that the pastor changes his dance partners.

"Patricia's dress is a bit low cut, isn't it?" Lillian Rose says to Betty, motioning toward a tall woman wearing a lopsided platinum wig that is cut in a longish Dutch boy.

"We were just bringing her food last week because her back was so bad. Must be a miracle cure. She hasn't missed a dance yet," Betty replies.

Lillian moves over to another woman as Betty and Art leave to dance a waltz. "This church has really done a lot for them," Lillian says as the Morrises waltz by. "Upwardly mobile, and they've been accepted."

The other woman nods. Betty and Art pass by and the other woman, Maude Miller, comments, "Hear that Betty's Martha made the *Who's Who*. Quite a girl."

Lillian looks to see if Betty and Art are out of hearing range. "There's another side to that kid. She's one thing when she's at home; it's another thing when she's away."

"Got some specifics?" Maude whispers.

"Just the feeling, and my feelings usually are right," Lillian says. "She's no angel. You remember the Len Morris adventure. Shush, here they are."

A group of women go to the rest room while Art and some other men stand around the table, which is loaded with pastries, a coffee urn and another urn with hot water for tea. They are gone quite a while, so that when Betty comes back, Art says, "Baby, you can't stay away so long; I miss you."

She pulls him aside and says softly, "Did you know that . . . I just can't believe . . ."

"What, baby, what?"

"Count the kids the people in this church have. I don't think most of them had sex any more times than they had to."

"Kinsey report?"

"Art, we're the champs. The Duluths never do it any more, and they're not even fifty. Women in their forties only do it when their husbands get so pissed off they have to. And even the Dupreys! They're young. When I told Francine we do it a couple times a week, she was shocked. Her Charlie comes home for a 'hot snack' at lunch once in a while but . . . Oh, Artie, we really do love each other. We really do have a wonderful marriage. And a family." Betty squeezes Art's hand tightly.

"Let me go home right now and improve the statistics. And don't go slipping me any of those muscle relaxants you've been taking. I don't want any muscles relaxed tonight."

"It's only ten thirty, Artie."

"A few more minutes. I can only wait a few more minutes." Art Neumeyer pulls his wife close to him.

"Lillian, did I tell you Martha is considering going into an inner-city program in Kansas City to do her practice teaching?" Betty says, talking louder and turning to her friend.

"That kid," Lillian says. "That's her problem. Most of the abortions we do at the hospital are for blacks. They breed like rabbits. Martha will see a lot of that."

"We're not pushing it," Art says. "Those kids in high school will be bigger than she is. She has to decide before Christmas, I think."

"Tell her to get some nice middle-class school and stop trying to save the world," Lillian says as she runs her hand along the side of her lacquered hairdo.

An hour later, Betty and Art are home. They have picked up Joan from the Dupreys and put her to bed, and now Betty is smoothing out the long dress before hanging it in the closet. They slide into bed and Art puts his arm around his wife. "No muscle relaxant tonight," he says.

"I notice," she says, smiling halfheartedly.

"Where's your mind right now?" Art asks.

Betty stares straight ahead as if she hasn't heard her husband.

"Where's your . . ."

As Betty turns toward him with her blank look, Art stops. Seconds go by before she replies.

"Where's Richard sleeping tonight?"

18

Be Honest

IN WILKES-BARRE, a harsh November wind blows brown leaves onto the floorboard of Richard's Mustang as he and Cary Fulbright get out under the streetlight. They stand silently for a moment in front of the rambling old house in which Richard has rented a room. Sometimes there are six, sometimes over a dozen people renting rooms from Cary's mother, a woman with a dazed, faraway look in her eyes who owns the house. She has never protested when her son brought home a parade of long-haired—some of them similarly dazed—young boys and girls who came to this city because they heard the town was "Freaksville." Some came to work, others to play, and some to just hang out.

One of those hanging-out places is the front porch of the house, and as Richard and Cary approach the group sitting and lying on the steps, one emaciated young girl says with a giggle, "Hey, Richie, the pigs've been here looking for you."

"OK, cut the shit, man." Richard almost snarls at her.

"No shit at all," another boy says. "They said you better call the station as soon as you get here. Left the number. What you into, man?"

"I'll bet you he's one of those people who use . . . who use . . ."—the girl giggles again—". . . dope."

Richard flicks nonexistent hair out of his eyes and looks at the faces on the porch. "Cary, let's go over to the booth." On the way to the corner, Richard looks back at the girl. "Flaky bitch.

Married twice, abandoned her kid, and she says she's got her shit together. What a joke. That bitch."

The phone at the police station is answered after the first ring. "Somebody was out to my place looking for me. What's up?" Richard asks, trying to sound both impatient and cocky.

"Somebody?" the voice comes over the line. "A police officer or what?"

"Yeah, and I want to know why," he says, standing up straight in the booth.

"Exactly who is this?" the voice returns irately.

Richard hesitates. His bottom jaw goes slack and he looks to Cary. Cary, his back to Richard, is kicking cinders toward the street. Richard looks at the receiver.

"Well, who is this?"

"Richard . . . Richard Neumeyer."

"Hold on, Richard Newcastle."

"Neumeyer. N-E-U-M-E-Y-E-R."

"Richard Neumeyer, right?" the voice comes back brusquely. "You from Mariposa?"

"Yeah."

"Call your mommy."

"What do you mean, man?"

"We got a call from the Mohawk County police that says a Mrs. Neumeyer of 97 Birchwood in Mariposa put in an emergency call that we should get ahold of you and have you call home. So *call!*"

"What does she want?"

"C'mon, kid, if I knew what you kids were up to or what your mothers wanted, I'd write a book about it."

Richard hangs up the telephone, takes another dime out of his pocket and dials home. His mother accepts the charges, and Richard hears another click on the line as the extension is picked up.

"I got your message."

"No other way to reach you in a hurry," his mother returns coolly.

"OK, what's up?"

"Don't start—" his father begins.

Betty cuts him off. "We just wanted to know if you were coming home for Thanksgiving."

"Thanksgiving? When is that?"

"I'll send you a calendar. It's two weeks away."

"Well, what are you asking me now for?"

"We just don't do things the last minute, Richard. If you are coming home, we have to make arrangements for another person. It's not so simple as you think."

"Got a job," Richard says curtly. "Don't want to miss any work."

"You could drive up Wednesday night and back Thursday night," Betty says, her tone softening.

"I just did that last weekend, remember?"

"Are you doing your own cooking, Richie?"

"Yeah."

"I've been saving those dishes for the first of you kids who sets up an apartment. I wanted you to take them back, but you left so quick."

"Wasn't my idea. I wanted to stay overnight."

There is silence on both ends of the line. "Got a good job, by the way," Richard says. "Good guy. Doesn't show up half the time, so I just do my work and go home."

"Go home," Betty says under her breath. Then louder, "Is it cold?"

"Unfinished buildings. Yeah, my hands get cold once in a while, but it's good. Anything else?"

"Sure you don't want to make it home for Thanksgiving?"

"Ma, I ain't driving all day and all night."

"OK, OK. Call us when you can."

"Yeah, the pigs'll let me know when I'm supposed to."

The conversation over in Mariposa, Art heads toward the kitchen and finds Betty with her back to him, staring out the window into the night. "Maybe you can get some stuff together at the office tomorrow. Send him a package, Artie, and I'll bake some bread."

Art looks at the floor. "Yeah, I'll send him a bunch of those bouillon packets. Good for when it gets cold."

In Wilkes-Barre the glass door of the booth rattles as Richard charges onto the gravel. "They aren't going to see my ass for one hell of a long time."

"What they want anyhow?"

"If those pigs would have come up to the room I'd be busted right on the spot. Had half a pound of it up there last week."

"How much you make on that anyhow?"

"About thirty bucks plus the ounce for us."

"Say, was that your supplier that got busted in Philly?"

"Shit, no, man." Richard smiles boyishly. "That dude had a hundred and fifty pounds of stock. In orange crates! My guy lives here. He's a small-timer."

"They're busting people here too, Rich."

"If I get busted, I get busted. Give my parents a good chance to pay their boy a visit."

"You'll be going home, man, don't give me that. Just like everybody else."

"Listen, Cary," Richard says, grabbing his friend's arm, "not only are they not going to see me for Thanksgiving. Not even for Christmas and . . . you still going to the Mardi Gras, right? They won't see Richie-boy for a long time."

On the Saturday before Thanksgiving, Betty stands at the top of the stairs with a list in her hand.

"OK, what's first?" Art says, pulling an old sweater over his T-shirt.

"I have seven things, Artie, and if you do them all you won't have time for church tomorrow. The only other thing is Joanie's cheerleading practice in about an hour. Rehearsing for the big competition or something. Start with this wall, Artie. It's all smudgy."

"Richie's hands are all over it every time he goes downstairs," Art says, going into his small workshop to open a can of white paint.

Joan's playing of "Fiddler on the Roof" is interrupted by the ring of the telephone. She leaps off the piano bench, but her mother is already at the phone. Betty's eyes look toward the ceiling as the caller begins talking. Joan covers her mouth, so her laugh will not be heard.

"She's right here," Betty says curtly. "Could you hold on? I'll ask her." Betty looks at her daughter and in a voice meant to be heard over the phone says, "Mrs. Padavano wants to know if you have sold your twenty boxes of leaf bags."

The smile is gone from Joan's face. "No," she whines.

"No, she hasn't," Betty says over the phone. Her eyes again look to the ceiling. I'll ask her. Joan, are you going to?"

Joan shrugs her shoulders.

"She'll sell what she can," Betty says, "and I'm in the middle of something so I've got to go." Betty slams the receiver into the cradle. She glares at her daughter. "Listen, are you going to be in Camp Fire whole-assed or half-assed?"

"Mommy, Mrs. Padavano wants my life and I'm tired of it," Joan says, close to tears.

"Look at you, hair hanging down; you look tired. You're just in too many things. Some of them have to go. We want some time with you, too."

"I'm here all the time, Mommy; isn't that enough?"

"You're never here too much, honey," Betty says, her voice thickening. "You're all we have now."

"But Martha's at school and Richie won't stay away long," Joan says innocently.

"You're all we have now." Betty repeats herself.

Betty had planned to take down the curtains today and wash them, but suddenly she feels tired. She is silent as she plops onto the couch to sit virtually motionless for five minutes. Then she puts on a Kate Smith record that was one of her father's favorites and covers herself with a comforter and, dozing off, listens to the strong, sure voice sing "God Bless America." When the record is almost over her eyes open wide and she throws off the cover.

Ten minutes later she is hanging up the telephone receiver as Art trudges up the stairs, wiping some paint from the back of his hand. "What's next?" he says. "Who was it this time?"

"I just got in the mood and called my brother to tell him I love him. And he said, 'That's funny, I was just thinking about you and the same thing. I love you.' People just don't say that enough any more, Artie," Betty says softly. "It's all take, take, take, more, more, more—"

"Betty." He cuts her off. "I love you. I love you, and Joan is going to be late for rehearsal if I don't take her soon."

Toward evening, Betty's quiet mood turns even more somber. She does not feel like cooking, so she asks Art to take her and Joan to Antonio's, a well-known local Italian restaurant. In the bedroom, as she applies a layer of lipstick to her thin lips, she looks at Art's reflection in the mirror. Her blank look, which edges on the sorrowful, causes Art to move toward his silent wife. He smiles, reaches out to her and just as he is about to speak, Betty says, "I just don't care any more, Artie. I just want to get loaded tonight. I just want to forget everything."

"Baby, whatever you want," Art says, putting his hands on her shoulders.

"And I want to start right now with a Scotch sour," she says with determination in her voice.

At the restaurant she has a second Scotch sour before her veal parmigiana. With the Irish coffee that ends the meal in her hand, she finally becomes more relaxed and laughs readily at the drunken mailman, still in uniform, who staggers away from the bar and at the nervous young couple they know from church whose children are not behaving.

"Why did you marry me anyhow?" Betty says with the casualness of asking for the bread sticks to be passed.

"You were the prettiest girl at the party, what'd you expect?" Art says jokingly. "How about you?"

Betty's face is a comic mixture of seriousness and alcohol-induced good humor. "I loved you," she says slowly. "I wanted security. And, Artie, there was another reason too. You know that I was—"

"Joan, your eyes are glassy." Art turns toward his daughter. "Betty, that's enough Irish coffee for her."

"Artie, what did we really want out of marriage?"

"Kids, Betty, and we got them," Art replies quickly.

"Kids," Betty says, looking down at her plump hands resting on the white tablecloth, now soiled with tomato sauce and coffee stains.

"So we got everything we wanted and more, honey."

Betty looks up at her husband. "And just where are those children, Artie? All the sacrifices, all the suffering. Look at us, Artie; just over forty years old and we're alone."

"You still got me," Joan says perkily.

Neither parent speaks until Art clears his throat and says, "Where's the check, anyhow?"

Five days later a fourteen-pound turkey bronzed by hours of cooking sits on the kitchen table, having only given up one breast to the people who are sitting in the living room. Dishes of turnips, sweet potatoes, Grandmother Santangelo's cranberry sauce, stuffing and gravy sit on the dining room table as the women—Betty, Bridget, Grandmother and Joan—pick at the dates and nuts on the ornate plates and, except for Joan, sip on crème de menthe. Art and George doze in front of the television set as one of a parade of Thanksgiving Day football games is played out.

Bridget and George arrived some four and a half hours ago, at noon. Before sitting down to eat the family visited the cemetery and, holding onto this ethnic tradition, placed a blanket of pine boughs, purchased at a florist, on the grave of Grandfather Santangelo. The rest of the time has been spent talking and eating, with no one but George possessing an appetite to match the quantity of food prepared. Collect telephone calls were received from Richard and Martha, but even these did not generate much excitement.

Richard was at a friend's house, having duck for his Thanksgiving dinner. Betty repeated "duck" as if it were a forbidden meat, but otherwise the short talk was uneventful. Richard was going to see *Easy Rider* tonight with a girl he'd met. Betty said, "That's nice; is that the Walt Disney movie?"

Martha told of the new station wagon Barry Lancer had gotten. Barry, Mark, Martha and Pat are going to drive to the semiannual student-teacher meeting. Betty asked how Mark and Pat were and if Barry's children liked the puppets he had brought them from his Mariposa trip.

"We better get moving," Bridget says, stifling a yawn. "Our baby has been alone in the house all day without a thing to eat."

"Bridget, you just got here," Betty says with little conviction in her voice. "Road Runner will be all right."

"We buy him the best dog food already but he won't eat it, so Georgie stuffs little bits of steak or chops into the bowl so he has to burrow down for them. Wants to eat just like his mommy and daddy. Spoiled rotten, that baby."

"Aunt Brij, our cheerleading team came in third," Joan says, coming over to sit on her lap. "Lost second by one point because we got a poor grade in coordination. One girl stood up when she wasn't supposed to."

"Speaking of cheerleaders, you ought to see these Southern babes," George says as he watches the set through slitted eyes.

"When you left me at the Dupreys' the other night, Mommy," Joan says, "the boys were watching football and they did it all night long and I couldn't watch anything I wanted."

"Don't whine, Joan," Betty says. "Like I told you, the next time you go over there, you take along the portable and watch what you want."

A smile comes over Grandmother Santangelo's face. "Imagine, this girl has never known what it was to have less than two TVs in the house. We were so excited when we had one radio."

"I don't see why I just can't stay home anyhow when you go out," Joan says. "I'm old enough."

"You might be scared," her mother says. "There might be noises in the house and it probably wouldn't be anybody but you might think it was somebody. I hear of lots of robberies around here, and I don't want you in the house alone."

"Here?" Bridget says. "Didn't think it was allowed."

"It isn't," Betty says, slouching into her chair. "Some people just don't obey the law."

"How's Richie doing, anyhow?" Bridget asks.

Betty straightens up and looks down at her hands. "Says he doesn't have heat where he lives. They got an electric heater. Hear about fires with those things all the time. . . ." Her voice trails off. "I'm really not up to talking about him today. Especially today."

"OK, Brij, let's go before Road Runner tears the place apart," George says, beginning to pry himself from the soft clutches of the sofa.

"Can you sleep overnight when you come for Christmas?" Joan asks excitedly, hugging her aunt.

"I can't promise, honey. We might be having some relatives from the other side," she replies. "We'll have to see."

"But you do it every year," Joan says. "You close up the store and come here for Christmas Eve, and then we open the presents when we wake up. Aunt Brij"—she draws out the words—"you always do."

"Things can't always be the same," Betty says, getting up from the chair and smoothing the tunic over her slacks. "Traditions can just go so we can accommodate everybody's new lives."

With the closing of the front door after Bridget and George leave, the one person who has shown some flashes of holiday spirit flickers into conformity with the subdued tenor of life in the house at 97 Birchwood. Joan goes to the basement with her little plastic record player, sits on Richard's bed and puts on the one 45 she brought along. "Hey, Mr. Tambourine Man, play a song for me. . . ." Bob Dylan's scratchy voice comes up to the living room.

By the time Art gets back from taking Grandmother Santangelo home, Betty has cleaned off the table and the dishwasher is sloshing clean their best plates and glasses. She tells him not to take off his coat and quickly pulls a coat from the closet, and the two of them go outside to walk the dog. It is a crisp autumn evening with the temperature of the still air in the low 30s as Art and Betty walk down the deserted street under the leaf-stripped trees. Their heads are down as they walk, gloved hand in gloved hand, past the elegant stone houses on the corner, past the Cadillac parked in the next driveway. Puffs of vaporized air stream regularly from their mouths as they exhale.

BETTY: I just don't want to be disappointed any more. I can't take it, I can't bear disappointment. I'm forty-three years old and I have to realize that we have as much as we're ever going to have in life, that two of our children are gone and that's it. I've always been a mother and now I'm being phased out like an old-model car. I'm not skilled enough, smart enough to make the transition. Anyhow, if I tried to live a different life now, there would be so many chances it wouldn't work out. So why be disappointed again?

What can I say about Thanksgiving, 1972, except that I see my life disintegrating? Somebody might say, Wait, in a couple years when everybody is settled and married, you'll be celebrating Thanksgiving someplace else with grandchildren and everything. I'm sorry, but right now I can't see it. For me children have been everything. I would not want to live without them. I could learn to live without Artie, but not without them. I had a cousin who named her second child Richard, just after our Richie was born. My mother said it was bad luck. And wouldn't you know it, her Richard was killed in a motorcycle accident. These nights I just don't sleep; I think of Richard driving around on some slippery road in those mountains. I just don't want to think about it any more. . . .

"Remember, Artie, when you were in the hospital?" Betty suddenly says, looking up at her husband. "How you were about the nurses and everything?"

"I was chasing them or what?" Art says as he pulls his wife closer to him.

"Don't be silly. You wouldn't let them touch you. You didn't want them to bathe you or do anything for you. You always waited for me. I was the only one that could care for you. Oh, Artie, we were so possessive in those days."

"We still are, Betty."

"Well, it's going to be like old days again," Betty says, as if she didn't hear her husband. "All we got is each other. Those two kids leave us so vulnerable. We're cutting them loose, Artie; we're going to live for each other. It's all we got." Betty stops short.

"Joanie's only in the sixth grade, baby; we still got a way to go."

305

"Only a matter of time, Artie, and we have to start preparing ourselves; nobody else is looking out for us." There is bitterness in her voice. "Our family is over; all we have left is our marriage."

ART: The biggest thing when people get married is sex. The question of whether or not your marriage is going to make it is when the sex wears off, loses its gloss. The reason our marriage has worked out is that private is private. Nothing that happens in this house goes out of it, and all the families in our church look at us as if we were the ideal couple and didn't have a problem in the world. Let them think so. They don't have to know what's going on right now. We'll get through. We've been in stews before and things always worked out.

Betty is just more pessimistic than I am; she worries about everything. She always thinks that times past were better. She's suburb-oriented now, and she'd hate it back in the city. She's oriented to going into stores and having big, beautiful, wide aisles to walk around. And having white people to look at and not having to worry if she walks out the front door and down this dark street. She feels safe here.

So what can I say about our life? We got more than we expected. We got a family. We love each other and we have a happy marriage. What more could anybody want?

BETTY: What do we have to look forward to: old age and no pension? But I still say I'm glad we scrimped for the kids, glad we did without. I want them to live life while they're young. If Joanie's braces cost nine hundred dollars we'll get them; I want her to have the perfect teeth the other kids didn't have. I'll give them as much as I can now and hope there's something when I die to leave them. I want to have pretty glass figurines and knickknacks, lace doilies—things I never had—so they can have them. I'd be happy to have them fight over my things when I'm dead. My teeth are rotting away, but would I get them fixed before we got Joan's piano? I'll be toothless before I'll deprive them.

But the house. The house! Supposed to be the dream castle, and all it did was keep me imprisoned. I'm free of responsibilities of children, but I'm not really free because I can't get to a job or to a course or anything. I don't know anybody who's so stupid she can't drive— except me. Artie said, "Don't worry, plenty of people around you will drive. You won't be isolated." What a joke! I don't really know a soul here. If I had an emergency and had to go someplace I'd have to call a cab.

"Maybe we'd have been a lot happier if we never left Tulip," Betty says as she and Art crunch across the cinders marking one driveway on their street. "Maybe we should have even stayed in the city; at least I was in my own element there. I could shrink right back into it now that I don't have any children."

"C'mon, Betty, you're talking crazy." Art reaches for his cigarettes. "You couldn't wait to get out here to the green grass and shrubs. You still got kids. This will pass over. And anyway, where we lived is a ghetto now."

"I'm just too young to be on the shelf already. If the kids would be leaving home in four years instead of now, I could be emotionally prepared for it."

"You'd never be prepared for it," he says. He feels his wife staring at him, so he adds, "And I wouldn't either. Look at it this way: our bills are going to be less and we'll be able to get things and go places we never could have when the kids were growing. This is the best time of our lives. We're just starting to live. You'll have it great."

BETTY: Artie, Artie, why didn't you give me real encouragement? You just left me to bitch about things, but you never gave me the push I needed. I don't know, maybe you know me better than I think. You probably know I'd rather not get involved in situations that might not work out, that might hurt me.

But with my children, I pushed them and I'm not ashamed to say it. I really worked on encouraging the kids to want more and more out of life. With Joanie, I think I perfected it. I wanted the kids to be secure. I wanted Martha to have pretty clothes because I had to wear ugly glasses and hand-me-down clothes all my life. It has everything to do with my insecurities. Even today I'd rather have my pretty dishes than go to the dentist.

I'm honest; I think that's a mark of getting ahead in the world.

So we've made it. It's just a little hollow on a day like this. I'm just happy I have God to pray to, because without that I'd never make it through.

Fifteen minutes after they left the house, the Neumeyers are back at 97 Birchwood. Betty trudges up the concrete steps and grabs onto the frail-looking iron railing on the small porch as if she were out of breath. She leans against the aluminum storm door and runs her hand over the initial "N" at its midsection. She looks at her husband, but her gaze is fixed not on his eyes but at a point some ten feet in back of his head.

"Let's go in, Betty," he says gently.

"Artie, just tell me one thing. I really need to know the honest answer. Did we make it all right? I mean . . . I mean, was it worth it all, Artie? Be honest," she pleads.

"Look at this beautiful house. Look at the three kids. We got health, we got more than our parents ever dreamed anybody could have. Sure, it was worth it. Some troubles along the way, like everybody else, but it was worth everything we put into it."

"Are you being honest?"

"Sure. What do you think? Let me turn the question around."

Betty reaches for the doorknob. "To be honest, Artie, tonight I just don't know if anything matters."

19

Getting Ready

"An Oklahoma pastor was driving through his town with an out-of-town preacher and his guest noticed that the Christmas decorations were up awfully early. 'Yes,' the pastor replied, 'our Chamber of Commerce loves that Christ child.'"

Laughter ripples over the congregation at Parkside United Methodist Church as Firth MacIntosh begins his sermon for the first Sunday in Advent. The smiles that Betty and Art Neumeyer exchange are soon replaced by more serious looks as the pastor delves into the real topic: boredom.

"There's going to be a man walking on the moon this week, and we're not even interested any more. . . . We are fighting a war we don't even believe in, but we don't care enough to end it. . . . We go to work at jobs that we hate, and yet we're scared to death of losing them. . . . But God isn't bored with us, hasn't been and won't be. . . . He sent his only begotten Son to earth, and he continually gets mixed up in our lives to show us that he still cares. . . ."

Near the end of the service, the worshipers shuffle silently over the red carpeting to the chancel railing to receive the tiny vials of grape juice and the cubes of bread that Betty, with a surgeon's precision, has prepared. As the congregation finishes "Ask Ye What Great Thing I Know," the final hymn, Betty turns to her husband. The tranquil "Sunday morning in church" look melts into a frown. "Still gets his half-hour sermon in, even on communion Sunday. Somebody has to let him know about that. It's quarter after."

After lunch on this bright but chilly day in early December Joan and Betty drop hints ("Bet the squirrels in the park are hungry today"—Joan) that evolve into a more direct attack ("The next man I marry isn't going to be sports-minded"—Betty) that Art should leave the televised football game and take them for a ride. Art smiles lazily at their prodding but stays planted on the sofa in front of the television set.

Later, as Betty salts and prepares the flank steak they are going to have for supper, she calls out to Art, "Remember, when Martha passed her driving test, we hung out the American flag? When Richie calls next time we should tell him we're hanging it out for him."

"And he got accepted because he was smart," Joan says proudly.

"No, honey," Betty says evenly, "it isn't because he's smart. He just had to apply. They have to accept him in the state university system."

"And he's lucky it's that way," Art says. "He's not exactly the sterling student. I don't know why he applied anyhow. If he's not ready to come home, he's not ready to settle down."

"I'm sorry I brought him up," Betty says, "so let's just drop it, OK?"

After dinner Joan brings out the Methodist hymnal and sets it on the tablecloth near the Advent wreath where four candles, shortened by a few years' use, stand in a wreath of artificial poinsettias. Since the children were young, the family has conducted short services on the four Sundays of Advent. When Martha and Richard were home, they would devise the service. Now the responsibility is Joan's. She does a few short readings listed for the First Sunday in Advent from the hymnal and then gives to her mother and father Sunday school booklets that have the hymn she's chosen.

Betty starts out strongly in her high voice, with the first stanza of "Holy, Holy, Holy, Lord God Almighty," and Art and Joan follow her lead. By the third stanza, the three voices have lost their fervor and by the fourth they are singing so softly the sound barely carries across the living room to the front door. Joan blows out the candle, the shortest, before heading for Martha's room to watch television. Betty sits quietly at the table as Art gets up and goes for a cigarette.

"Artie, did you take the leaf out of here?" she says pressing in on the sides of the table.

"It's out, Betty. That's as small as it gets."

"Too big any more," she says quietly. Then she walks over to the stereo and takes the family's seven Christmas albums from the back of the cabinet. She puts the stack of records on the spindle, and soon "White Christmas" fills the front half of the house. The First Sunday in Advent ends with a medley of Christmas songs and hymns.

On Tuesday afternoon, Betty accepts the collect call for anyone "from Mr. Richard Neumeyer." Joan runs to the extension to hear her mother' first words, reminding Richard that he was supposed to call in the evenings so his father could talk. "I just got down here, so while I thought of it, I called," Richard says, his voice straining with the same exhilaration his mother heard when he called from California more than half a year before. "By the way, I'm calling from Key West. Mom, you there? Key West in Florida."

Ten minutes later Betty puts down the phone. "It's funny, Joanie, I knew he was going to leave Pennsylvania, I just had that feeling. He's so far away now. Maybe he won't be home for Christmas." Betty Neumeyer looks out her kitchen window to a darkening December afternoon.

"Oh, Mommy, he said he was going to come home."

"He used the word 'try.' "

"He'll be home. Just like every year. Anyway, he sounded kind of lonely to me."

Betty looks around her kitchen—at the cupboards, the calendar, Martha's class schedule on the refrigerator door, the electric range —and is silent. A slight smile appears, first in the pouching of her full cheeks, then spreading slowly to her eyes and blossoming into a full-fledged grin. "Joanie, this is our last official Christmas together," she says suddenly as she takes her daughter by the shoul-

311

ders. "Next year Martha will be teaching in Kansas and who knows where Richie will be. But this year, he will come home. I know it! We are going to be together. No more blahs for your mommy. And we're going to make it the best Christmas ever. Ready?"

Joan jumps into her mother's arms, and Betty holds her cheek to cheek. "What's first, Mommy?" she asks, her eyes wide.

Art is surprised that night to have his wife and daughter meet him right inside the front door with kisses and hugs, telling him to hurry for dinner so they all can go shopping to launch the drive toward "our last Christmas together."

"Thought we had just decided," he says to Betty after Joan goes to give Black Beauty her evening feeding, "it was you and me—and Joanie—for a while. We were too vulnerable. We had to cut the kids loose and live for ourselves."

"What kind of foolish talk is that with Christmas coming up?" Betty says impatiently. "I was just in a down mood. It's going to be just like old times, Artie."

"And what if our darling Richie doesn't come home? Don't build yourself up and then be disappointed, Betty."

Betty turns to confront her husband face to face. "Go ahead," she says quietly, "stand there and tell me my boy isn't coming home for Christmas."

For the next few days Joan bows out of Camp Fire and other after-school programs and comes running breathlessly into the house at three thirty, eager to help her mother. Art digs out boxes of Christmas decorations as the infectious spirit of the household overcomes even his skepticism. After Betty tells her mother of the Christmas plans, Grandmother Santangelo promises to come by on Sunday and make some of the apple pies her grandchildren like so much.

By the weekend the upright freezer in the garage is packed. The newspapers that have filled its vacant spaces, thus saving electricity, have been put aside. There is eggplant parmigiana and lasagna with sweet Italian sausage, two of Richard's favorite dishes; frozen shrimp that will go into shrimp creole, one of

Martha's favorites; pot roast and rolled roast and ham and turkey; three frozen apple pies with grandmother's homemade crust to be thawed and baked the day before Christmas. In the cupboards are bags of potatoes and turnips; also the makings for spaghetti and meatball sauce, Christmas cookies—which are never baked until Martha comes home—and chicken soup, which Martha says she "loves as much as any good Jewish daughter."

Art has already wrapped the frilly aluminum-foil fringe around the banister and laced it with tiny white bulbs that send off twinkling, shimmering light. The revolving light is in the front window and the colored gels give a bright, multicolored proclamation to the outside world. The imitation Scotch pine Christmas tree is in place, the color-coded branches all in their proper order on the green-painted bark, each branch a trifle shorter than the one below so that the overall effect is that of a perfect tree. Art has painstakingly arranged over two hundred lights so that no part of the tree is over- or under-lit. Decorations, some dating back to their first Christmas together in the North End, are mixed in with those accumulated over the years, some of them made by the children, some of them bought. Other decorations are still in boxes; the Neumeyers used to have another tree in the recreation room, but for the last few years they haven't used it. The recreation room, which Betty once visualized as a family gathering spot, is now only used to house the pool table and an occasional guest.

Also by the weekend, Betty has completed mailing the eighty-five cards she's sending this year, and the Neumeyers have begun to receive cards from friends. Included in their mail Saturday was the telephone bill, a mail-order house circular, three cards, and a letter from Richard. It had been sent from Pennsylvania but was delayed by the holiday mail. Art takes the letter from the kitchen counter, looks at the address, "Family, 97 Birchwood, Mariposa," and reads it again.

> Cary, Sid and I are leaving for Florida tonight. We got word on Wednesday that everybody had to move out of the house because the neighbors say the place is a "hippie

pad" and they have been in touch with the police. I still hope to be home for Christmas, but don't worry about the technical problems.

Art quotes the last line to Betty from memory as he dumps out the box of old photographs onto the dining room table: "Please don't rationalize why I'm moving around. It's gonna be this way for a while, I am sure."

"And what is this place, the resting place before he launches off again? Eight months out of the last year that kid has been bumming around; what does he think is going on? *Betty*, are you listening to me?"

Betty and Joan are checking the cookie recipe to see if they have enough ingredients for several batches. "Yes, Artie, yes," she says absentmindedly. "Check the vanilla, Joan; we were low on that."

"Why doesn't somebody pay some attention to me around here once in a while?" Art says, tossing a grade-school picture of Richard back onto the pile.

"I am, I am, Artie," Betty says.

"Then come out here and tell me what you want up."

"Martha will be so excited, Artie," she says, wiping her hands on a paper towel. "Every Christmas as soon as she gets in the house she looks for what's different. We've always wanted a picture wall. Here, put this one up first, in the middle." It is Betty's father, a 1920-vintage sepia tone of an impressive young man with the same high forehead and slightly puffed cheeks that his son has today.

The selection of photos made, Art begins to pound tiny nails into the wall. When he comes to Richard's high school graduation picture—the only one they could find where he was smiling—Art says, "How about here, Betty?" He puts Richard's picture over the thermostat and turns it facing the wall.

Betty looks at him sadly. "Come on, Artie, you love him more than that."

Art looks at the picture of his son and lays it gently on the table.

314

"I even wonder if he's alive," Betty says.

"The car is registered to this address, so don't worry about it."

"He could be dead someplace and somebody else could be driving the car."

"Enough of this dead talk," Art says impatiently. "We're getting ready for Christmas. I feel like a yo-yo; don't know whether you're up or down any more."

"Next year it won't be so bad when there'll only be the three of us home, Artie," Betty continues in a somber tone. "My mother is getting on in years, and we're not so young ourselves. You never know. I'll just be ready for it next year if we say this year is it, the last Christmas together. Artie, we don't have a long life in front of—"

"Betty—" Art interrupts, but the ring of the telephone silences them both.

Betty grabs for the receiver. Her smile and "Yes I will" sends Art to the extension.

"School is out on Thursday so on Friday I'm going to Kansas City," Martha says excitedly shortly after the conversation begins. "Pat's going to look at where the kids live while they're in the program."

"Oh, that's nice," Betty says reservedly. "What—what kind of school will it be?"

"Mother, in the inner city of Kansas City it isn't exactly Mariposa High."

"Just be careful and ask a lot of questions as to what it involves, Martha," Betty says. "We're all ready with the cookie stuff. Do you know what time you'll be getting in?"

Betty hangs up a few minutes later. Art walks into the kitchen, shaking his head. "Why does she want to go and do something like that? What is she trying to prove?"

"I think it's a good idea, Artie," Betty says, looking him straight in the eyes. "It gets young teachers into the ghetto schools where they don't have everything instead of them going to a nice white school. Then they'd never want to go to the ghetto schools where they have less."

"I don't understand it. Tony Napoli's daughter's the same way. With all their money to send her to American University, she's teaching in a black school in Washington. I just don't see why Martha's got to go into a high school where the kids she'll be teaching will be bigger than she is."

"Artie, if you teach high school English, some of the students will be bigger no matter where."

"You know what I mean."

"You mean that Martha has some stuff in her," Betty says caustically. "If I had the gumption Martha has when I was twenty-two, I wouldn't be sitting across this table from you."

"She's twenty-one."

Betty's eyes narrow. "You know what I mean."

A few nights later Betty comes home from a church meeting to find a note from Art that she should wake him when she gets in. "Your son, the wandering coconut merchant, wants us to wire him fifty dollars tomorrow," Art says, his face buried in the pillow.

"Well, how are we supposed to do that?" Betty says irately.

"Damn it, I don't know." Art turns over to face his wife. "With the train strike on I already get up at five. When in the hell am I going to do it? Ungrateful little—"

"What did he say on the phone?"

"He hit another car, had to pay a fine and was out of money. He needs money for gas."

"To come home?"

"He seemed to imply that."

"Imply?"

"Betty, I did not tape-record the conversation," Art says, turning his face back into the pillow.

Betty slips out of her shoes and stands quietly, her arms crossed, looking at the far wall. "Where is the Western Union office?" she says.

"Up past Main Line, in the village."

"And then what?"

"Richie will check the Key West office tomorrow. Western Union said it would take three or four hours to get there."

"Oh, you called to check it out?" Betty says, running the zipper down the back of her dress. She is now smiling.

"Yes."

"Did he want us to send in the deposit for college?"

"Your son said he was not going to college. To quote him: 'Save your money; don't send it in.' Claims when he gets home he's going to get a job."

"Artie, who's going to hire a creep like that? He'll have hair down his back."

"He's going into the coconut business."

"What?"

"Says he can get coconuts three for a dollar down there. Going to load up the trunk of his car and make a killing up here."

"Wonderful, just wonderful," Betty says indignantly. "They're twenty-nine cents apiece in the stores."

The next morning, as Betty begins the two-mile walk to the Western Union office in Mariposa, Richard shakes the grass off his sleeping bag and hangs it in the hot sun to dry out the night's dampness. He runs his hand through his hair, then winces when a snarl stops him. His friend Cary offers him a doughnut and Richard bites hungrily into it, leaving crumbs and flakes of glaze on the scraggly growth of his mustache and beard.

When he left Pennsylvania over a week ago it marked still another dream gone awry. The mobs of people that he once enjoyed seeing at the rooming house had begun to annoy him. Richard would come home from a day of work to find his room filled with people, his food often gone and no time or space to prepare a decent meal. "It stinks, this town," he told Cary and Sid as they left Wilkes-Barre. The three boys drove all day and night to get to Tallahassee, where a girl they knew from Pennsylvania had an apartment that they were going to use. When he opened the front door to the apartment, Richard drew back. The stench from the excrement of the dogs and cats the girl had left behind was

317

staggering. The boys slept in the car that night before heading farther south.

A few hours out of Tallahassee, the temperature suddenly rose, orange groves and truck farms became numerous and Richard began to feel better about the trip. He and his friends picked fruit and vegetables along the road and gorged themselves all the way down to Key West. When they arrived there, it was 80 degrees. Richard began walking around the city in his bare feet to take in the sights. To him, it was another Hollywood. Sixty-year-old men sitting with their dogs by the piers passing a marijuana cigarette. Heavily made-up women, older than his grandmother, with sagging skin exposed by skimpy bikinis. Long-haired boys and girls dozing in the sun, high on dope.

Richard's euphoria in this new and exotic setting lasted three days. Once he paid the rent at a campground on one of the Florida keys, he had about $70 and his companions had less. Then the freak accident all but exhausted his bankroll. While pulling off the road to pick up a hitchhiker on his way back into Key West, Richard hit a parked car. Damages to the car and the traffic fine left him with less than $20, now fast diminishing.

"Let's go into Key West and see what's going on," Cary says.

"Naw, we don't want to have to go in twice," Richard says, screwing up his face.

"They going to send the money?"

"Better. It's mine. And listen, they'd do anything to get my ass home for Christmas."

"Going?"

"Thinking about it."

"Bullshit, man, you're going for sure."

"Don't bug me, Cary. If I go, I go. I'll see what's happening around here."

"C'mon, let's go for a drive or something. I just don't want to sit around another day."

"I'm not using up my gas just for a drive. I'm going into Western Union this afternoon. And no sooner. We'll go for a ride then."

"OK, OK."

"Listen, man, you were the one that said it was all happening down here. We drive all day, all night. So what's happening?"

"We met those chicks. That Merrylee is hot for you. What the hell you want, man?"

"I want something to happen."

"You were telling your old lady like you were having a ball."

"Yeah, a ball." Richard shrugs. "It's a drag. Hey, what day is today, anyhow? The date, what's the date, man?"

Art comes into the house after the long drive home from work on Friday, December 15, and looks up the stairs. He can smell Betty's "football casserole"—a dish with pork and beans, ground beef, brown sugar and spices—which is sitting on top of the range, but his wife is not in the kitchen. Black Beauty's tail beating against the wall as she wags it furiously is the only sound he hears. He puts his book down, takes off his coat and goes into the bedroom. "Betty," he calls out. "Betty!"

"Be right up." A small voice comes up from the basement. Betty slowly trudges up the stairs and into the kitchen.

"What were you doing down there?"

"Don't really know, Artie. Went to get something and I just sat down. I've had a terrible day. Pam Brown—"

"Try being cooped up with Frank after spending a day listening to Mort give his opinions on everything from the President to dirty movies. Frank. I'll be glad when the strike is over and he goes on his train and I'm on mine. Some people shouldn't be together too much."

"The same thing. I was thinking the same thing. Pam . . ."

"Frank . . ." Their frustrated voices block out each other.

"Go ahead, Artie, you always tell your story shorter."

"Frank was on this big kick about education. It was a waste of time. It was a waste of money. Why go to college when you can't get a job when you get out? I told him that a person could go to college and take liberal arts for four years and then work in a gas station and he would be better off. And if he wanted to

319

be an engineer, it would only be two more years. The Browns were too cheap to send their kids to school; now they want to knock us. I even told him that regardless of a job a person got, that knowledge had its own value. That's exactly what I said: knowledge has its own value."

"Oh, Artie, I'm so proud of you," Betty says, throwing her arms around her husband. "And you should have reminded him about the two thousand dollars they're spending on Sylvia's wedding just to keep up with the Joneses. He's just miffed because Martha isn't going to spend over three hundred dollars for travel, a gown, flowers and some fancy restaurant rehearsal dinner just to be in the grand wedding."

"She's not coming back for sure?"

"Hell, no, she's not. And in five years Sylvia's going to have two kids and a suitcase that was used once. Martha will have an education behind her. Maybe she'll have a husband or a man. Maybe a family. The Browns? There's just one layer to them. There's no complexity to their lives. They programmed themselves and their kids to believe just a certain way. Those kids are not going to fall very far from the tree."

"They're so happy that Sylvia and Bart are going to have three-hundred-dollar-a-month payments on a house right off the bat. That's supposed to settle them down. Ha! They talk about Sylvia and Bart like they were the couple of the century. Every night he's off he's on a barstool up at the Jade Room. He's a real boozer. They're just putting their heads in the sand."

"Now it's my turn, Artie," Betty says, rubbing her hands along her arm. "I think I'm going through an identity crisis with Pam. Remember when she was going through that bad time with her sister?" Art looks at her blankly. "You know, her sister is very competitive and she was trying to outdo Pam for her mother's love. Anyway, I was very sympathetic. She always said she couldn't have made it through that without me. So I started talking about Rich a little bit and that things were a little rough with the children getting older and everything. Like we talked about the other night. Well, did she rub my nose in it! I told her if Rich got home for Christmas he wouldn't have time to shop for everybody, and she turned around and told me about the nice sewing basket Gerard is giving Sylvia.

"She brought out those sugar ball cookies and told me to have some, that they were delicious, so delicious. I don't know what got into me, Artie, but I said, so snotty, 'Yes, I know it's my recipe.' Then she brought out this book report their youngest did at home because he didn't have time in school. Used the encyclopedia and everything. It just kept on building in me, and without even thinking I snapped back that Joan didn't have to bring things home. Her teacher was more efficient and they're able to do everything in school. What is it, Artie?" Betty says, going into the kitchen to get the casserole. "Have our children taken our lives in such different directions?"

"Just proves to me to keep family problems to ourselves."

"That was nothing. Got a call from Brij today. Oh, Artie, this Christmas just isn't going to work out!" Betty's voice is becoming congested, which is usually a prelude to tears.

"Why do things have to be so complicated?" Art says, his face contorted, a mixture of mounting anger and frustration.

"They can't get anybody to sit with their precious dog and they can't leave him overnight, so they're not coming Christmas Eve. Now Brij wants to leave up there at five in the morning and get here at seven. All the cooking I've been doing. For what? All we can have is a big breakfast. What kind of Christmas meal is that? I told her not to make it before eight. The hell with them. We're not getting up in the middle of the night just to fit into their schedule."

"That damned, worthless dog."

"I'm glad Martha's coming home tomorrow. She'll be quite the lady this time. A senior. I need somebody to talk to."

Martha arrives at the airport the next afternoon to find a tearful mother, a younger sister bubbling with enthusiasm for the holiday ahead and a father who at first maintains his distance but who eventually walks out to the parking lot with his arm over his daughter's shoulder.

On Saturday, Sunday and Monday, cookies are made, mounds of

turnips eaten by Martha, old friends called and gossip exchanged. Late Monday night, with the rest of the family in bed, Martha brings her mother up to date on her life since August.

"We've had some snowball fights and good old Martha gets rolled most of the time. . . . Everybody's been a little crazy this year, I don't know why. . . . Had a fifties dance; God, it was fantastic. Big Bopper music like 'Chantilly Lace.' Everybody was wearing white socks and saddle shoes and the guys had baggy pants. This one guy had a jar of Vaseline in his pocket and kept gopping it on and slicking down his hair."

Betty looks up from her empty teacup, glances at the clock and then fixes her gaze on her daughter. "What about that boy . . . that man, the adviser, the one who came here this summer."

Martha's eyes, which had been dancing with the excitement of the happier times of the semester, are immediately dulled by her mother's halting words.

"I really got to see inside the teacher group this term," she begins slowly. "Backbiting, infighting, really ugly things. . . . Barry and Lacey really had the hots for each other, and then this other guy who wanted Barry's job started spreading even more filth about them. So Barry broke that off and said he would have to, and I quote, 'maintain some distance from the students.' And then Mr. Mark Hard tells me, and I quote, 'If we can't be lovers, then I don't want to be friends.' Mommy, I'm just sick of the whole bunch of them. Nobody is what they say they are. I'm looking forward so much to practice teaching."

Betty looks up again at the clock. It is close to midnight. "Your father isn't too happy about the Kansas City business, but—"

"Yeah, about that—" Martha cuts in, then stops abruptly.

"—but if you think you'll be safe. Don't forget, Pat is teaching grade school and you're going to be in high school with boys bigger than you are."

"Been thinking about all that," Martha says, biting her knuckle. "I'm not going to go into the program."

Betty is silent for a moment. "It's probably better, honey. Really. You really might have gotten into something just too much."

322

"I hate myself for it, Mommy. All the big talk about helping people, and here I am."

"Honey, even the white students need help. You'll be helping them just as much."

"When I watched McGovern get beat by your friend Nixon, I cried that night. And I cried after I decided not to go into the program. I really bawled, Mother."

"It's late; let's go to bed. It'll look better in the morning."

Martha Neumeyer sits at the kitchen table alone, in silence. Her hands are on her face, which this last semester has cleared and tonight gives evidence of only a few fading blemishes. Her fingers run slowly through her new shag haircut.

MARTHA: Barry and Lacey were screwing all through the convention, and then good old Martha goes back to Kansas in August and where does she end up? At Barry's house, of course. With his wife and two kids too. One night she went out and Barry and I took the kids out for ice cream, gave them baths. It was like playing house. I really had a good time, and I knew the next morning that soon I wasn't going to be satisfied with just playing house. I could really see why he was bored with his wife. Totally unenthusiastic person he married when he was in college. He moved on to other things and she stayed the same.

I found myself hoping he'd start talking seriously about a divorce. And I knew it was time to bow out or get into real trouble. Imagine what that one would do at home. I'm out there getting my dumb education—which is an escape in a way anyhow—and then I link up with a married man to boot. How can I get into situations like this? And I knew I was the latest in a string of seven or eight chippies he had met through the association, and I said enough. It's tough because he's a great guy. I even found out I liked drying dishes with him.

By midweek, Martha has done her shopping and the final Christmas preparations have been made. Presents have been wrapped and hidden throughout the house so other members of the family will not be tempted to rattle or poke them in hopes of finding out what is within. Although the Neumeyer children are now older, presents are still kept out of sight until Christmas morning.

Also, by midweek, most of the plans Martha has made for the holiday time at home have not materialized. One friend is now engaged and isn't interested in going out to a local bar with Martha. Another has come up with a flurry of excuses: trimming the tree, too tired, going out with her mother. On Thursday night, after finishing the last of a pack of cigarettes she bought that morning and tossing aside a book she has been reading, Martha says to her mother, "Maybe I'll go back to Kansas for New Year's. If I'm stuck home on New Year's Eve, I'm going to commit suicide."

Betty puts down the newspaper. "Why does it have to be this way?" she says, a hurt tone in her voice. "Christmas, New Year's, used to be so good." The front door opens and Art comes in after his second night of bowling this week, having been called in to substitute in the church league. "Martha's going back right after Christmas, Artie."

"*Mother!* Don't blow things out of proportion. I just said I might go back a couple days early. Good God, you misunderstand everything."

Tears fill Betty's eyes. "Why don't you go back tonight if you're in such a hurry? If you think it's so boring to be with your family. We don't need either of you kids. We'll take you right to the airport now, won't we, Artie?"

"Come on, come on, everybody, calm down," Art says. "Betty, it's late, let's go to bed. Tomorrow it will all look better."

"That's your answer every time, Artie. Put it off."

"I'm not going anyplace, Mother," Martha says softly. "Let's all go to bed."

On Friday, a phone call early in the day brings good news. Bridget's mother and father have to work Christmas Eve at the children's home where they live and can take care of Road Runner. Bridget and Frank will come on Christmas Eve, as has been the custom.

Later in the afternoon a collect call comes from either Virginia or Delaware, Betty forgets which, she is so elated. Richard is on his way home. He says he will probably be home sometime tomorrow, December 23. As she puts down the receiver, she calms herself for a moment, long enough to close her eyes and say a short prayer. Then she shrieks, "Martha, Joan! He's coming!"

20

"Our Last
Christmas Together"

ON FRIDAY, DECEMBER 23, Betty lingers at home until she has just enough time to walk to her one-o'clock appointment at the hairdresser. Once there she has been shampooed and rinsed when she hears Miriam, one of the beauticians, telling a caller that Betty can't come to the phone. But before the caller has a chance to leave a number, Betty, her hair dripping from beneath a towel, grabs the receiver.

It is, as she has hoped, Richard.

Miriam hurries Betty through a set and drying and less than half an hour later Richard is outside to pick up his mother.

"I hugged him and he hugged me back," she excitedly tells Art that evening when he comes home from work.

Art looks down at the smudge on the rug at the top of the stairs and proceeds to hang up his coat. "You can tell he's home," he says flatly.

Joan and Martha screamed with delight when they first saw their brother that afternoon. Their mother cried. But tonight as Art walks about the living room and kitchen and his son remains a floor away, lying passively on his bed, reading a health food magazine, each knows the other is in the house; neither is willing to make the first move.

Finally, it is time for dinner. Betty motions to Art with her head and a smile. He knows what she is trying to tell him, so he lights a cigarette and goes into the basement. The sound of rubber heels on linoleum is audible in Richard's bedroom, but he does not look up as his father approaches the room and stands in the doorway. Art inhales deeply. "Supper's on, Richie. Hungry?" he says in a monotone.

"Yeah, wow, starving," Richard says, leaping out of bed and coming toward the door. Art reaches for his son's hand. They shake hands in silence. Richard moves past his father, ready to bound up the stairs.

"Same rules," his father says dryly. "Put a shirt on for supper."

As the family digs into the steaming mounds of spaghetti spread with Betty's mildly flavored sauce and topped with meatballs, the talk dances about the week's events as if Richard had never been gone.

"Thought we were going to see a walkout on Sunday during the pastor's prayer about the war," Betty says.

"Should stay out of politics," Art responds.

"I read we dropped more bombs in a month on Vietnam than we did in the whole Second World War," Martha says. "Geez, we're just making bigger holes over there. Nothing left to bomb."

"Creep Nixon," Richard says with a sly smile on his face.

"You should talk about creeps, Richie," Art says. "You didn't even bother to come back to vote for your wonderful McGovern."

Betty quickly switches to Christmas shopping and relates how Francine Duprey noticed that "nobody spoke English" at Sav-Mor, a discount department store. "She said they were Puerto Ricans and every different kind of race. Where are they all coming from?"

"Wipe that smirk off your face, Richard." Art almost shouts at his son. "Now that you're home, show a little respect for people."

"Merry Christmas," Richard says softly.

After the meal, with Richard downstairs, the three women of the family spontaneously converge on Art. Joan's plea is first. "Daddy, if you're mean to Richie, he's going to go away and we won't have Christmas together."

"I didn't come home for all these hassles, Daddy, and if it's like this I'm . . . I'm taking the next plane back."

"See, Daddy, see?" Joan says plaintively.

Betty has tried to speak, but after her daughters are finished she does nothing more than look at her husband and then turn away, a hurt look on her face.

"I think you're being very obnoxious to him," Martha adds. She takes Joan by the shoulder, and they go downstairs to talk to their brother.

Art lights his after-dinner cigarette, thinks for a moment, then looks at his wife. "I'm not saying anything about his long, filthy hair. I'm not saying anything that he blew hundreds of dollars and then had to cry for help from home. But if he's going to live here—even for a while—he's going to live by our rules and he's going to talk with respect."

"OK, Artie, OK, but can't we just take it easy until Christmas is over at least? Please, honey." Betty drags out the words. "This is our last Christmas together. Let's make it one that everybody remembers with a warm spot in their hearts."

"Do you see the clothes—the rags—he's wearing? Just tell me what he's going to wear tomorrow night. He's not going out with us like that."

"Do you want him to go to church or not?" Betty says, looking out the kitchen window into the darkness outside.

"Of course."

On the day before Christmas, Art, Betty and Martha take Joan to the Dupreys for a piñata party and return home by midafternoon. Art takes the television set to the recreation room to watch a football game while the female members of the family make final preparations for that night and the next day. One of Grandmother's presents is still to be wrapped. A huge baking dish of lasagna and an apple pie are taken out of the freezer to thaw. Joan will sing in the choir tonight, so Martha helps her wash her brown hair, which almost reaches to her waist.

Betty, on her way upstairs from the freezer, smiles at Richard as he comes out of his room. "Look at those ribs. I'll bet you don't weigh a pound over a hundred."

"You want to bet? I'm not that skinny." He smiles boyishly back at her.

"Get out the scale. I'll give you a dollar for every pound over a hundred."

Richard pulls the scale out from under his bed and steps on. The needle flickers, then settles at 140.

"Wait a minute," Betty says, playfully pushing him off. She gets on the scale herself but as Richard looks down to check her weight she jumps off as if the scale were electrically charged. "Oh, no, you don't. I'm porky but I don't weigh that much. This shag rug is throwing it off. Put it out on the linoleum."

Richard is laughing loudly as he puts the scale on the floor outside the recreation room. He gets on and the needle stops at 120. "That will be twenty dollars, please."

"Is my credit good?" Betty says.

"Not for long."

Richard bounds up the stairs and Betty is left standing by the scale with a huge smile on her face. She glances at Art to find him looking at her over the television set. He shakes his head slowly. "How could you get rooked into a deal like that?"

Betty's smile is her answer.

Since they moved to the suburbs, the Neumeyers have made it a practice to have their Christmas Eve meal in a restaurant. This year, because Joan must be at church before the seven-o'clock service, Art has told his wife and family they must leave at five. With the early hour he has not felt it necessary to make reservations at Billie's, a more expensive restaurant they only go to on special occasions.

It is four thirty and Joan and Martha are dressed, Betty is almost ready and Art, who has already picked up Grandmother Santangelo, stands at the Christmas tree, trying to find the burned-out bulb on a darkened strand. Richard trudges slowly up the stairs, his jeans hanging loosely off his bony hips, a towel over his shoulder.

Art wheels around. "Are you going to take a shower now?" The tone of his question stops the chatter between Joan and Martha and their grandmother.

"Yes, sir," Richard says cavalierly. He walks slowly toward the bathroom and locks the door behind him.

Betty, who came out of the bedroom when she heard the tone of Art's voice, immediately heads for her husband. "Art, this is Christmas. Let's all relax and enjoy—"

"So we can sit around and wait for him to take a shower," Art says, the words spilling out of his mouth. "He sits around all day; why does he have to take a shower now? Why? And what is he going to wear, Betty? Those crummy jeans?"

A few minutes before five Richard saunters across the living room running a towel through his hair. Art glares at his son but says nothing.

"We're going to Billie's, Rich; come over as soon as you're ready, OK?" Betty says. "And get a move on so we can eat together."

Richard nods and goes down the stairs.

Art, Betty, Martha, Joan and Grandmother Santangelo silently get into the red Chevrolet and head for the restaurant, about a five-minute drive away. As they approach it Art can see there are just three cars in the parking lot and the restaurant seems dark. He leaves the car engine running as he parks in front of the restaurant and starts to get out of the car.

"Don't bother, Daddy," Martha says from the back seat. " 'Closed Christmas Eve,' the sign reads."

"And now we have to wait for your son before we find another place to eat," Art says, slamming the door behind him.

"He won't be long," Betty says brightly. "He was almost ready when we left. Joanie, how many songs will you be singing tonight?"

Five minutes later Art sees the Mustang, which has only one headlight plus a bashed-in fender from the accident, and he pulls out. Martha rolls down her window and shouts, "See you at the Mariposa." Because of the shortness of time, the family has agreed to eat at their old standby, the Mariposa Diner.

Art and the family are settled at a table when Richard comes into the dining room, which has but a half dozen of its fifty tables occupied. Art takes one look at his son and returns to studying the menu. Richard is wearing dark red velvet trousers, a flowered shirt, a blue sweater vest and a short blue suede jacket. Also he is wearing purple-tinted granny glasses.

Art continues to study the menu, holding his hand to the side of his face as if he were shielding himself from something. Richard leans back precariously in his chair and gazes around the nearly empty room. The four females talk among themselves paying little attention to either Art or Richard. They talk about the Christmas Eve service last year; they wonder if Bridget and Frank will arrive while they are at church; they tease Joan about not getting any presents because she has been a bad girl this year.

When the waitress comes to the table for the third time, Art says, "Would everybody please order so we can eat and get there on time."

"I'm not very hungry," Martha says.

"It's so early, Daddy, and I had so much stuff at the party," Joan adds.

"Lovely things here, Artie, but I'm not too hungry either, I'm afraid," Grandmother Santangelo says, widening her ever-present smile.

"If nobody is hungry, I am," Art says. "And I plan to eat." His voice grows calmer. "Now everybody pick out whatever they like so this lady can get to her other customers."

"Well, I'll have a cheeseburger," Grandmother says.

Art winces slightly.

"Give me a pastrami sandwich," Richard says.

"Roast beef for me," Martha says.

"I'll have a cheeseburger too," says Joan, smiling at her grandmother.

"The shrimp salad, please," Betty says.

Art points to the large featured item on the menu, a prime rib dinner. "I'll start off with cherrystone clams," Art begins his order.

After the meal, Martha gets into the car with Richard for the ride to church. When the faded blue Mustang and the red Chevrolet arrive in the parking lot at six thirty, the two older Neumeyer children tell their parents they will go inside later. Martha

331

offers her brother a Salem. "Fucking cigarettes taste like shit," Richard says blowing out the smoke loudly. "Been smoking nothing but grass down South, Martha—Panama Red—really the best stuff. Much healthier for you. Dynamite."

"Daddy is really pissed at you, if you haven't noticed."

"That's his problem. They'd do anything to have me home, so I'm not going to change just for them."

"Just try to be a little bit civilized. I know it's not always easy."

"Fuck it, Martha. I'm my own man now. I'll be the way I want to. I was living off bitches down in Florida. Old broads too."

"For how long?" she asks with no inflection in her voice.

"Well, for a time," he stammers. "Anyway, I'm not taking their shit."

"You had to call home for money, and they sent it. I'm going inside; it's cold out here."

"I'll be right there. Randy Short said he was coming. The place'll probably crumble when he walks in."

Martha walks through upper fellowship hall, which is bustling with people, on her way to the sanctuary. It is reminiscent of Easter, with effusive hellos from old acquaintances followed by strained smiling silences. Betty and her mother have already been seated in a row on the right side of the church, and Art, who is ushering, hands his daughter a program and leads her to them. Just before the processional hymn, Richard and Randy slip into the row from the other side. To the triumphant organ strains of "Hark! the Herald Angels Sing," Parkside's senior and junior choirs start up the center aisle, followed by Paster Firth MacIntosh, his deep baritone voice resounding as he moves slowly toward the front of the church. Pots of poinsettias take up much of the room behind the communion railing so the choir members and pastor carefully work their way through the holiday obstacle course, going to their assigned positions.

Parkside United Methodist Church is almost filled this evening, recalling the days when the church was troubled over where to put people rather than how to keep and attract them. The dim overhead lighting and the soft radiance from the candles lining the aisles lend a homey yet religious atmosphere and also mask the need for the paint job that still remains in committee. Throughout the church, the family portrait is repeated: neatly dressed father, mother and children stepping down in size from the oldest to the youngest. Some college students are home; some newly married couples are worshiping with their parents. In the middle of the church are the Neumeyers, who will be joined by Art after the collection is taken and his duties are completed.

Betty smiles broadly at no one in general as the congregation sits down. The pastor dispenses with the conventional Bible reading of the birth of Christ and reads a fourteenth-century monk's poetic version. Betty looks over her shoulder and winks at Art. Art, who has been looking her way, winks back.

> ART: It's a typical Christmas, I guess. It's different in that when the kids were younger we didn't trim the tree until they were in bed. Christmas is a big holiday for us, but it looks now that Martha probably won't be able to spend too much time with us at Christmas, and who knows about Rich? I guess I can accept the fact easier than Betty that children grow up and go away from home. Women are more emotional than men.
>
> We've always made a big thing of holidays, and Richie has that in him, so I knew he'd be home. Anybody can see he's trying to be extra nice to his mother because if a person is raised that way it always comes out. But I'm pretty damn tense about some things about him. I just don't want to leave for work in the morning and still have him laying around in bed. He's got to find a job. I want Betty to have a nice Christmas, so I'm trying to keep my mouth shut. But wait. The holiday spirit will wear off and her nerves will get frazzled. It will change.

One of the older boys in the Carson family, all of whose members have musical talent, steps out from the choir and stands in front of the lectern, a guitar in his hand. In a low voice that seems incongruous with his seventeen-year-old face, he begins to sing a folk song about a cherry tree that bent down to present its fruit to Mother Mary on the first Christmas night. Betty settles into her seat, the warm smile beginning to fade from her face.

BETTY: The way Richie lives, I don't know if his body can stand another year of the abuse he's giving it, living so transient without anybody taking care of him. God was very good to give us this nice Christmas, with Richard wanting to do what he did. He didn't have to come to church but he did it to please me; I know that. For Martha, it's easier; for Richard it was an extreme sacrifice and a gesture of love. So if something does happen, it's so much easier to end on a pleasant note, happy memories. It's important to Joan, too, because we tell her God is love, and if anything happened, we'd be able to tell her: Remember Christmas and everything was good?

The frustrating thing is we weren't able to get Richie things he needs. We never put the accent on giving a lot of unnecessary things, but good articles they can use. But I wouldn't want to give Richie anything he had to carry around. He left his radio in one place and he broke his watch so we're finished with that kind of stuff now.

I can see him twitching over there, tapping his feet on the floor and beating his fingers on his knees. But it seems as the service goes on, he's more relaxed. It makes me proud he brought Randy too. Rich is like a missionary. It's not a lecture; he's just showing Randy by his example that you do some things because they make other people happy and that's what makes the world go around.

The events leading up to Christmas were so nice. To have everybody in the house doing things. Martha doing, Joan doing. Regardless of what Martha says, she loves all the commotion around a holiday. And underneath it all she's glad to be here in church. When she looks back on it, the church was her whole thing at one time because she wasn't so active at school, except for being in athletics. She belittles church now, but how many kids had earthshaking things happen to them at fourteen or fifteen? She learned how to teach in Sunday school; she forgets that. She just forgets the enthusiasm she had for church.

The candles that line the aisles flicker as a draft from an open door wafts through the church. The younger children in the congregation especially are drawn to the dancing flames that had been so still they could have been electric imitations. But soon their attention, as well as that of the older members, is drawn to a story of a rabbit and a field mouse on a cold winter's night. Told by a boy of about fifteen, whose shoulder-length brown hair bobs in the soft light at the lectern, it takes the worshipers to a touching ending where the rabbit wraps himself around the mouse for body warmth, saving that life but losing his own.

Sitting next to her mother, Martha starts to slowly chew on her calloused thumb, hiding it from view by swirling the ends of her hair forward with a slight movement of her head.

MARTHA: I guess it's been coming for a long time, but this is the first time going to church for Christmas was totally nothing. Almost a painful thing to have to go through. And that bothers me.

I always assumed I was a religious person, always read all those little doctrines of the church and thought I believed them. I went to church, stood up for prayers, stood up for hymns, but I never internalized any of it. It was funny when I went to make my confirmation. I expected the skies to open up when I first took communion that day. A whole new me. Rebirth. Something really fantastic. That was such a disappointment because I sat down and, other than the taste in my mouth, I didn't have anything to remember.

I don't even know if I believe in God now, and that's the scariest part of it all. And just yesterday the pastor asked me to speak on Youth Recognition Sunday. Should I really say what I think? I found out I wasn't really a church person when I went away to college and realized they were saying the same old crap I had heard here. Right out of the Bible. Be a Christian but never think that Vietnam or racism or politics have anything to do with religion. I probably think more about religion now than I ever did before—then it was just a case of buying whatever my mother and father said.

It wasn't till I went away to college and stopped going to church that I formed any religious beliefs at all. Right now I don't know about a God, but I believe there's some sort of force, some power in the world that is basically good, and there's real good in each man to some extent. I'm living in a scientific age, and if it can't be explained somehow, it's hard for me to believe it. But I want something to hold onto.

Art and three other ushers march with military precision up the aisle to the front of the church. They fan out in front of the pastor, who hands them shining collection plates lined with felt. Richard leans over to Randy to say something, and smiles come over both their faces. Richard digs into his tight-fitting trousers for some change. The plate is passed, and soon Art is handing it to the first person in Richard's row.

RICHARD: This is kind of cool. Not the idea of church or anything, but it's a pretty service with the flowers and candles and everything. I like churches. I've seen a lot of them traveling around. I haven't gone inside any, but I dig the architecture and stuff so I really can get into it like I never did before.

I makes my mother happy that I'm here and it doesn't hurt me, so it's OK. I guess my father likes it too. They don't know it, but I'm not going to be around long. Probably about a month. Then I'll split. I might not be back till next Christmas. My old man is pretty uptight about me—do this, don't do this, take your feet off the furniture—so I'll just split sooner if he leans on me. Now that I've been around and know I can go any time, his shit doesn't penetrate any more. It's a good place to visit, but I wouldn't want to live at home.

I get the feeling that my folks think I just came home from around the block. They don't want to hear about it. They don't pursue anything about where I've been or what I've seen or what I've done. Same way when I came home from California. It's just that I'm home, that's important, not all the experiences I had. I'd dig it if they said they wanted to sit down for a couple hours and listen to what I did. They just walk away; Joanie's the only one who listens. They just think I was out there for kicks. You do what you please, but it just ain't all kicks, that's for sure. Why aren't they interested enough to listen to me?

I don't want anything for Christmas especially, just

336

for them to be friendly to me. But I'm glad my mother lent me the money for Christmas presents. It feels pretty good to give shit to people. The only trouble I'm having right now is that I have this boil on my ass and it hurts like hell on these pews.

At the end of the service, all the church lights are turned off as the pastor lights a small white candle and then offers the flame to the first person in the first row. Slowly, Parkside United Methodist Church takes on a mellow glow as the small candles everyone was given at the beginning of the service are lit. In the choir, Joan giggles as she drips some wax, waiting for the candle of the girl next to her to catch.

JOAN: All Christmases are the same because everybody is here. But next year Martha and Richie aren't coming home; I'm sure of that. Martha will probably be teaching and they don't get any money for that, and I don't know if my mother and father will treat her. Richie will probably be someplace else.

I like Christmas because we play games and tell jokes and talk and my aunt and uncle come. It's a couple of days that we celebrate that Christ was born. Presents really don't matter that much. Seeing the new ornaments we get every year, that's fun, and they're all going to be mine when I get married. Yeah, and when I get married everybody's going to come to my house, just like Grandma does now.

After the service, holiday greetings are exchanged by various members of the Neumeyer family with people they hadn't seen beforehand—all except Martha, who excuses herself and almost runs to the church basement. She catches up with her family before they get into the cars and join the stream of vehicles leaving the church parking lot.

As Art approaches his house, he sees an unfamiliar station wagon parked in front. The car's radio is blaring through the open windows on this mild winter night. Someone laughs inside the car and an empty beer can is tossed out, first landing softly on the grass

337

close to the street, then giving off a tinny rattle as it skitters onto the sidewalk.

Inside the red Chevrolet there is silence as the family watches. They get out of the car in the driveway and walk into the house, averting their eyes from the station wagon. Richard parks on the street, slams his car door shut and walks jauntily toward the house.

"Richie, what's happening, man?" A voice comes from the station wagon.

"Not much, man," he replies, recognizing the voice. "Just got back from Florida. All the tourists go there for Christmas, but I come north." He smiles, obviously proud of his quip. Randy, who has just pulled up, follows Richard into the house.

As Richard comes in he sees his father looking out the front window from behind the curtain. The grass next to the station wagon is littered with beer cans, cigarette butts and waxed paper and cups from a McDonald's drive-in.

Betty puts her hand on her husband's shoulder. "Artie, let them be. They're troublemakers."

"Bums," he says, his eyes narrowing.

"Artie, I've seen Eric carry dead squirrels and rabbits up the block that he shot on the golf course. Sick, he had a sick look on his face when he was doing it. All the kids in that family have been arrested for drugs."

"Who is it, Betty?" Grandmother Santangelo asks.

"One of the Murdock kids; they live four houses up."

"I'd like to call the police," Art says.

"The only one who can get hurt out of this is Joanie," Betty says. "They might do something to her. Come away from the window. Artie, it's Christmas," she pleads.

As Richard and Randy go downstairs to play pool, Joan is told to get into her nightgown. The house is momentarily quiet when Martha walks slowly into the living room, her head down.

"What's wrong, baby?" her father asks, only half seriously.

"Nothing."

"Come on, baby."

"Daddy, quit it." She walks into the kitchen and says softly. "It just so happens I threw up after church. That's all."

338

"Are you all right?" Betty says. "Do you want an Alka-Seltzer? Something wrong?"

"Just forget it, Mother. You know I throw up all the time; I have for years."

Art shakes his head and goes into the kitchen to fix daiquiris for himself and his wife. Betty calls downstairs, "You boys want a beer? We have some wine too."

"Yeah, just bring the bottle of wine down," Richard hollers back.

"No," Art says in a loud voice. "You have a glass like other civilized people."

"Artie, the boy's been out for three months and could have had anything he wanted," she says quietly. "Now you're worried about a little wine. Come up and help yourself, Richie," she calls out.

About nine thirty the doorbell rings and Joan runs to the door, shrieking a high-pitched "Whee-e-e!" She leaps into her uncle's arms and reaches over to give her aunt a hug and then a kiss.

Black Beauty yelps as exuberant greetings are exchanged between Betty and Bridget, George and Martha, George and his mother. Art waits at the top of the stairs to shake hands with George and then to give Bridget a kiss. "Where's Richie?" Art asks.

"We saw him outside," Bridget says. "He's out there with his friend in the car."

Art glares at the already closed front door. "Did they come for him?" he asks Joan.

"No, he and Randy went out a little while ago," Joan says. "And they're drinking beer and everything out there." In the silence that follows, the rattle of a beer can hitting the sidewalk is heard.

Betty gets Art aside and whispers, "They look so tired, don't they?"

Art looks at George, whose eyes have faint red circles around them. That color is accented by the pallor of his face, which Art has branded "grocery-store yellow." Bridget has dark half-circles under her eyes. Her blond hairpiece hangs askew at the back of her head. Because she parts her hair in the middle and hasn't had it peroxided recently, a brown line at the roots is all the more noticeable.

George loosens his tie and falls onto the sofa, coming down with such force that the legs move from the indented spots on the carpet. "What a day! Started out slow; then it was dynamite. They were buying cold cuts like they were starving. Bologna, salami, liverwurst! Cleaned off the bread rack. We should have had roller skates, right, Brij? Got a new display for pet stuff: bird seed, doggie bones, all that stuff. Nice display, doesn't take any floor space. They were in today buying gifts for their pets. Brij, what would you say? Didn't we do fifteen bucks in pets' presents?"

"I don't know, George," she says in an exhausted tone. "All I know is that holidays for everybody else are madness for us." '

"Madness, Brij? What're you talking about? I'll bet we did . . . well, we did plenty today."

"You got to take more time off, Georgie, you look so tired," Grandmother Santangelo says. "Even your father didn't work Sundays."

"I will, Ma, I will. We're going to take Wednesdays off as soon as things settle down."

"Been saying that for the last three years," Art says blandly.

It is after ten o'clock and Richard is back in the house—having been greeted by a father's glare and a mother's smile—when Betty tells Joan it is time for bed. The youngest member of the Neumeyer family puts some of the Christmas cookies she and Martha made on a plate, pours a glass of milk and leaves them on the kitchen table as a snack for Santa Claus. Then she thumbtacks the red felt Christmas stocking with her name on it to the newel post at the top of the stairs and calls to her brother and sister for them to do the same. As Martha pins hers up, there is a strained look on her face. Richard, who has had several cans of beer and glasses of wine, lets a cigarette dangle out of his mouth as he puts his stocking up. He laughs. "Santa, Santa, fill it full of the stuff I need."

"Stuff we need." Randy laughs too.

Soon after, Randy leaves and the family makes final preparations for the morning. Christmas presents emerge from all corners of the house, from George and Bridget's car, from the garage. A pile of presents builds for every member of the family. When all the presents are set out, Joan's is by far the biggest mound. The two smallest piles contain the few gifts for Road Runner and Black Beauty. Even the gifts for the dogs are handsomely wrapped and tied with ribbon.

After this chore is done, the family members sit down to talk in the living room. Richard, who is shirtless, lies with his body half under the dining room table, lazily sipping on a can of beer, but his father says nothing to him. It is not long after the conversation begins that George's eyes begin to droop and Betty demands that everyone go to bed. By one o'clock all the beds and sofas in the house at 97 Birchwood Drive are occupied. Everyone sleeps except Martha, who has been assigned Richard's room. She lies awake into the night.

Christmas, 1972, dawns bright and crisp. A light breeze plays with the branches of the pines and nudges the waxed papers in front of the Neumeyer house. Inside, Joan is the first to get up. After she puts on her robe, she runs through the house, knocking on doors and shaking sleeping bodies on the sofas. "Get up, get up, it's Christmas!" She dances about, jumping up and down, clapping her hands. "Oh, oh, oh!" she exclaims as she sees her stack of presents.

One by one, family members find their way to the living room. Richard is the last to make his appearance, coming up from the recreation room only after repeated calls. Betty scans the living room, the people, the tree, the presents and the decorations and cuddles up to her husband. She leans her head on his chest and then wraps her arms around him and closes her eyes.

"Artie, I'm so happy."

"OK, everybody dig in," Art says.

Ribbons are eased off, paper crinkles and the range of voices and emotions go from Joan's "Oh, just what I wanted" to Richard's "I don't wear socks any more." Joan jumps with glee over Barbie doll dresses and a digital clock radio. Betty hugs Art and puts on the beige woolen cape that bears a note, "To the best wife, from Santa Claus." Art kisses her on the cheek as he looks at the certificate that says he's the owner of a new bowling ball. Martha tries to look appreciative of a tastefully made nightie. The only problem is its color: lavender again, like the one she got at Easter. It is a color that went out with Mark Hard. Bridget tries on slippers and finds them too small. Art and George open boxes to find sweaters or shirts. Richard tries on the snorkel coat from his parents and pronounces the sleeves too wide and bulky. Betty puts Joan's handmade wall hanging "Sing Praise to the Lord" on a doorknob and smothers her with a hug.

The weeks of preparation, the hours of shopping and wrapping have culminated in this morning. And, an hour after the present opening begins, that phase of Christmas is over. A gigantic heap of wrapping paper sits in the middle of the living room rug.

"You keep gabbing," Art says to the suddenly quiet, almost pensive group, "and I'll fix breakfast." In forty-five minutes a huge plate mounded with sausages and steaming ham is brought to the table, followed by a continuous stream of pancakes fresh off the griddle. It is the "big breakfast" Betty has settled on as the Christmas meal for this year. In the conversation that ensues over cups of coffee, Christmas itself is left behind except to negotiate which presents have to be taken back because they won't be used or are the wrong size.

Two people are silent. For one of them, Art, it is a natural way of reacting at a family gathering. For the other, Joan, it is not typical. She looks often at the kitchen clock, knowing that at noon her aunt and uncle will leave. She sits by her mountain of presents and listlessly handles two necklaces she's received. Betty notices this. As Grandmother and Art set up for bingo, she goes to her daughter and, without saying a word, gives her a hug. The tremendous buildup for this "last Christmas together" has peaked, and Joan already is anticipating that the coming down will be sudden and not as enjoyable.

As family members gather around the dining room table, bingo cards are purchased for three cents apiece and Grandmother Santangelo begins to call the numbers. After four games, George is winning, having amassed twenty-four cents. But also after four games, it is noon. George and Bridget begin to gather up their presents and to offer profuse thank-yous. Fifteen minutes later they are gone.

Richard goes downstairs to call a newly found girl friend in Delaware and spends the next twenty minutes reminiscing about their time in Florida and coming back in the car. ("How about that chick who was a diabetic? Sold her works to that junkie and we had money for pot, gas and food.") Once the phone is free, Art makes the perfunctory holiday call to his mother and sister. One by one, Betty, Martha, Richard and Joan take the phone to thank Art's side of the family for the presents Betty swore would not be reciprocated this year. But after Betty's blowup at the wedding, she said nothing about her vow not to send presents and went forward with the shopping as if nothing had happened.

Throughout the afternoon the older members of the family doze on chairs and the living room sofa, Joan plays quietly in her room, Martha reads and Richard goes back to bed. At four o'clock the women gather in the kitchen to begin to prepare the evening meal, which mostly involves the heating of frozen dishes.

The evening Christmas meal is a feast, and where Thanksgiving saw plentiful food and no appetites, there are a group of eager eaters today. Antipasto with salami, peppers, artichoke hearts, anchovies, olives and Italian bread that George brought is first, and the platter is nearly cleaned off. Lasagna, followed by chestnuts, mints and coffee, completes a meal Art calls "the best you've ever made, Betty. I think it's about time we got married. I don't want to lose a good cook like you."

After supper, Betty suggests a game of Yahtzee and Joan perks up. Martha is less than enthusiastic about the idea, but she puts down *The Other*, a paperback book she's been reading, and goes to the kitchen table where the game is played. Joan scores three Yahtzees by rolling five of a kind three times and demolishes the competition by a margin of one hundred points.

It is nine o'clock when Joan says she is tired and wants to go to bed. Martha is reading her book once more. Randy, Ron and Richard are downstairs, talking. A few minutes after nine, after a lull in their conversation, Richard goes to the plastic Army tank he made in grade school that sits on a shelf over his stereo. He lifts off the turret and takes out a small foil-wrapped object, no bigger than a piece of sugarcoated chewing gum. He places it carefully in the pocket of his flannel shirt as if it were either very valuable or explosive. The boys leave the house. Soon they are sitting in a car alongside the golf course. Using the pipe Randy has under his seat, Richard lights a chunk of the hashish. They sit in silence for the better part of an hour, passing the pipe back and forth, staring out through steamed windows as Christmas day comes to a close. It is only when the bright lights of an oncoming car suddenly shine into his heavy-lidded eyes that Randy finally speaks up. "I'm tired. I'm going home."

At 97 Birchwood Betty has her shoes off and her feet on the coffee table. She exhales loudly and her husband turns away from last night's paper to look into her eyes, also tired and droopy.

"Everybody was here, Artie. I'm so happy," she says.

"Was it everything you expected?"

"Everybody was so happy. They all had such a great time."

"I asked, 'Was it what you wanted?'"

"Of course not." She hesitates. "It only lasted a couple of hours. I want Christmas every day. To last forever."

21

In Public

As Pastor Firth MacIntosh reads the announcements on Sunday, December 31, Martha Neumeyer reaches beneath her glasses to rub her right eye. She hesitates a fraction of an inch from the itchy eye and slowly her hand goes back to rest on the four sheets of paper in her lap. She then looks up at the minister, just a few feet away from her in the chancel of Parkside United Methodist Church. Martha spent fifteen minutes this morning applying makeup to a face that only had the benefit of four hours' sleep; she does not want to disrupt the several layers that conceal the dark circles under her eyes.

As the pastor tells about members in the hospital, a Sunday school teacher's meeting and the other affairs of church life, Martha looks down at the four pieces of paper and quickly shuffles through them as if cramming in the last moments before an exam. Those pages are the result of a fair amount of soul-searching, a mild amount of ambivalence and at least one night's abbreviated sleep. It wasn't until four thirty this morning that Martha completed her preparation for her talk on Youth Recognition Sunday.

". . . privileged and happy to have Martha with us to share . . ."

With the pastor's words, Martha's head suddenly jerks up from the pages. She looks out into the congregation and smiles vaguely toward the place where her parents are sitting, more to the front than is their custom. Betty Neumeyer smiles broadly in return and moves to wrap an arm around Joan, who is sitting between her parents.

Martha walks to the lectern, as the pastor finishes his introduction, and looks intently at the top page of her speech. Several sentences spill out before she raises her eyes to look out at her audience ". . . And I could stand here this morning telling you that I'm very active in the church at college and that it keeps me going from day to day . . ."

Betty looks to the lectern, her face still in a serene smile.

". . . but I won't. Because I just don't fit into any religious circle right now. I have some nice memories of this church and Sunday school and choir and MYF, but I also have some very bitter ones. Bitter feelings about the ministers you criticized and got rid of because they believed in racial justice and didn't believe in war. I feel that that is the quickest way to drive young people out of the church today. . . ."

Art and Joan are still looking at Martha, but Betty's eyes are now focused firmly on her hands. Her face has been wiped clean of emotion.

". . . Too often churches get sidetracked on what their real mission is. The building becomes more important; paying the bills is the whole object. I can remember as the representative of MYF the meetings I sat in on where people got into heated discussions about painting a wall or whether or not to get a new set of dishes for the kitchen. . . ."

The lines slowly form on Betty's smooth forehead. Her shoulders sag and her head hangs limply as she stares at the visitor's card and the sharpened pencil in the rack in front of her.

". . . Since the beginning of time there's always been some kind of worship. Man has always needed to acknowledge God or some Spirit or Buddha or whatever. But every church must meet the needs of its people and not get sidetracked on all the details. Many kids going to school today were born into the *Future Shock* age and they are taught to trust facts, facts, facts. So when you're teaching them religion, give them a reason behind it or at least help them to find the reason."

Martha Neumeyer looks at the bottom of the last sheet and

then out into the congregation. She plants her palms firmly on the lectern as her voice grows firmer, yet lower.

"And regardless of all the facts or the reasons or the faiths that are taught, the old saying still goes: Actions speak louder than words. And I have to face up to that too."

After the service, Martha walks out with Pastor MacIntosh and takes her place alongside him in the vestibule to greet the worshipers as they leave. Once the organ postlude is completed, the tall, red-bearded man in the long black robe turns to Martha and grabs for her hand.

"Fantastic. Couldn't have written it better myself. I just hope they were listening, Martha. Gosh, you're good."

Martha looks up the main aisle of the church to see people easing out of their pews, exchanging greetings and then slowly walking toward her and the pastor. She takes a nibble at her calloused thumb, then puts both hands behind her back as she awaits the verdict.

As the people come closer their ill-defined faces come into focus, and Martha can see they are smiling toward her.

"Wonderful talk, Martha," the first woman says.

"Wish we had more like you."

"Couldn't sleep during your sermon," says an elderly man who pats her hand.

Martha Neumeyer looks up at the pastor and beams. She presses her palm against her stomach to stop the gurgling sound that has begun, a by-product of the queasy feeling she has felt all morning.

"You ought to be mighty proud of this girl of yours," the pastor says as he puts his arm around Martha. Her eyes move quickly down the line of people waiting to greet her and rest on Joan, who is jumping with excitement, obviously eager to reach her sister. Martha's eyes go up from her sister, along the buttons on a familiar tweed coat and then to her mother's face. The wide smile that Martha has developed to receive her congratulations is wiped off instantly as she meets her mother's cold, even stare.

A few more people pass by, but Martha has difficulty saying anything to them. Soon she is facing her family and the pastor is repeating to the Neumeyers how proud they should be of their daughter. People who are lingering in the vestibule also congratulate the Neumeyers—some enthusiastically, others perfunctorily—as they stand in front of their daughter and their pastor.

"Good talker, just like her father," Art says, putting his arm around his daughter.

"You were super, just super," Joan says, squeezing her sister's hand. "Everybody was really listening."

Betty Neumeyer's lips are beginning to move. "Pastor, it was a lovely service, as usual."

A few minutes later Art, Betty and Joan are in the red Chevrolet waiting near the front of the church as Martha says good-bye to the pastor and runs down the steps.

"Let's get home so we can eat sometime today," Betty says in her clipped tone as soon as Martha opens the door. "Some people aren't as considerate of time as they should be. Art, sure you feel OK?"

"Cold's a cold," he replies.

"Well, what about it?" Martha says softly.

"What about *what!*" her mother shouts at her, swiveling violently in her seat as she turns toward her daughter.

"Mother, you haven't said a word about the talk."

"Pastor thought it was wonderful," Betty says in a singsongy voice. "All the people said you were great. Who cares if you make fun of everything we believe in, make fun of our life?" Her words begin to tumble out faster. "Of course they all loved it; now they can tell everybody about what our darling daughter had to say about her family. You go back to school. We have to face them every week."

"Mo . . . ther"—Martha draws out the word—"it was not personal. Pastor said I should be honest and I was. Why didn't you tell him right then how horrible I was? Anyway, I wasn't saying all those things to you. If religion makes you happy, that's fine; but it doesn't make me happy." Her voice lowers. "At least the way they practice it at Parkside."

"Nobody expected you to get up there and gush that it was the whole world, but you didn't have to put it down. It was everything when you were a teenager."

348

"And when I was a teenager the best minister we ever had was run out of town. Everybody sits there so pretty and holy on Sunday and they hate blacks and they want war. Mother, that's called hypocrisy!"

"And look at you! Savior of the minorities, and you aren't going to the ghetto, either."

Martha lowers her eyes and her hand goes to her mouth. Her lips brush against the calloused knuckle. Then she drops her hand angrily to her side.

"It's the holidays," Art says as the car pulls into the driveway at 97 Birchwood.

"You were so proud I was going to talk in church," Martha says softly. "You just didn't want me to say anything. You just take everything like it was aimed at you."

Betty and Art walk to their bedroom, and Betty closes the door behind them. She takes off her glasses, sits down on the bed and begins to rub her temples in an attempt to ward off the headache that is coming on.

"It's all so crazy," Betty says.

Art looks at her and says nothing.

"We invested everything in Martha. Maybe we even invested hope in her. And now look what she's done. In public. God, what did we do to deserve that kind of embarrassment?"

"Betty, I didn't think it was all that bad," he says, before blowing his nose in a tissue.

"Martha, the perfect one. *Who's Who*. College. Our dreams come true. How? Why?" Betty suddenly gets up from the bed. "Well, I guess it's better this way. We talked about turning them loose. And Martha has just said she doesn't want to have anything to do with us."

"Betty, I don't see—"

"It's crazy." She cuts him off. "And look at the way Rich is now."

"Tell me about it," Art says, putting his hands on his hips.

"Talks about getting a job, a steady job with a strong union. Keeps his room clean. The rebel has had his year of rebellion and now he wants to settle down."

Art's frown turns into a tiny smile that wrinkles the scars left by the acne. He puts his arm around his wife. "Baby, I'm so confused I won't even say a word. Except that I wish everything was as black and white as you see it."

Betty's gaze moves from the tiny lines on her pink hands to the dresser, the pictures on the wall and then back to her hands. "To me it always seems like the best time was some other time." She is speaking so softly her husband puts his ear directly in front of her mouth to hear her. "But I never realized it while the good times were happening. Is there something wrong with me, Artie?"

Other than the septic tank being clogged again, the passing of a year and the embarking on a new one were uneventful at 97 Birchwood.

Joan went back to school two days after New Year's, eager to go to work on the science project Mrs. Ferris had promised they could think up, design and execute if behavior was better than it had been before the holidays. But behavior worsened and the open class was abolished, and Joan and her classmates went back to straight rows and alphabetical seating. Ironically, even some of the parents who were the most vehement against open classrooms protested the change. They, like Betty Neumeyer, felt their children were doing better in the more free setting.

A modern dance class was offered at school, and Joan enrolled. She enjoyed leaving the house early on dance mornings, wearing a leotard under her school clothing and running out to the waiting taxicab. Her mother gladly paid the fare, saying it was a small investment for the poise Joan would learn. Joan remained interested in the dance class for several weeks, but she lost much of her zeal for school. When Betty offered a "sick day," Joan accepted it, and mother and daughter, as they had done in school years before, went shopping one weekday.

Richard took a job driving a truck for an auto parts store and surprised his father one evening by telling him that the union he would be joining provided $150 a week retirement payments after fifteen years of work. Richard gave up smoking regular cigarettes soon after the holidays, drank much less and became interested in health foods. He ate very little meat at home. He bought a new poster for his room: "If a man does not keep pace with his companions, perhaps there's a different drum and steps in the music which he hears, however measured or far away." He still went out most evenings, but often to Randy's house where he would smoke marijuana or, when he could afford it—usually on Friday, which was payday—hashish.

Sitting in Randy's bedroom, listening to hard rock music, the sweet smell of marijuana in the air, Richard talked about going on unemployment and also about going back out on the road. But in the daylight he worked steadily and even got a weekend job to help him pay off the education loan. Soon he began to complain that he was "digging himself in deep again" with debts for a newer van he had bought. Although his mother hoped he would "settle down with a nice girl," he drifted into the year without a steady girl.

An uneasy peace existed between Richard and his father. Hostilities flared up often, especially when the boy would come home after work and announce he was going out immediately and would not have dinner with his family. But at lunchtime Richard would often drive his delivery truck home and his mother would have a meal waiting for him. Betty bought more fresh vegetables and yogurt to cater to his new tastes.

Martha, who admitted this was the most boring vacation at home, was forced to stay almost two weeks longer than she planned. A fuel oil shortage and a cold wave in the Midwest forced a delay in the reopening of Hillcrest. During the additional time at home Martha became increasingly lethargic, reading extensively and spending more time in the kitchen, cooking and baking. She made her first Bundt cake, chocolate and coconut macaroon, and sardonically told her mother she was practicing so she could "get a husband."

Len Morris, who had written Martha at the start of the semester saying he loved her and wanted to marry her, phoned several times for a date. Martha said she would go out for coffee and talk, but she did not want to get home at 3 or 4 A.M., their usual hour. For Martha, "it wasn't worth the hassle of going through the smoke my parents would put up." Martha saw Len at a New Year's Eve party she went to without a date, but he was stoned on marijuana and they didn't talk. Martha left the party early after she found that some of the people were sniffing cocaine.

When Martha returned to Hillcrest, she did her student teaching at a high school in a better section of the city. Soon it was time to apply for teaching positions for the next year, and she made application to Kansas City schools, realizing that if she were hired she would be going into one of the ghetto schools she had spurned just a few months before. She also applied to school districts in a number of small and middle-sized cities in the Midwest, most of them with primarily white student bodies.

Betty was outraged when she had to pay $1.49 for stewing beef and told Art that it didn't seem so long ago that it was 49 cents a pound. She found that the $50 a week she was budgeted for food, which used to stretch enough for a pair of shoes or a blouse every so often, no longer was enough. She told Art she needed more money to feed the family of four. She again vowed she was going to get a job. But with Martha's graduation coming in May, she said she didn't want to get started on a job and then have to leave it. She and Art planned to drive to Kansas for the graduation, and Betty was to stay on campus for a period afterward and then fly back.

Betty finally had her ears pierced and confided to Art she should have had it done twenty years ago. Her only concern was that she might get an infection. The same day she had her ears pierced, she bought Martha a black nightgown. It was in memoriam: Martha had written home that Mark Hard was to be married on February 24.

In her conversations with Pam Brown and other friends, Betty found that marriages she once thought were stable were heading toward divorce. Two couples on Tulip Lane—a couple from the North End, married for twenty-two years, and another couple with eight children—were already separated. A piano teacher on Tulip Lane who Betty always thought was a flirt, constantly had cars in front of her house, she learned from Pam. In addition to giving lessons, the woman also engaged in prostitution.

With the train strike still on, Art continued to drive into the city with Frank Brown. Art complained about Frank's excessive smoking in the car. Frank told him he was only allowed to smoke in the basement or outside the house, and that when he got into another person's car he enjoyed cigarettes a great deal. Art rolled down his window before picking Frank up and the car was noticeably cold, but Frank never got the message.

A thirteen-part television series, "An American Family," began early in the year. It was a documentary about the lives of a California family named Loud. The first part gave an overall look into the lives of the parents and their five children and showed that, by the end of the seven months the film crew had lived with the family, the couple was getting a divorce. The second segment centered on the Louds' homosexual son, Lance, and his life in New York. Pronouncing the family "exhibitionists" and "actors," saying that what viewers were seeing was not a real family, Art said he was not interested in seeing any more of the series.

Afterword

"How DID YOU FIND the family?" "What was it like to be with them for a whole year?" These two questions were often asked as people found out about my year-long study of an average American family. And the Neumeyers of Mariposa became so much a part of my life it almost seemed as if I had always known them.

My first thought was to do a book about a year in the life of an ethnic city family, showing how old country ways were being discarded or adapted by the children and grandchildren of immigrants as the first generation was dying out. I was fascinated by this, especially after visiting my old neighborhood on the East Side of Cleveland (heavily Slovak and Hungarian), to write an article that appeared in the *New York Times Magazine*. In further conversations with two people who are here thanked gratefully for their kindness, advice, prodding and encouragement, Genevieve Young, my editor at Lippincott, and Theron Raines, my agent, we began to see that perhaps an even more interesting subject would be one "average American family."

From the Census Bureau I found out that in 1970 an average family consisted of a father, 45; a mother, 42; and children 19 and 17. They lived in a mortgaged house in a suburb of a metropolitan area, had one air conditioner and 1¼ cars, among other earthly possessions. The parents had twelve years of schooling. The father was a "craftsman, foreman, or operative," the Census Bureau said, and in 1970 he made about $10,000.

Those were my guidelines, although from the start I knew I would not slavishly adhere to them. Inflation had driven wages up in two years, so for my family I thought a $10,000 to $13,000 range would be reasonable. When I put down other qualifications on a sheet that I planned to leave with contacts, they read like this:

—parents in early to mid-40s.
—Protestant or Catholic or mixed marriage (Jewish would be atypical).
—two to four children, at least one still in local public schools
—wife might work but not necessarily.
—family lives in mortgaged house.
—ideally, couple was raised in an urban area.

Before going out to find the family, I talked to some experts in various areas of people-study. I had written a number of magazine profiles of the famous and the ordinary, and my technique was rather simple: I asked direct questions only after research for the story was almost over. I watched how people acted before I asked them what they thought. For me, it was the best way to get an accurate picture, and I planned to use the same technique once I found my family. But I wanted to find out from sociologists and anthropologists if they thought the project itself was worthwhile and possible and how I should go about finding the family that existed only as a short set of qualifications.

Arthur Vidich at the New School of Social Research and Meyer Barash at Hofstra University encouraged me and were helpful in pointing out how I might find the family. Herbert J. Gans at Columbia University discouraged me, but even with his misgivings that the study of a single family and an arbitrarily "average" one was too limited, he gave me some sound advice.

I was especially worried about finding a family, working with them for three or four months and then having them say they wanted no more. Each of these men said that this could happen, but if a firm, honest approach was made to the family members, explaining what they could expect over the year, it was less likely. They told me to pick carefully and to make sure the family and I had some "chemistry" or else I might be in for a big disappointment.

It took me two months to get to the point where I could begin looking for the family. It would be two more months before I walked for the first time into the living room at 97 Birchwood.

I narrowed down the geographical search to seven suburban communities, all of which were heterogeneous ethnically and had large numbers of wage earners in the bracket I was looking for. I then began to talk to people in these communities: teachers, principals, personnel managers, neighborhood activists, busybodies, college professors and their students, editors and writers on suburban papers. I also talked with priests and ministers who served these suburbs; they were by far the most helpful. I told each person I talked to what I wanted to do—"study American family life"—and how I intended to do it—"by following one family for a year." Could they recommend a family that fit the criteria I had on my sheet of paper?

Many people suggested families, but most wanted to get in touch with them before giving me their names. I was thankful for that. It was much easier to talk with families to whom I had been introduced by someone they knew. Also, it gave people a chance to back away from the idea, saving their time and mine. I was not worried about the "right" family getting away. I was sure it would be quite easy to find any number of average families; my concern was, would they want to be the subjects of a book? I was wrong on both counts. Average families were hard to find, but once I began to find possibilities, almost all were eager to be the subjects.

From my contacts, I had a list of over fifty families. With a series of phone calls, I began a process of elimination—too many children, children too young, too old; a second marriage; too high an income, too skilled a job; too much education—and soon had a list of fifteen families that roughly fit my outline. I was beginning to be a bit nervous. This was no easy task.

I interviewed each of the fifteen families at length, asking about their background and their thoughts about being studied. What came out during those interviews amazes me. The stories of mental illness, pregnant daughters, drugs and unfaithfulness led me quickly to realize that these people were yearning to talk. It was not that I was especially empathetic or good as an interviewer. All I had to be was interested in them.

Those families in which I found severe problems, even in the first interview, I decided I would not use. I was not looking for a "Peyton Place" family. I wanted people that, at least on the surface, seemed to be coping with life. I was sure that they, like all of us, would have their share of problems as well as their triumphs. I did not want to spend a year writing about an already ravaged family.

On the evening of January 6, 1972, I had an appointment to meet a family that had been recommended by the Methodist pastor in a town I have called Mariposa. Their daughter was home on Christmas vacation and their two other children would be there, so I had a chance to see the entire family together. They were the Neumeyers.

Their pastor had said they were a hard-working family, not particularly beset with any overwhelming problems he knew of, Republican and conservative in the small "c" sense of that word, for law and order, against blacks and welfare, but what he considered open-minded people.

The Neumeyers were warm, friendly and reasonably open in that first meeting. Betty had baked some brownies and brewed one of the best cups of coffee I had had for a long time. She was the most talkative member of the family and mentioned that she felt it an honor to be "chosen."

Art was quieter, yet he was straightforward in answering the questions I asked. All the members, including Joan, were excited at the prospect of being the subjects of a book. But it was Art who touched me and made me realize that they were going to get something out of the book too. "If anything can make us see ourselves better, it'll be good for us." Many people had wondered why any family would want to be studied. Art had just given his reason. Also, as I was to learn, the lives of the Neumeyers were not very exciting, and the other members thought having me around might be a novelty.

As the evening went on and we touched on politics and the Vietnam war and race, the generational differences came through. Martha especially was vocal in her comments about the "lily-white neighborhood" and "holier-than-thou hypocrites" at the church. Art told his side of the story, of having to escape from the city because blacks were moving into his neighborhood. But I found out that night that Art Neumeyer was not a closed-minded bigot and was no more a hypocrite than most of us, including me. That night he mentioned offhandedly that he and some other men from the church had helped guard a house under construction that was being vandalized because a black family was building it. Art *wanted* to be fair.

As we talked, it became clear that I had found the family I wanted to study. But would they be willing to go along, once I told them what it involved? I munched on still another home-made brownie, asked for a second cup of Betty's coffee and told them what to expect.

I would be in and out of their lives for the next year. I would go to church with them, go to the beach with them, go out with Richard, visit Martha at her college in Kansas, spend days with Joan in her schoolroom, with Betty at home, with Art at work. I would be there for Easter and Christmas; I would be there in the mornings and at night. Because I lived so far away, I would hope to stay at the house, when possible. When things were happening, I would move with those happenings. When life was slow, I would just be there and not expect conversation or attention. I would not melt into the wallpaper—that would be impossible— rather, I would try, insofar as it was comfortable for them, to incorporate myself into the family. When it was convenient, I would sit down with family members and gather information on their past lives and the events of the year.

I didn't press for an answer. I told them it was a major allotment of time for me and them, and they should discuss it without me breathing down their necks. Also, I offered them a ten-day free home trial. If I "chose" them and they said yes, I would come out and be with them over a ten-day period, and after that we would talk over the arrangement and see if we should proceed. I also said I would have to ask them to sign a release that would state they were cooperating fully and would have no editorial control over what might be written about them. I promised to protect their privacy by changing names and places. I never mentioned paying them and they never asked. This whole business of payment had troubled me. I wondered if anyone would cooperate without being paid, and whether I had the right to ask them. But after talking with Vidich, Barash and Gans, I was convinced that anyone who was paid would then feel obligated to "perform" for the fee. That satisfied me in one way, but I still felt the family should have something besides the book—which they said was quite an honor itself—when the study was completed. Unknown to the Neumeyers I had a clause written into my publishing contract that the family I selected would receive $1,000 as soon as the book was completed.

By the time I called Art and Betty back, about a week later, I had interviewed the last of the fifteen families. The Neumeyers were my first choice. So when they said yes to the project, I was indeed happy and eager to get moving.

In the next ten days, I spent time with Art at the factory and with Betty at home and at church. I visited Joan's school. I rode around with Richard in the evening. During those ten days I did not take a single note in front of the Neumeyers, a practice I continued throughout the year. They may have thought I had weak kidneys, for I did make many trips to the bathroom, where I would jot down my observations. I found it handy to remember key words about interchanges or events I wanted to get down. "Postcard," "sleep on bed," "lettuce" were expanded on in my bathroom notes and then further embellished that night or the next morning, when I would either type or tape-record my notes. I found I could remember no more than three items, so when three key words were in my brain, off to the bathroom I'd go.

During those ten days I tried to be a willing friend rather than an idle observer. If Betty needed help shredding the cheese for supper or Joan needed a ride to Camp Fire, I would offer. I saw myself as a pleasant but not-too-bright cousin, who liked to hang around, ready to help and listen but with few opinions of his own. I'm sure I was bland company at times, but I did not want to intrude on their lives any more than I already was just by being there. And I surely didn't want to reshape them to my way of thinking. The Neumeyers told their close friends who I was and that I was doing a book on them. Of course this caused a stir initially and people were somewhat nervous, saying things like "Don't put that in the book." I would smile as if I hadn't heard whatever they wanted to cover up and would try to change the subject as quickly as possible. To casual acquaintances of the Neumeyers I was Paul, a friend.

After the ten days together, I sat down with Betty and Art and asked if I could continue. They said they saw no reason why I shouldn't. Betty's concern had been that she would have to entertain me, make conversation with me, and would not be able to live her own life. She said that hadn't been the case, that she and Art thought I was a decent enough person, not hard to be with. Two months later when I asked them to sign the release, it was a formality.

As I became more a part of their lives, I was always careful to be friendly, never familiar. Betty's friends often joked about this young writer (only eight years younger than she) being in the house; the jokes had sexual overtones. I disregarded these but was especially careful not to be cute or familiar with Betty or with Martha. If Art had ever felt I had designs on his wife or his daughter, the project would have been terminated immediately. I had no such designs, and I had invested so much of myself in this family I did not want our mutual efforts wasted.

How was it to be with the family? I am an urban creature, so my year in suburbia was both educational and fun; at other times it was downright boring. I was fascinated by Betty's busyness but I was equally fascinated with the woman who lived inside

Betty, struggling to get out but often pacified by hours on the phone, a nap, or some over-orchestrated task. Joan's school, its staff and her reactions showed me first hand how the educational system can pigeonhole youngsters, much to the youngsters' loss. Richard's aimlessness, his dreams and his reality are a fundamental part of the book, and being with him, while interesting, was difficult. He is a very nervous young man, not unkind but, as Betty says, "jitsy." Martha was probably the most open member of the family, providing insights and facts that startled me. The interviews with her really helped me get below the seemingly tranquil surface of this family. Art was a gentleman, at times distant and difficult to talk with at length but, as I look back, a person who was consistently behind the project. I found out only recently that the family had voted on being studied. Art had cast the only "no," but he abided by the majority's wishes.

We had our ups and downs. There were times when Betty shared deep-seated frustrations, and there were times when she felt she had had enough of me. This happened especially when there was friction around the house—usually because of Richard. At one time when Richard was in Pennsylvania he called me at my home but refused to contact his parents. This put me in a particularly touchy situation, and when I didn't tell Art and Betty I had heard from their son, they were hurt and also angry with me when they found out through Richard. A week went by. I called them and offered to come out and talk things over. They voiced their concern about their son. I told them I could not be the intermediary. I understood their feelings and they understood my position, and soon we were on better terms.

Observing the family only when they were all together would have yielded, I felt, a one-dimensional and rather shallow view of what they are like. For that reason I conducted extensive tape-recorded interviews with each family member. For the most part, these were done individually to allow free expression that might not occur if another member were present, although some interviews were with both Art and Betty so that they could comment on each other's thoughts and feelings. The transcripts of the conversations run to over four thousand pages and helped give background and perspective to this particular year in the Neumeyers' lives.

Once the year was over and I had to begin writing, I kept in touch with the family. I still call or see them at least monthly. At this writing, Art is still working at his job. Betty is back to being a full-time homemaker after working three months as a waitress. They have given up looking for a new house, citing high interest rates but also acknowledging a lack of desire.

Martha could not get a teaching position and spent the 1973–74 school year at home, substitute-teaching in Mohawk County schools and otherwise working for a promotion company. Her job was to sell blocks of tickets for sporting events over the phone. In midsummer, 1974, she returned to Kansas City, took a temporary job teaching retarded children and again made application to teach there. She and her college roommate Pat share an apartment. Before she left Mariposa, she wrote a card *"To Mom and Dad: Everybody needs somebody—especially parents who will always be there no matter what."*

Richard worked for almost a year as truck driver for the auto parts store. He then quit and moved into the city to be the custodian of an apartment complex. He shuttled back and forth to Mariposa, spending many nights at home, although he had his own apartment for six months. After beginning a course in masonry and other construction skills at a school in Mohawk County, he finally got tired of the commuting. Richard is once more living at home. He has a job with a roofing company, but he and Ron Bronowski are talking of going to Mexico. He is also a confirmed vegetarian.

Joan is in junior high school, likes it, and is proud of finally becoming a teenager.

As I wrote about the Neumeyers, I often wanted to inject my opinions or comments or otherwise try to tie in the family with what was going on in America, or even in Mariposa. I have clippings on everything from unemployment and the hopes and

363

fears of Americans to the high price of beef, and I would have loved to have used many of them. But, as much as the Neumeyers are products of this culture and their ideas and ideals are formed by the world around them, they talked little of current events or trends or movements. To somehow make them into representatives of the "silent majority" would have been false.

But perhaps a few summary paragraphs on the family I spent so much time observing and living with might help to identify for them and for ourselves some of the main threads of their lives.

To me it is apparent that Art and Betty are locked into their roles—but for the most part they are comfortable with this stereotyping. Art views himself as the breadwinner and his wife will be the housewife; she should never cross over into his preserve. Art has a great need to feel authoritative, although it seemed to me that Betty was the real power in this family. Yet Betty would consistently do things to make Art feel like the head of the household, like having dinner ready when he walked in the door, almost as if she would be punished if she were late. Betty in a sense was bred to be a housewife and mother and she has found great rewards in the home, but she knows she has had to sublimate her own life in the process. Her hostility toward herself and her family often came surging to the surface when things were not going her way or she felt unappreciated.

Art and Betty, both of whom came from relatively poor families, want the best they can afford for their children, but they also want a repayment. Although Betty says she just wants her children to be happy, she also wants them to be educated, successful and intelligent and to occupy an acceptable place in society. Art and Betty gave a lot to their children in terms of time and interest, and they also shoved a good deal down their throats. Perhaps they pushed too hard; perhaps their comparisons of Richard with Martha will damage Richard for the rest of his life. More likely, Richard and Martha and Joan will have the usual garden-variety kinds of psychological problems and may thank their parents some day for pushing them.

Perhaps more distressing and potentially more hurtful is the way

364

in which Betty and Art—but Betty, especially—gives. There is often a hook in the gift. Betty tells Joan she may go out on a date; then she holds it against her—and will use it at a convenient time—that she did it when Martha was home from college and Joan therefore obviously didn't care enough about her sister to stay home. Betty tells Martha to be independent, yet when Martha doesn't call home at the expected intervals, she is either angry or hurt. Betty tells Richard to come home for lunch, yet she complains that she has to buy special foods for him. Art's comments about Betty's being a woman impossible to satisfy have a certain truth to them.

There could be many reasons why Betty is like this—her own insecurity as a child, a certain jealousy of the freedom her children have that she never had, the fact that she often feels overburdened and underrewarded—perhaps all these reasons apply. I think it more significant that Betty is, plain and simple, underutilized. She is an intelligent woman who has too much time on her hands to do too few things. She therefore is a compulsive overorganizer, and she also has a need for her efforts to be rewarded immediately. After all, she has thought a lot about what she's giving and has invested so much in seemingly small situations that when they don't pay off she feels slighted.

What constantly struck me during the year were the quick reversals that I kept seeing. Betty was never going to send presents to Art's family after the incident with the long dress; a few weeks later she shopped for the presents without a word. Martha was absolutely going to practice-teach in the inner city, and then she abandoned the plan. On Christmas Eve Richard was ready to leave in a few days to go back out on the road; by the first of January he was talking about job security in his new work. Betty was "living for ourselves" one day and doing everything to keep the children close and indebted to her the next.

This book shows the ragged, often unresolved, way people go through a year in their lives. It is not a neat package. Life isn't either.

In closing I want to thank Bertha Hoopes, who transcribed thousands of pages of my notes and tape-recorded interviews, Louise Fisher, who typed the finished manuscript and subsequent revisions, and Janet Baker, who so professionally copy edited the final version. My wife, Joy, was patient with me and willing to share me with the Neumeyers for a year, and I love her for it.

I save for last the thanks that go to the Neumeyers of Mariposa. They are not portrayed here as particularly heroic or famous. They are kind people, and they were courageous to allow themselves to be studied for so long a period. My hope is that this book gives an accurate picture of them and, as importantly, *for* them.

Brooklyn, New York
October, 1974